D0960102

WHO DARES WINS

WHO DARES WINS

SPECIAL FORCES HEROES OF THE SAS

PETE SCHOLEY

First published in Great Britain in 2008 by Osprey Publishing,
Midland House, West Way, Botley, Oxford OX2 0PH, United Kingdom.
443 Park Avenue South, New York, NY 10016, USA.
Email: info@ospreypublishing.com

A CIP catalog record for this book is available from the British Library

ISBN 978 1 84603 311 7

Page layout by Ken Vail Graphic Design, Cambridge, UK
Index by Glyn Sutcliffe
Typeset in Adobe Garamond
Originated by PPS Grasmere Digital Ltd, Leeds, UK
Printed and bound in China through World Print Ltd

08 09 10 11 12 10 9 8 7 6 5 4 3 2 1

For a catalog of all books published by Osprey please contact:

NORTH AMERICA

Osprey Direct, c/o Random House Distribution Center,
400 Hahn Road, Westminster, MD 21157, USA
E-mail: info@ospreydirect.com

ALL OTHER REGIONS

Osprey Direct UK, P.O. Box 140, Wellingborough, Northants, NN8 2FA, UK
E-mail: info@ospreydirect.co.uk
www.ospreypublishing.com

Front cover artwork: Ian Palmer
Back cover image: Iranian Embassy siege courtesy of Pete Scholey

DEDICATION

I dedicate this book to HM Forces, who have always given a good account of themselves on the field of battle. All the soldiers were valiant.

> We are the Pilgrims, master; we shall go
> Always a little further; it may be
> Beyond that last blue mountain barred with snow,
> Across that angry or that glimmering sea.

(From The Golden Journey to Samarkand *by James Elroy Flecker, inscribed on the SAS memorial clock tower.)*

CONTENTS

ACKNOWLEDGEMENTS

My thanks to Rod Green, Mal Peachey, John Conway, Richard Belfield and Anita Baker for their help and advice during the writing of this book.

My appreciation, also, to the families of those mentioned in the book for their support and loan of photographs.

Special thanks go to Colin Wallace, Mark Haworth, John Partridge, Bob Podesta, Pete Winner, Don Large, Mike Colton and Paul Griffiths for their encouragement and help throughout this project.

Lastly, I am indebted to my wife, Carolyn, unpaid secretary and computer wizard.

FOREWORD

Like many people in Britain, I recall 5 May 1980 with perfect clarity. Half the country was riveted to the World Professional Snooker Championship on TV. It had reached a crucial stage. Cliff Thorburn and Hurricane Higgins were tied at 17 frames each; the world crown hung on the 35th frame. Then the screen blanked and turned to a blizzard of white dots that eventually dissolved into a street scene.

The language in my own sitting room went as blue as the sky outside. Then I recognized the building on which the cameras were fixed. It was the Iranian Embassy, which for a week had been infested by a group of terrorists, holding the entire staff, a BBC sound man and a London policeman hostage. As we watched, spidery figures in black outfits rappelled down from the roof, crashed through the windows and disappeared inside to the chorus of stun grenades. Within a few moments, the embassy had been liberated, the hostages freed and five of the six terrorists 'slotted' – as the Special Air Service (SAS) later came to refer to the act of killing.

It was on that day that the SAS Regiment was transformed from a shadowy and vaguely mentioned group of special forces soldiers into a national and eventually international obsession. Today it would be hard to count the number of mentions of the 'SAS' initials in media and fiction. Impelled by a fevered public interest, various journalists and writers have explored the history of the SAS from its beginnings in the Western Desert in 1941, as the much-mocked idea of a young Scots Guards officer called David Stirling, to the present day. Some accounts are accurate, some fanciful and not a few are enough to cause derisive laughter in a certain barracks complex outside Hereford.

We knew of course that the SAS played a covert but highly significant role in the 33-year struggle against the Irish Republican Army (IRA). We have learned of the long and sweaty campaign against Indonesian forces who tried to take over North Borneo (part of the Malaysian Federation and thus of the Commonwealth). We have heard of the seven-year secret war waged to deter fanatical guerrillas infiltrating into Oman from communist Yemen, and to keep Sultan Qaboos on his throne. We know vaguely about the presence of teams from the SAS who train special forces all over the world, protecting the lives of monarchs and presidents; of hostages 'sprung' and terrorists slotted; of high-altitude drops by parachute far behind enemy lines; of ships with illegal and deadly cargoes boarded at sea by dead of night; of prisoners liberated in Sierra Leone from the grips of drug-crazed madmen; and of missions deep inside Iraq during the Gulf War of 1990–91.

Some of us have learned from those who were there how the liberation of a hijacked German airliner at Mogadishu nearly went catastrophically wrong until two SAS men, who were only there to advise their German colleagues, stepped in and wasted three of the four terrorists. And there were tales that never hit the press at all, such as the affair of the president of The Gambia, toppled in a coup while playing golf at Gleneagles, restored 48 hours later and his captured family liberated. This feat was performed by two SAS non-commissioned officers (NCOs), who motored into Banjul from Senegal in a car hired at the airport.

Lastly, we have come to know that these three initials are synonymous with extreme physical hardness, relentless stamina, cool nerve and, on occasion, fearsome aggression. The most controversial operation of recent times was the 'taking down' of three IRA killers on the Rock of Gibraltar. The three were planning a bloodbath in front of the governor's mansion with a massive bomb in the boot of a parked car. As their ill-luck would have it, the day they died they were on an unarmed dry run, a reconnaissance, casing the joint with an empty car ... but the SAS men tailing them could not know that. The dummy car was parked to reserve a space for the next day. The three IRA operatives (two men and a woman) headed on foot back to the Spanish border. The SAS watchers could not know they did not have any detonator button on their persons. The order was given: they must not leave the Rock. They didn't.

The real car and the Semtex explosive were eventually found across the border in a Spanish car park, but the usual media elements attacked the SAS because the three IRA elements had been taken down while unarmed. Such coverage explains why the SAS really hates having to operate in front of crowds of civilians. They prefer to slip in, do the job and slip out again.

So what are they like? Really like? The only way to know is to ask someone who knew many of them, and well. Pete Scholey did; he was one of them. Pete is no spring chicken. Today a whole new generation of 'Ruperts' (officers), NCOs and troopers fill the ranks. In this book, however, Pete Scholey gives a pen portrait of 20 of those SAS soldiers who became legends, but only inside their own tiny brotherhood. This book is a glance behind a curtain that very few can draw aside.

Frederick Forsyth
April 2007

INTRODUCTION

Here is a very personal book. It is written as a tribute not only to the men featured in these pages, but to all of those who have served with the SAS. On many occasions since leaving the forces, a few of us old SAS veterans have got together over a beer or two and inevitably reminisced about our time in uniform. We remember all the happy times, of course, the pranks and the laughs, but also those moments when we experienced the excitement, the fear and the horror of combat. That's something that, with only a few words, you know you can share with someone who has been there, who has gone through those experiences alongside you. It's something that is often very difficult to explain, or even to talk about, with anyone who has not been through it. During these reunions, many of the same old stories are unearthed and given an airing not just to relive old times but also, I suspect, as a kind of cathartic exercise, a way of keeping old demons at bay. It's also a way of remembering those colleagues who are no longer with us, some who lost their lives in action and a few who died in training. All were heroes but none would have regarded themselves as such and none needed a medal pinned on his chest for his bravery to manifest itself. I hope that in writing this book I can help those outside the Regiment to appreciate the dedication and courage of these heroes.

The men I have chosen to write about are special in many ways, not least because many of them are among the last of their breed: SAS 'lifers' who spent the best part of their military careers – sometimes more than 20 years – with the Regiment. I was honoured to serve with most of them and count many of them among my closest friends. Soldiers like Don Large, Alfie Tasker, John

Partridge and Pete Loveday served with the Regiment during its renaissance in the jungles of Malaya in the 1950s before going on to Oman, Borneo and Aden. Pete would not ultimately retire for good until 1996, having spent 45 years with the army, 43 of those years with the SAS. Some of the men I have included, like Paddy Mayne, who was one of the founder members of the Regiment during World War II and took over joint command when David Stirling was captured, are legendary figures within the SAS. Lieutenant-Colonel Mayne was, unfortunately, before my time and I never had the opportunity to meet him, but I did come to know Len Owens, one of the survivors of a perilous mission behind enemy lines in the Vosges mountains in France in 1944 – his is a quite remarkable story. The only other man I have featured with whom I did not serve is Vince Phillips, a brave man who died on the ill-fated Bravo Two Zero patrol during the Gulf War in 1991.

Others in this book, good friends whom I came to know during my time in the Regiment through the 1960s, 1970s and into the 1980s, served in theatres from Borneo and Aden to Northern Ireland and the Falklands. They saw the Regiment emerge from beneath its traditional cloak of secrecy, fighting a clandestine war in Oman, to become hot news in the tabloid press and on television with the storming of the Iranian Embassy in London in 1980. They lived through the changing tactics and expanding role of the Regiment and helped to develop the weapons and techniques of the Counter-Revolutionary Warfare (CRW) team, the world's foremost counter-terrorist unit. The stories of these heroes, therefore, cover most of the history of the Regiment. Wherever they found themselves being sent around the world, I have tried to explain – as it was explained to us – why they were sent there.

This book is not, however, a history of the Regiment. It is the stories of some ordinary men who accepted an extraordinary challenge to become members of the SAS. In doing so, they chose to become part of a very special 'family' whose members are forever linked by bonds that are forged not only through their experiences in combat, their memories of journeys all over the world or their escapades during training, but by the common experience that every member of the Regiment must endure – Selection.

To understand the SAS, you first have to separate the realities of the Regiment from the myths. SAS soldiers are not supermen, they are not all budding James Bonds or Rambos and they are not infallible. So much nonsense has been generated around the SAS name in books, on TV and even in computer games, that it is worth remembering that SAS soldiers are just that – soldiers. But these are no ordinary soldiers. Whatever the myths and legends, one fact is not in dispute: the SAS is certainly the foremost military unit in the world, the elite of the elite, respected and feared in equal measure.

The rigorous Selection process ensures that only the very best are accepted into the Regiment, no matter from what unit or from which branch of the armed forces the Selection candidate has come. He must have been in the armed forces for at least three years and already be a highly proficient soldier before even considering volunteering for Selection. A potential SAS recruit in my day would have heard of the Regiment through the military grapevine, and known that it was the pinnacle of soldiering, but he volunteered for something he knew virtually nothing about. I applied to join the SAS after serving for eight years, first in the Royal Artillery and then in 2nd Battalion, The Parachute Regiment. Today, every soldier knows what the SAS is and has a pretty good idea of what the Regiment does. This understanding, however, will not make it any easier to pass the SAS Selection course.

The gruelling marches carrying heavy loads of equipment over the Brecon Beacons (a stretch of punishing mountains in South Wales) that form part of the Selection process are designed to wear the candidates down, day by day, hour by hour, throughout the first three weeks of Selection. The candidates have to prove that they can carry on; that they have the stamina and determination to keep going; that they can still think and function as soldiers when they are struggling through appalling weather, soaked to the skin, fighting off fatigue and with every muscle screaming for rest. No one ever forgets facing up to the challenge of Selection. I can remember every exhausted step I took over those hills, every trick the instructors pulled to try to persuade us to give up, every blister and every muscle strain. Just like everyone else who goes on to earn the right to wear the Regiment's beige beret and 'winged dagger' badge, however, what I remember most of all is the elation at being told that I had passed. That is a feeling that you share with very few others. Only nine out of the 120 candidates on my course passed – and that's normal. The standard is that high.

As a professional soldier, going on to Continuation Training with the Regiment was, for me, a huge opportunity to improve my skills and learn many more new ones. It was the equivalent of attending the finest university, with the additional bonus of studying in North and South America, the Caribbean, Europe, the Arctic, Africa and the Middle and Far East. Along the way I acquired a variety of specialist skills. We constantly trained for war, but as well as learning how to take life, the SAS also trained me to preserve it. I learned to work as a paramedic, capable of treating my own or my comrades' wounds – gunshots, blast injuries and fractures – and acquired a working knowledge of disease and tropical medicine. The skills of an SAS medic are sufficient to treat minor casualties and stabilize major ones until they can be evacuated, even if it takes as long as three days. I was also involved in bodyguard and VIP protection, by then already a complex and still-evolving art. VIP protection in the UK was pioneered by the SAS; SAS soldiers started the process that sophisticated VIP protection offers today.

One of the reasons why SAS men are so effective in so many different situations is that we apply the lessons learned in training not just in combat but to our entire lives. Continuous self-criticism is a way of life in the Regiment. We're always looking for ways to improve our performance, and in planning for any mission we attempt to cover every conceivable eventuality. It's meticulous, exhaustive and often unconventional, but gives us the best possible chance to second-guess our opponents.

In SAS training, the soldier spends much of the time looking at things that might be targets and trying to find the weak spots. The viewpoint is similar to that of a criminal plotting to bypass or defeat security systems to pull off a robbery. The SAS soldier studies the defences and uses his knowledge of human capabilities to predict the likely response to any of his actions. Turning that on its head, once he knows how to find the weak spots, he also knows how to defend them. SAS men are the archetypal poachers-turned-gamekeepers, with the added twist that they are required to turn back into poachers again when necessary. Furthermore, when an

SAS unit decides on a plan of action, it doesn't stick blindly to it if the situation changes – it has to be flexible.

Many of the lessons SAS soldiers learn in training are lessons that can be applied outside the military environment, particularly awareness. The SAS soldier is always aware of his surroundings. He is constantly switched on, paying attention to what's going on around him and what the likely dangers are. Amid the confusion and noise of explosions, gunfire, smoke, flames and CS gas, awareness helped the SAS assault team storming the Iranian Embassy to distinguish instantly between terrorist and hostage, friend and foe. If a soldier is aware, he is better able to anticipate dangerous developments. Before any mission, the SAS plans ahead, using intelligence reports, knowledge of the terrain and any information about the opponents to predict their probable responses to any given action. SAS soldiers anticipate problems before they arise, and hence are better able to avoid getting into conflict. That's not cowardice, it's simple common sense, and it's exactly what the SAS practises.

After the Regiment's successful campaign against Indonesia in Borneo during the 1960s, Major-General Sir Walter Walker, commander of British Forces Borneo Territories (BFBT), described ten SAS soldiers as being 'equal to 70 conventional troops'. The Regiment's intelligence-gathering and its 'hearts and minds' work with the civilian population saved many lives through battles won without a shot being fired. The SAS extends its zone of security by deploying patrols to listen, observe and gather intelligence. When operating overseas, the Regiment enlists the help of indigenous communities, offering medical treatment and help with projects beneficial to them. In return, the native population gives advice on local food and medicinal plants, and information on the movement of enemy troops. An effective 'hearts and minds' campaign is a far better way of dealing with a situation than simply imposing your will on people by force of arms.

Contrary to popular myth, SAS personnel will go to great lengths to avoid confrontation. Whenever a patrol is confronted by an obstacle like a guard post or a gun emplacement, the first reaction is to 'box it' – going 500 yards (457m) north, then 500 yards west, for example – before resuming its track. Getting involved in firefights and skirmishes is counter-productive for them, because it delays or prevents them from achieving their primary objectives.

Self-reliance and self-confidence are part of what makes the SAS so formidable. In any other section of the armed forces, the commander can get down to the lowliest unit on a voice-link within minutes. Things get done because the big stick is being waved. It's the opposite in the SAS: things get done despite – or possibly because – of the fact that there is no officer on your back. In the Regiment, once a soldier gets his instructions and begins the mission, there's frequently no way for the commanders to influence what's going on; if the soldier doesn't do it, it won't get done. It's very easy to duck out of things in situations like that, but in all my time in the Regiment, no one ever turned to me and said, 'We don't need to do this.' It was always, 'How are we going to get this done?'

On SAS operations in which I was involved, there was always a lot of talk about the best way to achieve our objectives. That discussion was often heated and sometimes furious, but when the leader closed the discussion and told us what he felt we should do, everyone accepted his decision without question. At the end of the day, there were only three things you could do: lead, follow or get out of the way. There was no complaining, whingeing or 'I told you so' during the mission; only when it was over and we were safely back at base would a post-mortem begin. There was always a certain satisfaction in having unsuccessfully argued a different approach and subsequently being proved right, but that was something from which to learn, not something to crow over.

SAS soldiers come to realize that everyone is responsible for his own actions and his own life and is accountable to himself. In the Regiment, we're trained to avoid situations where all our options are closed down. We try never to be in a situation where someone else can dictate to us, because then we have abdicated control. For example, SAS patrols prepare a hide so thoroughly that people can walk right up to it without detecting its presence. We'll be inside it, defending it, but we always have an escape route that we've planned beforehand, just in case – although the hide is unlikely to be discovered, we never put ourselves in a position where we haven't got a back door. At its crudest, we always want to be able to fight or run. If we are cornered, we have no option but to fight. Although it's much easier said than done, keeping a cool head no matter what the danger is the surest way for an SAS soldier to escape unscathed from any threatening situation. Fear and anger are always detrimental, because they lead the soldier into rash and hasty actions. By keeping his cool, most of his problems can be solved.

Soldiers who go through the enormous trial and immense traumas of Selection stand only at the threshold of the SAS family. Progressing through more advanced training and gaining operational experience draws them ever closer into the fold until they become completely immersed in the culture of the Regiment. Each person has different skills and talents, different strengths and weaknesses, but very few possess the determination and courage that I have seen displayed so often by so many of the men of the SAS. In my eyes, every one of them is a hero.

dead of night carrying a satchel full of bombs to place on the parked planes, ripping out the cockpit controls with his bare hands when he ran out of explosives, I wondered why we hadn't finished off the Germans a lot sooner with invincible warriors like Paddy on our side.

A great deal has been written about Paddy Mayne's exploits, fact sliding into fiction to create a legend surrounding the man. He stands, however, as one of my heroes not simply for the way he fought on the field of battle – his bravery was recognized with a series of awards that made him the most decorated British serviceman of World War II – but also for the way he fought for the Regiment from behind a desk. Without Paddy, the SAS would not have survived the war.

Born on 11 January 1915, five months after the start of World War I, Robert Blair Mayne was named after his mother's cousin, Captain Robert Blair of the 5th Battalion, Border Regiment, who was killed in action the following year and awarded a posthumous Distinguished Service Order (DSO). Young Robert was one of seven children, with two older brothers, Thomas and William, a younger brother, Douglas, and three sisters, Molly, Barbara and Frances. His father, William, was a successful businessman, owning property and running a retail business in Newtonards, County Down, and the family lived in a large house, Mount Pleasant, set in around 40 acres (16 hectares) of grounds overlooking the town. In the countryside around his home, young Paddy took to the outdoors life, becoming a marksman with his .22 rifle as well as taking up fly-fishing, golf, horse riding and deer stalking. He attended a local grammar school, Regent House, where he excelled at cricket and rugby, playing for Ards Rugby Football Club Second XV when he was just 17, becoming team captain the following season and captaining the First XV the next year. By the time Paddy came to study law at Queen's University, Belfast, he was powerfully built, 6ft 2in (1.88m) tall and weighed in at well over 15 stone (95kg), although he boasted a speed and agility that belied his impressive bulk. It was while at university that Paddy won his boxing honours and first represented Ireland as an international rugby player. He would go on to win six caps for Ireland and was selected for the British Lions on a tour of South Africa in 1938, playing in 18 of the side's 24 matches, including all three tests. His rugby career was, however, cut short by the incredibly unsporting Herr Hitler.

As war in Europe grew ever more likely, young men of military age were encouraged to join their local Territorial Army (TA) regiments to gain some basic military training, and in February 1939 Paddy was commissioned into the 5th Light Anti-Aircraft Regiment, Royal Artillery TA, Newtonards. When war was declared, he was called up for service, but spent several frustrating months kicking his heels in Ulster, about as far away from the action as you could get without actually leaving Europe. In April 1940 he transferred to the Royal Ulster Rifles, hoping to be able to get into the war at last, but still found himself based in Ulster. Within weeks he volunteered for secondment to the Cameronians and was transferred to Scotland – hardly the sort of overseas posting which he wanted. In the summer of 1940, however, he joined 11 Scottish Commando, training to launch raids into enemy territory to destroy installations or capture strategic positions to pave the way for the advance of a more conventional force. This was work where he at last felt he could make a valuable contribution, but after months of arduous training and cancelled operations he was still waiting impatiently for the chance to have a crack at the enemy.

That opportunity did not eventually arise until a commando force, which included 11 Commando, set sail from Scotland for the Middle East at the end of January 1941 – two years after Lieutenant Robert Blair Mayne had first donned his uniform. In March they arrived in Egypt and after another period of frustration, delay and inactivity, 11 Commando was posted to Cyprus at the end of April for garrison duties. It was reported that there was general unrest among the commandos at that time, created by what was perceived as the high command's failure to utilize the commandos' specific skills properly. Several officers were said to have offered their resignations or applied for transfers to other units in order to take a more active part in the war, and for someone like Paddy Mayne the situation was almost intolerable. He was a complex character, a bewildering mixture of diametrically opposed qualities. In a foreword to *Rogue Warrior of the SAS: The Blair Mayne Legend* by Roy Bradford and Martin Dillon (Mainstream Publishing, 2003), Colonel David Stirling, the founder of the SAS, described Paddy's temperament.

> It is always hard to pin down the qualities that go to make up an exceptional man and Paddy could be exasperatingly elusive because his character was such a mixture of contrasting attributes. On the one hand there was this great capacity for friendship; his compassion and gentleness displayed during the war in his deep concern for the welfare of all his men and expressing itself in peacetime in his voluntary work with juvenile delinquents and boys clubs and as a regular prison visitor; his love of the countryside and the attention he lavished on his rose garden; and his essentially happy family life. Qualities like these would seem to demonstrate his belief in God. On the other hand, there was a reverse side to his character which revealed itself in outbursts of satanic ferocity.

That 'satanic ferocity' was not always confined to the rugby pitch, the boxing ring or the battlefield. When Paddy had been drinking, his fiery temper could sometimes burn out of control and swapping monotony in Ulster for frustration in Scotland followed by boredom in Egypt and tedium in Cyprus led to an incident in a Nicosia nightclub. At the end of the evening, Paddy and his best friend Eoin McGonigal were the last of their party to leave. On checking the bill, Paddy believed (probably with some justification) that they were being overcharged. He demanded to see the manager who, rather unwisely, was not only unhelpful but downright rude. Paddy forced the man into the middle of the dancefloor, produced his revolver and emptied it into the floor around the terrified man's feet. He was arrested and remained under open arrest under the supervision of another officer for 48 hours. After a month or so in Cyprus, Paddy had had enough of 11 Commando and requested a transfer to a unit in the Far East. In the meantime, however, the type of operation for which he had been longing began to take shape.

Following the fall of France in June 1940, German forces occupied the northern part of the country, the Italians claimed part of the south-east, and most of the south of the country was administered by a collaborationist French government based in the town of Vichy. In fact, the Vichy government was technically still in control of the whole country, although the tendency of the German army of occupation to override the civilian authorities whenever they chose made any effort at central government almost impossible. Nevertheless, not only was the Vichy government in charge throughout France – and officially recognized as such by the Americans and Canadians – it also had control of French territories and French military forces abroad. By 1941 this meant that the German Luftwaffe could use French bases in Syria and Lebanon to bomb the British in Iraq, cause problems in Palestine and pose a major threat to the entire British eastern flank in Egypt. The decision was taken, therefore, to launch an offensive into Syria and Lebanon. The commandos in Cyprus were tasked with capturing a bridge over the Litani River, an important crossing point on the road for forces heading into Lebanon from Palestine, and neutralizing enemy strongholds in the vicinity of the crossing to allow the Australian 21st Infantry Brigade to advance across the river.

Paddy was in command of 7 Troop, 11 Scottish Commando, part of three separate raiding parties that landed near the mouth of the Litani at first light on 9 June 1941. A number of problems were encountered by the raiders (not least being shot at by the Australians), but Paddy's performance was outstanding, his troop attacking several positions manned by French colonial troops and capturing around 70 prisoners. (It is somewhat ironic that Paddy's first major action was against the French, who would later bestow upon him their highest awards for gallantry, the *Croix de Guerre* and *Légion d'Honneur)*. For his efforts at Litani, Paddy received a Mention In Dispatches (MID), but after two days of excitement and three days of rest and recuperation in Haifa, it was back to garrison duty in Cyprus with the prospect of the commando force being disbanded altogether.

It was at this point that one of the most fateful episodes in his military service created what was to become a major part of the Paddy Mayne legend. Within a week of returning to Cyprus, Mayne was to leave 11 Commando. Some stories have it that this was the result of an altercation with his Acting Commanding Officer, Geoffrey Keyes. It was no secret that Paddy and Keyes did not see eye to eye and their antagonism came to a head when Keyes interrupted a game of chess Paddy was enjoying in the mess one evening. The more exaggerated accounts have Keyes flipping the board over and Paddy leaping to his feet, knocking Keyes out with a single punch and being placed under arrest pending a court martial. The more likely scenario is that Keyes passed comment on the game and Paddy pushed him away, knocking him over. Even this, of course, is a very serious business when a senior officer is involved. In an excellent and assiduously researched recent biography entitled *Paddy Mayne*, author Hamish Ross could find no evidence that Paddy was placed under arrest following his altercation with Keyes or ever had to face the prospect of a court martial. What is known is that Paddy left Cyprus and returned to Egypt where he was hospitalized in Geneifa with malaria.

The legend would have it, however, that Paddy was languishing in some rat-infested prison cell in utter disgrace, awaiting his court martial, when he was approached by David Stirling, who wanted to recruit him for his new SAS unit. Stirling then had the charges against Mayne dropped and Paddy became one of the founder members of the Regiment. Even David Stirling has been quoted as saying that he went to see Paddy in jail in Geneifa, although it seems more probable that the meeting actually took place in the hospital. When creating a legend, though, I suppose the truth should never get in the way of a good story. You can guess which version old Harry Warner preferred to tell me back in Brighton.

Whichever story you choose to believe, Paddy became part of the new unit that Stirling had been given permission to form. Known as 'L' Detachment prior to being granted regimental status as 1 SAS in 1942, its primary role was to attack airfields and lines of communication deep in enemy territory, parachuting in close to its objectives before completing its mission and making its way to a predesignated rendezvous, where trucks would be waiting to take the troops home. The new recruits to the unit begged, borrowed or stole the equipment they needed and went through a two-month training period, including parachute training, before they embarked on their first operation on 16 November 1941. The plan was to attack airfields at Timini and Gazala, Libya, in advance of an Allied offensive, Operation *Crusader*, with five teams of 10–12 men dropping by parachute at night to disable as many aircraft as possible. Prior to the attack, Stirling was warned that high winds were expected over the drop zones (DZs), making parachute landings extremely hazardous. Cancelling the unit's first ever operation, however, was not something Stirling was prepared to contemplate. 'L' Detachment had to prove its worth or political pressure from within the army hierarchy would ensure that the outfit was never given the chance to shine – army bureaucrats have a deep suspicion of special forces, who don't always follow normal procedures, and they will pounce on every opportunity to highlight any shortcomings. Calling off the mission was almost unthinkable. In the end, however, it would have been the better option.

When the men of 'L' Detachment exited their lumbering Bristol Bombay aircraft on the night of the operation, they jumped into pitch darkness and a howling gale. The worst storm in 30 years was raging. I have always loved parachuting, but even though the equipment and the aircraft we used in my day was far better than that available in North Africa in 1941, a night drop into near gale-force winds over hostile terrain in enemy territory would rank among my worst nightmares. For 'L' Detachment, it was a complete disaster. On hitting the ground they found it impossible to spill the air out of their parachutes and release their harnesses, the wind dragging them across the floor of the desert over punishing rocks and through razor-sharp camel-thorn bushes. Paddy Mayne's troop suffered two casualties who were too badly injured to continue and the other groups fared even worse. Some soldiers were dropped miles from their intended landing areas and losses of men and equipment made the operation completely unviable, although Paddy did make it to his target airfield with his troop and just enough ordnance to do the job. Unfortunately, it began to pour with rain, turning the ground into a quagmire and filling the desert wadis with near impassable torrents of water. Paddy also discovered that the fuses for the bombs they were supposed to place on the aircraft were, like the men, soaked through. The soldiers had no means of detonating the explosives. Abandoning their mission, they began a long, miserable trek to their rendezvous in freezing conditions. The operation was a complete failure and of the 55 men who embarked on the mission, only 21 returned – the rest were either dead, missing or captured. Paddy's group, however, had come close to hitting its target and, had the abominable weather not intervened, another group would also have done so. Next time, they would not be so unfortunate.

Three weeks later, Paddy led a raid on an airfield at Wadi Tamet, Libya. Instead of relying on risky parachute jumps to reach their target, they were driven into the area by the Long Range Desert Group (LRDG), a reconnaissance unit whose vehicles had been used to extract the raiders on the previous mission. It was only logical that if the LRDG could get 'L' Detachment out of the target area, they could also get them in. Paddy's six-man team placed bombs on 14 aircraft, destroyed the instrument panels of a further ten, blew up a bomb store and a petrol dump, destroyed a few telegraph poles and attacked a building manned by 30 Italian troops. They then returned to their LRDG transport and were ferried back to the unit's new base at Jalo Oasis, shared by the LRDG and 'L' Detachment. Two weeks later they went back to the same airfield and destroyed a further 27 aircraft, and were fighting their way out of the now heavily guarded facility when one of their bombs went off prematurely, betraying their presence. Once again, they sustained no casualties while inflicting a crushing blow upon the enemy. Following this raid, Paddy was promoted to captain and awarded his first DSO.

Of course, Paddy wasn't the only officer leading raids on enemy airfields. There were others enjoying almost as much success, but by the time SAS operations in North Africa drew to a close in 1943, Paddy was credited with having personally destroyed well over 100 aircraft – far more than any Allied fighter ace! Throughout the two years that they fought in North Africa, the SAS developed new techniques and tactics for launching their attacks. They worked closely with the LRDG but began using their own vehicles – heavily armed jeeps fitted with Lewis guns that had been used on Gladiator fighter planes. They learned how to navigate themselves across the desert and developed convoy drills that we were still practising when we were training in the same Libyan Desert almost 25 years later, albeit with Land Rovers instead of the old Wilys jeep. Paddy remained at the forefront of the Regiment's endeavours, not least when David Stirling was captured in February 1943. Stirling's brother, Bill, was in the process of establishing and training a second SAS regiment but it was Paddy, now Major Mayne, who took over command of 1 SAS. This is an interesting point to note. Had Paddy been the kind of maverick that some stories would have us believe, a loose cannon of a man barely in control of his own psychopathic temper, there is no way that he would ever have been allowed to assume control of any regiment in the British Army, even one as unconventional as the SAS. The high command would not have presented that sort of authority to anyone they thought might cause them a problem.

There were elements in the upper echelons of the army, however, that did not believe that there was any further use for the SAS desert raiders. The desert war was won and there was pressure to disband the Regiment or merge it with another unit. It was now Paddy's job to fight for the survival of the SAS. The kind of courage and determination that were required in the field under fire, the quick thinking and decisiveness that were needed to press home an attack or get his men out of a tricky situation, now had to be adapted for use in the boardroom battles of army staff meetings where the Regiment's future was at stake. Had he been a complete hothead, Paddy would not have been able to appreciate that negotiation and compromise were the tactics he had to adopt. But this was a man who had trained as a solicitor while studying law at university. He knew how to argue his case, he had practised the art of negotiation, he understood when he should give ground in order to achieve his ultimate goal and, although changes were made – the Regiment's name was changed from 1 SAS to the Special Raiding Squadron (SRS) and the overall command structure into which it fitted was altered – Paddy kept the Regiment together as a unit. The man whom many would have us believe was an undisciplined adventurer also earned a fearsome reputation for insisting on strict discipline and instigated a vigorous training regime for his men to prepare them for the new role they were about to play.

On 10 July 1943 the SRS was tasked with undertaking an amphibious landing at Capo Murro Di Porco in Sicily in order to destroy coastal defence batteries that threatened the main force poised to invade the island in Operation *Husky*. The mission turned into a demonstration by Paddy and his men of how well they could adapt to different challenges. They captured the target battery plus three others, taking 450 prisoners and killing over 200 Italian troops. Two days later Paddy led the way as the SRS stormed ashore during another amphibious landing to take the town of Augusta. For his actions in Sicily, Paddy was awarded a bar to his DSO with the citation from Colonel H. J. Cator stating that:

> In both these operations it was Major Mayne's courage, determination and superb leadership which proved the key to success. He personally led his men from the landing craft in the face of heavy machine gun fire and, in the case of the Augusta raid, mortar fire.

The SRS continued to serve under Paddy during the campaign in Italy until January 1944, when they returned to the UK to a base in Scotland. After a period of leave they were to begin retraining for yet another new role – one more akin to the raids they had conducted behind enemy lines in North Africa. With the newly promoted Lieutenant-Colonel Mayne in charge, the SRS became 1 SAS Regiment once more, part of a far larger SAS brigade. Their new training regime was to prepare them to take part in the invasion of France in June. They would be expected to parachute deep into France and work with local resistance groups to sabotage rail networks and other lines of communication in order to prevent reinforcements reaching the battlegrounds in Normandy. When the time came, 1 SAS mounted several such operations, but Paddy, as the commander of the Regiment, was barred by military policy from infiltrating behind enemy lines – the British Army did not want the commander of one of its regiments to be killed or captured in enemy territory. Paddy argued long and hard to be allowed to join his regiment in the field and was eventually granted permission with the provision that he fulfilled a command role and stayed out of the firing line. They might as well have told the rain not to fall.

On 7 August 1944 he was dropped into the area west of Dijon that was the base for Operation *Houndsworth* (the invasion of France had been launched two months previously). As the Allies advanced out of Normandy, the SAS was kept very busy, with Paddy crossing and recrossing the German and American lines by jeep in broad daylight on several occasions to guide reinforcements to his unit. Brigadier R.W. McLeod, officer commanding the SAS Brigade at the time, stated that 'It was entirely due to Lt. Col. Mayne's fine leadership and example, and due to his utter disregard of danger that the unit was able to achieve such striking success', these words appearing in McLeod's recommendation for the award of a second bar to Paddy's DSO.

By the spring of 1945, the Allies were pushing into Germany and it was here that the Paddy Mayne legend took on the aura of a Hollywood film script. An incident at Oldenburg graphically illustrates the attributes that went towards making him a true hero and demonstrates his astonishing intuition and inspiration in battle. He was cold-hearted and ruthless in action, yet harboured a deep affection and loyalty towards those who served under him that could easily justify putting his own life on the line whenever he felt it was necessary. That was just what he did at Oldenburg. The citation for what became the third bar to his DSO reads as follows:

> On Monday, April 9, 1945, Lt-Col. Mayne was ordered by the General Officer Commanding Canadian 4 Armoured Division to lead his Regiment, then consisting of two Armoured Jeep Squadrons, through the German lines. His general axis of advance was north-east through the city of Oldenburg with the special task to clear a path for the Canadian armoured cars and tanks and to cause alarm and disorganisation behind the enemy lines. As subsequent events proved, the task of Lt-Col. Mayne's force was entirely and completely successful. This success, however, was solely due to the brilliant leadership of Lt-Col. Mayne who, by a single act of supreme bravery, drove the enemy from a strongly held key village, thereby breaking the crust of the enemy defences in the whole of this sector.
>
> The following is a detailed account of the Colonel's individual action which called for unsurpassed heroism and cool, clear-sighted military knowledge.
>
> Lt-Col. Mayne, on receiving a wireless message from the leading Squadron reporting that it was heavily engaged by enemy fire and that the Squadron Commander had been killed, immediately drove forward to the scene of the action. From the time of his arrival until the end of the action, Lt-Col. Mayne was in full view of the enemy and exposed to fire from small-arms, machine-guns and snipers' rifles. On arrival he summed up the situation in a matter of seconds and entered the nearest house alone and ensured that the enemy here had either withdrawn or been killed. He then seized a Bren-gun and magazine and, single handed, fired burst after burst into the second house killing and wounding all the enemy here and also opening fire on the woods.
>
> He then ordered a jeep to come forward and take over his fire position, he himself returning to the forward section where he disposed the men to best

advantage and ordered another jeep to come forward. He got in the jeep and with another officer as rear gunner, drove past the position where the Squadron Commander had been killed a few minutes previously and continued to a point a hundred yards ahead where a further section of jeeps were halted by intense and accurate enemy fire. This section had suffered casualties in killed and wounded owing to the heavy enemy fire and the survivors were unable at the time to influence the action in any way until the arrival of Lt-Col. Mayne. The Colonel continued along the road all the time engaging the enemy with fire from his own jeep. Having swept the area very thoroughly with close-range fire he turned his jeep round and drove back down the road still in full view of the enemy.

By this time the enemy had suffered heavy casualties, and were starting to withdraw. Nevertheless, they maintained an accurate fire on the road and it appeared almost impossible to extricate the wounded who were in the ditch near the forward jeep. Any attempt at rescuing these men under these conditions appeared virtually suicidal owing to the highly concentrated and accurate fire of the Germans. Though he fully realised the risk he was taking, Colonel Mayne turned his jeep round once again and returned to try and rescue these wounded. Then by superlative determination and by displaying gallantry of the very highest degree and in the face of intense enemy machine-gun fire, he lifted the wounded one by one, into the jeep, turned round and drove back to the main body.

The entire enemy position had been wiped out. The majority of the enemy had been killed or wounded leaving a very small remnant who were now in full retreat. The Squadron, having suffered no further casualties, were able to continue their advance and drive deeper behind the enemy lines to complete their task of sabotage and destruction of the enemy. Finally, they reached a point twenty miles ahead of the advance guard of the advancing Canadian Division, thus threatening the rear of the Germans, who finally withdrew. From the time of the arrival of Colonel Mayne, his cool and determined action and his complete command of the situation, together with his unsurpassed gallantry, inspired all ranks. Not only did he save the lives of the wounded, but also completely defeated and destroyed the enemy.

The citation was submitted by Brigadier J. M. Calvert as a recommendation for the Victoria Cross (VC) and it was signed by him, Major-General Vokes, who commanded the IV Canadian Armoured Corps; Lieutenant-General Simonds, General Officer Commanding II Canadian Corps; General Crerar, Commander First Canadian Army; and Field Marshal Montgomery, 21st Army Group. Eyewitness accounts from those who took part in that engagement vary in terms of detail, but it is clear that the citation was an attempt by those who knew him best to have Paddy's cumulative and outstandingly brave and effective leadership on so many occasions recognized by recommending him for the award of the VC. The award was, however, ultimately downgraded to a third bar to his DSO.

Colonel Stirling maintained his view that it was a 'monstrous injustice' that Paddy was not awarded the VC for his outstanding bravery during World War II. 'It was the faceless men who didn't want Paddy and the SAS to be given the distinction', he wrote. Colonel Stirling's views were supported by the then Chief of Combined Operations, Major-General Sir Robert Laycock, who wrote a personal letter to Paddy Mayne when the war ended.

> My Dear Paddy,
>
> I feel I must drop you a line just to tell you how very deeply I appreciate the great honour of being able to address, as my friend, an officer who has succeeded in accomplishing the practically unprecedented task of collecting no less than four DSOs.
>
> You deserve all and more, and, in my opinion, the appropriate authorities do not really know their job. If they did they would have given you a VC as well.
>
> Please do not dream of answering this letter, which brings with it my sincerest admiration and a deep sense of honour in having, at one time, been associated with you.
>
> Yours ever,
>
> Bob Laycock

The reason why Paddy was denied the VC is probably down to a technicality. The VC is awarded for individual acts of bravery in the face of the enemy, but Paddy actually called for a volunteer to man the twin Vickers guns on his jeep before he set off. Lieutenant Scott stepped forward to join Paddy in the jeep and, while some accounts also have Paddy firing a Bren gun as he drove, it was Scott who poured fire on the enemy from the Vickers and covered Paddy as he picked up the wounded. Nevertheless, this was a supreme act of bravery and even King George VI was reported as wondering why the VC had 'so strangely eluded' Paddy. In 2005, 60 years after the Oldenburg incident, 100 MPs signed a motion in the House of Commons calling for Paddy to be given the VC during the 150th anniversary year of the award, but their pleas fell on deaf ears.

Yet Paddy counts as one of my heroes not because of any injustice that may have been done to him over the VC, but because of all that he achieved. He established beyond doubt that the SAS was capable of adapting to different situations and bringing its specialist skills to bear in a number of diverse roles. That fundamental flexibility has become the bedrock of the Regiment's philosophy – the SAS has to be as special when it comes to covert operations behind the lines or raiding enemy facilities as it is at storming terrorist-held buildings or protecting vulnerable diplomats. All of us who later served in the Regiment owe a debt of gratitude to Paddy Mayne. I would love to have served under him. I might have had a few smacks in the mouth for being cheeky, but I'd have been proud of those bruises.

To have survived his years of fighting without a scratch would seem to support the view that Paddy led a charmed life, although it later transpired that he had sustained a back injury, probably during the disastrous Timini jump, that grew worse as the war progressed. He told no one about it during his service with the SAS, but it plagued him so much when he embarked on a voyage with an Antarctic survey team after leaving the army that he had to be hospitalized.

The last ten years of Paddy's life were spent without real purpose, searching for a role. His job as secretary to the Northern Ireland Law Society neither held his interest nor filled his days. He tried poultry breeding like his father before him and took real pleasure in his garden. He played golf when he had the time as well as chess and cards. He was good at bridge, better at poker. He idolized his mother; when playing rugby before the war, it was his mother, not his father, who used to accompany him in the car to watch the game and who drove home with him. After the war, he spent much of his time looking after her when she was an invalid in the family home.

Those who knew him during his latter days could be divided into two distinct groups: those who were proud to be in his company and those who were afraid to be. His riotous nature still had a tendency to prevail when he had had a few drinks and he could be a dangerous man to be around. Having survived the carnage of war relatively unscathed, it was all the more tragic that Paddy Mayne should be killed in a peacetime car accident. At around 4.00am on 15 December 1955 he was driving home when his red Riley sports car struck a lorry parked at the roadside. The car careered across the road and rammed into a pole carrying electricity lines. He was killed instantly.

Paddy is buried in the family grave in Movilla churchyard in his native Newtownards. In the wider world, the most decorated and outstanding British soldier of World War II is almost totally unknown, but he has not been forgotten by the SAS. In 1969 some members of D Squadron, who were then serving on operations in Northern Ireland, visited his grave and laid a wreath on behalf of the members of his other 'family' – the Special Air Service Regiment.

Chapter 2

SERGEANT LEN OWENS

As I was only a youngster during World War II, I never had the opportunity to serve with Paddy Mayne, but I know a man who did – and you would struggle to find two men more fundamentally different.

Len Owens is a slightly built, short, modest and quiet sort of man, a far cry from the hell-raising Irish giant who was Paddy Mayne. The one thing that they certainly had in common was their courage. Len may be small in stature but he has got a big heart, something that he has proved time and time again not only during his wartime service, but for the more than sixty years since World War II ended. Len is a special kind of man and when he was in uniform, he had a very special role to play.

There was not much to talk about for the soldiers sitting in the belly of an aircraft shoulder to shoulder with around 20 other men, buttoned, zipped, fastened and strapped into so much kit that they could barely stand, even if there had been any room to walk about. For Len and the men of 2 SAS, conversation was pretty much redundant anyway. The noise inside the converted Stirling bomber meant that anything that was said had to be shouted at the top of the voice to be heard. Not that anyone was in the mood for a chat. The atmosphere was tense, to say the least. They were heading south over the English Channel, crossing the Allied lines to be dropped into eastern France deep inside enemy-held territory as part of Operation *Loyton*. It was early August 1944, two months after the momentous D-Day landings in Normandy. The Allies, having fought their way off the beaches and gained a strong foothold inland, were now poised to break out of the Normandy area. Various special forces units were operating within France behind the German lines, training and arming local resistance groups, gathering intelligence on German troop movements and, particularly in the case of the SAS, attacking the enemy lines of communication to help prevent reinforcements reaching the Normandy battlegrounds.

The Allies had almost complete control of the air, but that was little consolation for the men packed into the fuselage of the Stirling. The aircraft had been designed as a heavy bomber in the dark days at the beginning of the war and had entered service in 1941, the first of the RAF's four-engined bombers. While it soon became apparent that the Stirling's limitations in range, payload and service ceiling meant it fell short of the standards that could be achieved by the new Lancaster bombers, its rugged construction and manoeuvrability made it ideal as a vehicle for paratroops or as a glider tug. Inside the Stirling, however, there were no thoughts among the paratroops of its toughness or agility. Lone Allied aircraft flying fairly low at night were tempting targets for nervous gunners on Allied ships in the English Channel or manning anti-aircraft guns protecting the Allied beachhead. Everyone had heard stories about planes being fired on by 'friendly' gunners on the ground. Once over German lines, of course, the soldiers could expect some fireworks if they were spotted and there was always the remote possibility that a prowling Luftwaffe night fighter might pick them up. The first thing they would know about that was when the deadly tracer and cannon rounds came ripping through the Stirling's thin metal fuselage or exploded into the fuel tanks in the wings, sending a billowing surge of fire roaring through the aircraft. Every time the constant vibration in the Stirling gave way to a clattering lurch as the aircraft passed through a pocket of turbulence, Len and his comrades suppressed all thoughts of alarm. No-one wanted to look like he was about to burst into a panic. No-one wanted to look like he couldn't take the strain. And for everybody, the dangers of the flight were easily dispelled by thoughts of what was yet to come.

A constant stream of messages was passed over the intercom between the four crew members and the pilot as they identified what landmarks they could in the darkness below to help keep the flight on course, but the first instruction Len and the rest of the 2 SAS passengers received was when a message came through to one of the senior sergeants: 'Twenty minutes to go.' The flight's wireless operator then made his way towards the rear of the plane to act as dispatcher and the men were given the signal to 'Stand up, hook up'. Procedure and training now banished any nervousness. They stood in two lines, known as 'sticks', facing the rear of the aircraft and each man hooked his static line to a pulley that ran along the roof of the fuselage. When he jumped, the static line would remain attached to the aircraft, pulling open his pack and releasing his parachute. They then ran through their equipment check, each man sounding off as he ensured that the man in front of him in his stick had his parachute and static line properly fastened. As they did this, the dispatcher lowered the strop guard and locked it in place. This was a metal frame that dropped down outside the aircraft to prevent the trailing static lines and their parachute bags from flapping against the fuselage or fouling the control surfaces on the tail.

With the Stirling having descended to below 800ft (244m), the bolts at the front and rear of the two doors in the floor were slid back and the doors opened inwards, restraining clips holding them back against the walls of the fuselage. There was now a gaping black rectangular hole in the floor about the size of a large bath ... or an open grave. The signal came back: 'Five minutes to go' and, after the longest 4 minutes 55 seconds imaginable, the five-second red 'Action Stations' light flicked on followed by the green jump light. One by one in quick succession the men stepped forward to the floor hatch and dropped out of the belly of the Stirling into the night sky over France.

As Len exited the hatch the first thing that hit him was a blast of windrush and momentary buffeting from the aircraft's slipstream that took his breath away. The Stirling's inboard engines had been throttled back to reduce the effect, but it was over in a split second in any case. Then, as his canopy snapped open and the roar of the aero engines faded, he was overwhelmed by silence. After hours cooped up in the Stirling with the constant engine drone and ever-present vibration, these few moments of quiet as he drifted to earth were a godsend. They also meant that no one below was shooting at him. The next thing he noticed was the smell, the aromatic scent on the night air that reminded him of his first operational jump into France, for this was not Len's first mission behind the lines. There was little time to dwell on thoughts of past adventures, though, as he knew the earth was rushing towards him, and he couldn't actually see the ground in the darkness. He kept his knees bent and feet together – if a paratrooper can't judge exactly when the impact is coming, then he just feels for it. The French countryside slammed into the soles of his boots and Len collapsed into a heap, absorbing as much of the collision as he could with his best attempt at a parachute roll.

Len had landed safely. He checked himself over. No broken bones and, more importantly, the precious Jedburgh radio that he carried strapped to his chest appeared intact. As he gathered his parachute, the reception committee at the drop zone helped assemble everyone from the two sticks and the Stirling circled to drop their canisters of equipment. There were a few concerned glances towards Len to check that he was okay. Len, you see, was one of a very select few. Len was a 'Phantom'.

The Phantoms, officially designated as GHQ (General Headquarters) Liaison Regiment, consisted of experienced, specially selected men who had been drawn from other army units to provide an essential service. Their job was to work with frontline troops and reconnaissance units, even to operate behind enemy lines, in order to gather intelligence about enemy troop deployments and the actual positions of Allied troops so that the 'bomb lines' (areas where artillery or air strikes could be directed without endangering friendly forces) could be mapped as accurately as possible. The Phantoms, whose regimental badge was a white letter 'P' on a black background, provided a constant stream of encoded radio reports, using Morse keys rather than voice communications, transmitted directly from the enemy's back yard. The unit was formed soon after the outbreak of the war by Major-General Hopkinson (who was subsequently killed while leading the 1st Airborne Division in Italy in 1943), and although there were moves to disband the Phantoms after the retreat from Dunkirk in 1940, Hopkinson persuaded the high command that there was still a need for his outfit. Phantom sections were posted all round the coast of Britain during

1940 to send instant reports of any signs of the arrival of a German invasion fleet. They also served in Greece, North Africa and Italy before playing a vital role in the invasion of France.

St James's Park in London, a delightfully landscaped garden park with duck ponds and extensive lawns, hardly seems like the sort of place that a highly secret military unit would choose as its headquarters, but it was here that the Phantoms' base radio sets were located and here that the pigeon lofts for the carrier pigeons also used by the Regiment were built. A note tied to the leg of a pigeon might not have been as sophisticated or as fast as a coded message tapped out on a Morse key, but the birds were a reasonably reliable last resort. Another London park, Richmond to the west of the city, was closed to the public during the war and used as a training ground for, among others, the Phantoms. It was here that Major-General (then Lieutenant-Colonel) Hopkinson, known as 'Hoppy', put his men through a rigorous training regime. They learned how to drive fast and also cross-country, they ran for miles round the park, swam through its freezing cold lakes in the depths of winter and would work for two days or more without a break to simulate the conditions that they would encounter on active service. Above all, they had to be expert in the use of the unit's codes and cipher systems and be able to transmit Morse messages at no fewer than 30 words per minute. They used state-of-the-art lightweight radios. The compact Jedburgh set, powerful enough to contact London from anywhere in Europe under the right conditions, was used for transmissions, while the MCR-1 receiver dealt with incoming signals. These men were highly trained, highly specialized, highly professional soldiers; the best the army could muster. So what on earth was Len doing there? He had never even wanted to be in the army – he wanted to be a sailor.

When Len was called up for military service, his first thought was to join the Royal Navy. A life on the ocean waves away from the grime and mud of an infantryman's existence was what he fancied, but the navy just didn't seem to want him. The army, however, liked him just fine and claimed him for the Royal Corps of Signals. Ironically, almost the first thing the army did once they had trained Len as a soldier and signaller was to put him on a ship.

Len served in North Africa, enjoying his time on the troop transport far more than he did trudging around the desert, or being cooped up for hours on end in a radio shack. By 1943, he found himself back on board a ship again bound for the invasion of Sicily. That made his mind up to apply for a transfer to the Royal Navy, but again he was turned down. Desperate for a job that would give him a bit more adventure, a bit more of a challenge, he spotted a notice in Regimental Orders asking for volunteers for work of a hazardous nature. Len lost no time in applying and the army lost no time in sticking him on another ship, this time bound for the UK. He was put through a series of aptitude and skills tests, passed with flying colours and found himself a member of the GHQ Liaison Regiment.

The hours of tedium and routine in North Africa, although punctuated by spells of intense activity and extreme danger when the opposing forces got down to the business of fighting the war, were a world away from the frantic pace of Len's life as a Phantom. He was whisked off to Scotland to train with the Combined Operations Group (COG) and 2 SAS, to whom he was being seconded. Such was the reputation that the Phantoms had earned for themselves that just about every other unit wanted their own Phantom detachment. Phantoms had accompanied the Canadians on the ill-fated Dieppe raid in August 1942 and they had been in North Africa when Len was there with the Royal Corps of Signals. They had been listening in to German communications and passing on information about casualty rates and unit deployments, every scrap of intelligence being analyzed to try to give the Allied commanders some kind of edge over Rommel's Afrika Korps. Now, in the early part of 1944, volunteers were requested to undergo parachute instruction and training for amphibious landings. In the army, they say that you should never volunteer, but Len stepped up to the mark once again and, with even more British Army irony, training for amphibious assaults meant that he was back in a boat yet again.

Phantom teams were parachuted into France immediately prior to the D-Day landings on 6 June 1944 and others went in with the main assault groups. So good was the intelligence they passed back to Britain that when General Eisenhower visited the British Second Army HQ in Portsmouth during the early stages of the Normandy campaign, he was so impressed with the work of the Phantom patrols that he ordered Phantom detachments to start working with American units straight away. Len's unit, F Squadron, was deployed with 1 and 2 SAS on their operations behind the lines in France. His first operational parachute jump came with Operation *Dunhill*, four weeks after the initial D-Day assault, when five patrols from 2 SAS were dropped into the area between Rennes and Laval in eastern Brittany to report on enemy activity prior to the American breakout from their Normandy battlefront. In the end, however, they were on the ground for only a few days before the Americans under General Patton, as Len puts it, 'overran the area'. The British soldiers were quickly airlifted out and awarded seven days' leave, which was immediately cancelled as they began preparing for their next foray into occupied France.

The men with whom Len jumped from the Stirling into the Vosges mountains in eastern France on Operation *Loyton* in August 1944 were part of a much larger force that arrived in a series of drops over a period of two weeks. In all, the group would eventually total over 100 men. The first to arrive were 14 men of an advance party whose job it was to find a suitable drop zone to accommodate the larger parties that were waiting back in England. The advance party also had to foster relations with the local resistance, the Maquis, some of whom were operating as guerrilla fighters in the area. The SAS team brought with them weapons intended as bribes to secure the Maquis's cooperation, for the situation in eastern France was complicated by the bitter rivalry and divided loyalties of the various resistance groups. There were around two dozen different factions involved with the French underground movement, one of the strongest of which drew on elements from the French Communist Party whose hardliners were committed to fighting fascists, whether they were German invaders or French nationalists. The subversive atmosphere of cloak-and-dagger clandestine operations in France was intensified by the perfidy and deceit practised by many of those who had a secondary agenda to follow. In the Vosges area, the situation was further complicated by the fact that the region, close to the border between France and Germany, had been part of both countries during the lifetime of many of its inhabitants. The Germans had claimed it in 1871 following the defeat of Napoleon III and the French had taken it back at the end of World War I in 1918. When the Germans returned in 1940, most of the population saw them as invaders, but there were others of German descent who felt quite differently.

Worse still, while other SAS operations to the west had been conducted in the midst of the confused German retreat, in the Vosges area the Germans were preparing to make a stand against Patton, moving reinforcements into the area to bring the American advance to a halt. All that makes it sound as if the area was so teeming with troops that anyone descending by parachute would immediately be spotted by hordes of soldiers on the ground, or that any aircraft flying into the area would easily be heard and seen by the Germans. It should be noted, however, that the distance between Nancy and Strasbourg (which roughly straddle the Vosges region) is about the same as the distance between London and Southampton, about 50 miles (80km). Furthermore, unlike the great swathes of Surrey and Hampshire that separate Southampton from the capital, the countryside in the Vosges is not intensely populated nor criss-crossed by motorways. It is, in fact, an area of hill forests and pastures with small, isolated villages strung out along remote valleys. It is the sort of country where you could hide an entire army in the depths of the woodland, let alone a small force of mobile raiders like the SAS.

The *Loyton* parachute drops, however, were not without incident. The weapons carried by the advance party were spirited away by the Maquis before they could be used as any kind of bargaining tool. There were skirmishes with German patrols prior to the arrival of Lieutenant-Colonel Brian Franks with the last of *Loyton*'s personnel on 30 August, and on that same night a Frenchman, whom the Maquis claimed was an informer but who maintained that he was simply out looking for mushrooms, was caught lurking around the SAS camp. It was decided to hold him prisoner until the colonel arrived. Franks was not best pleased with his reception. The Maquis were making enough noise to allow any German within miles to home in on the forest clearing chosen as their drop zone, and of the parachute-dropped canisters containing their equipment, one that was packed with ammunition exploded on impact. The ensuing fireworks caused enough of a distraction for the French prisoner to snatch a Sten submachine-gun

(SMG) and make a run for it. He was shot dead. Then a horrendous howling was heard from the darkness on the far side of the drop zone, where one of the resistance fighters had managed to open a container and, spotting what he thought was some kind of cheese, had hungrily scoffed a few handfuls. His cheese turned out to be plastic explosive, which contained arsenic. He died shortly afterwards.

Far from allowing the operation to descend into chaos, however, the SAS teams continued to tackle the job at hand. Len, by then Sergeant Owens, was part of a patrol under the command of Lieutenant Peter Johnsen. By scouting the area, setting up observation posts and gathering intelligence, it soon became clear that there were far more German troops moving through the area than anyone had thought. They were able to confirm Maquis reports that up to 5,000 German troops were advancing up a valley just a few miles from the main SAS camp in a forest near the village of Moussey. General Patton's army had halted at Nancy rather than pushing on east to Strasbourg, as they were in danger of outrunning their supply lines. This gave the Germans a breathing space of which they appeared determined to take full advantage by moving in substantial reinforcements, which included an SS Panzer division. SAS sabotage attacks and firefights with enemy patrols, meanwhile, led the Germans to believe that they were dealing with a far larger force in the Vosges countryside, possibly an advance unit of Patton's main army. They began to mount patrols in strength, combing the countryside in search of the elusive raiders.

The activities of the SAS were to be augmented by the arrival of three armed jeeps on 19 September. Each jeep was parachuted in on a special palette designed to act as a kind of shock absorber and minimize the impact to the jeep on landing. The vehicles were partially dismantled – the steering wheel and the fuel tanks, for example, had to be reinstalled by SAS fitters to make the vehicles operational. Of the first three jeeps to be dropped, one landed on target, one landed way off target in a field and one ended up in a tree. It was eventually recovered and two nights later three more jeeps were dropped along with 20 men as reinforcements. Operation *Loyton* had been under way for almost six weeks, but now the SAS was able to change tactics and attack German vehicles on the roads in the area with the formidable firepower of the jeeps' Vickers and Browning machine-guns. They shot up convoys, destroyed several staff cars and on one occasion even ventured into the village of Moussey, coming across an SS unit assembling by the roadside. They drove straight through, blasting the Germans with their machine-guns before disappearing back into the hills.

The Germans realized that the SAS could not be operating without the knowledge of those who lived in the area. They knew that the unit had to be cooperating with the local Maquis and suspected, quite rightly, that the locals were being given things like soap (which was in very short supply in occupied France) by the British in return for fresh food or even as a reward for hiding members of SAS patrols being hunted down by German troops. What the Germans did not know was the precise location of the main SAS base. They decided to find out by asking the villagers of Moussey. All of the men and boys of the village between the ages of 16 and 60 were arrested and taken for 'questioning' at various locations in the area, including the Château de Belval, just a couple of miles outside the village, which now bears a plaque to that effect. Even under the most brutal of torture, none of Moussey's men would talk. They were threatened with execution but still remained silent. Eventually, all 210 of them were transported to concentration camps. Nine months later, when the war was finally over, only 70 of their number returned to Moussey alive. Some of these were so ill, disabled by the deprivation in the camps, that they also died soon after. The valley in which Moussey nestles is still referred to by some as 'The Vale of the Widows'.

By the end of the first week in October, it was decided that Operation *Loyton* should be brought to an end. There was little chance that General Patton would be in a position to relieve the British any time in the immediate future and the operation that had been intended to last just two weeks had now stretched on to ten. Lieutenant-Colonel Franks ordered his men to split up into patrols of three or four men and make their way individually towards the American lines. That meant a journey of around 40 miles (64km) westward towards Nancy through enemy-held territory. The weather, too, was turning against them and the prospect of a forced march, lying up by day and travelling by night through the cold and rain, held little appeal for Len. Nevertheless, he set off with one small group, moving as quickly and as quietly through the countryside as they could, making full use of all available cover, ever alert for German patrols. Every man knew by then what it meant to be captured by the Germans. Hitler's infamous 'Commando order' had been issued in October 1942, demanding that any raiders or saboteurs, whether in uniform or not, even if unarmed or attempting to surrender, should be immediately shot. Some commanders in the field, including Rommel, took the brave decision to ignore the order, but the SS troops who were sweeping the countryside searching for the SAS would gleefully comply with the Führer's command.

Len was separated from Lieutenant Peter Johnsen, his immediate superior, who took with him Privates Peter Bannerman and George Johnston, choosing a slightly different route. His group was ultimately ambushed by a German patrol just a stone's throw from the American lines. All three were hit: Bannerman and Johnston were killed but the lieutenant, with wounds to one arm and one leg, managed to escape. He was one of the lucky ones. In the systematic search the Germans were now conducting, 31 of the Phantom and SAS troops, among them some of Len's closest friends, were captured and tortured by the Germans before being executed. Len is still haunted today by the memory of first hearing about their appalling treatment at the hands of the Germans, knowing that those brave men endured great cruelty and humiliation, fully aware throughout that the best they had to look forward to was the inevitable bullet in the back of the head. The villagers of Moussey buried ten in their churchyard. At the same time, four young women, members of the Special Operations Executive (SOE), were also captured. They were interrogated before being sent to concentration camps. They were given knockout injections and were then burnt alive. One of them, however, regained consciousness as she was about to be bundled into the incinerator. She clawed her guard's face so badly that at the end of the war an unofficial SAS team hunting war criminals was able to identify him from the marks. He was arrested, stood trial and was hanged.

Len joined Lieutenant-Colonel Franks and Major Peter le Power during their escape attempt, making their way through the German lines and arriving on the Americans' front doorstep to looks of utter disbelief. The Americans couldn't believe that such high-ranking officers were operating behind enemy lines. Once safely in friendly territory, they mustered as many of 2 SAS as they could and managed to hitch lifts on various trucks and jeeps heading back in the general direction of the English Channel. From there they intended to join a troop ship for the trip back to England. Len remembers seeing the Mulberry Harbour, the great prefabricated temporary docking facility used to feed supplies in to the D-Day beaches. He should remember it. He had several days to take in every detail because the landing craft that was ferrying his party out to the troop ship hit an underwater obstacle and was stranded there, unable to move. Its passengers spent five days baling out the water in shifts, waiting for a crane ship to arrive to lift them off. By now, as you might imagine, Len's burning desire to join the navy was just about extinguished.

The end of Operation *Loyton* did not spell the end of Len's active service during the war; far from it. In April 1945 he and the fully recovered Lieutenant Johnsen were forging a route into Germany with Lieutenant-Colonel Paddy Mayne, blazing a trail for the 4th Canadian Armoured Division. As a Phantom, Len's job was to relay messages between the mobile units as well as maintaining communication with the Canadians and the War Office back in London.

The 40 jeeps of B and C Squadrons travelled in two columns, packing a powerful punch with their massed arrays of machine-guns, yet they were nonetheless plagued by ambushes. The terrain around the area of their advance near Oldenburg was a maze of narrow roads, streams and canals, making for dangerously slow progress. As the lead four jeeps of B Squadron passed through one crossroads, they came under fire from machine-guns and *Panzerfaust* anti-tank weapons. The rest of B Squadron's jeeps, including the one from which Lenny was now reporting the contact by radio to C Squadron's column, deployed at the crossroads and began pouring covering fire into the enemy positions. The crews of the lead jeeps who had survived the initial onslaught threw themselves into roadside ditches and two managed to crawl back to the crossroads to report that the squadron commander, Major Bond, had been killed.

The Germans, well entrenched in a wood to one side of the road as well as in a small group of farm buildings slightly closer to the crossroads, kept the ambush survivors pinned down in the ditches. It was then that Lenny heard the roar of an approaching jeep. The vehicle shuddered to a halt at the crossroads and Paddy Mayne leapt out from behind the wheel. Len watched as Mayne calmly took in the situation, barked a few orders then sprinted off towards the nearest of the farm buildings. Len and his companion in their jeep, Dave Danger, opened up with their twin Vickers to provide covering fire for Mayne. Although Danger fired short bursts to avoid overheating the Vickers, the machine-gun's thunderous roar deafened Len to the sound of the spent brass shells tinkling to the floor of the jeep, but he could see the .303 rounds hammering into the farm building where the machine-gun nest was sited, gouging out chunks of masonry around the window.

Mayne reached the first of the buildings in seconds and took only a moment to confirm that this one was unoccupied. He then dashed back towards Len at the crossroads, with Len continuing to plaster the building that housed the German ambushers. Grabbing a Bren gun and a clutch of magazines, Mayne then ran back to the empty building. Len watched as he paused under cover at the corner of the structure, checked his weapon and then began moving forward, firing the Bren gun from hip and shoulder into the building where lurked the Germans. While Len and Danger did their best to help keep the Germans' heads down, Mayne pressed on, firing bursts and changing through the Bren's magazines until he had taken the stronghold, having killed or wounded all of those inside. Mayne then signalled for a jeep to come forward and take over this fire position. The next task he set himself, as detailed in chapter 1, was to drive forward along the road, engage the enemy in the woods and rescue the men pinned down in the ditches. Len counted himself privileged to have witnessed Paddy Mayne in action and winning the third bar to his DSO.

Len has a fine display of medals himself, including the Military Medal (MM), a decoration that was awarded to warrant officers, NCOs and lower ranks for distinguished conduct in the field. Len wears his MM and his impressive array of campaign medals for some of those special occasions where old soldiers feel it is appropriate, but he is actually far more proud of his father's medals from World War I, which he generally wears at the same time as a mark of respect.

As far as I am concerned, Len's bravery, his great fortitude and undiminished energy rank far higher than any award that could be bestowed upon him. He is one of my heroes not only because of the things he did during his service in World War II, but also because of the things he has achieved since. He worked hard as a farmer, married a wonderful woman and raised a family, but he never forgot his friends who were left behind in the Vosges mountains.

In early 2003, Len asked the Allied Special Forces Association (ASFA) if they might know how he could get a sizeable piece of coral granite from a quarry near Moussey up to the Phantom Memorial Garden situated within the National Memorial Arboretum in Alrewas, Staffordshire. Members of ASFA Richard Marshall, Scarf Jones and the secretary, Mike Colton, promptly went over to Moussey and organized the shipment of a large granite block that is now in place in the Phantom Memorial Garden. The granite represents the solid resolve of the French resistance not to betray the Phantoms and SAS men. The memorial commemorates those friends of Len who did not return from Moussey:

Sergeant Gerald Donovan Davis
Signalman George Gourlay Johnston
Signalman Peter Bannerman
31 men of 2 SAS Regiment
One British and two French servicewomen
140 men and women of the French resistance

Pete Bannerman, Gerry Davis and George Johnston each have a tree dedicated to them. Plaques have been prepared commemorating the SOE and SAS personnel and 140 rosemary bushes have been planted in a 'P' formation, one for each of the men and boys from Moussey who were killed. Len's late wife, Tess, was a member of SOE and a seat has been placed in the garden in memory of her. The garden was entirely funded by Len, the late Lieutenant Peter Johnsen and other surviving members of Phantom. It was designed and built by Robert, Len's son, with help from all the family and was opened on 14 June 2003 with a memorial service for those who lost their lives in Operation *Loyton*. Sadly, Peter Johnsen passed away a few days before the ceremony.

At the sprightly age of 85, Len is now raising funds to pay for two flagpoles to be erected in honour of the bond between the French people and the Allied armies during the war in eastern France. He has more life in him than a man less than half his age and makes the most of every day, having long since earned the hero's right to live a long and happy life.

Chapter 3

MAJOR MICHAEL 'BRONCO' LANE

We used to joke with 'Bronco' Lane, teasing him mercilessly on the firing range if he had a stoppage with his weapon, as we all did from time to time, that his rifle wasn't jammed, it just wasn't firing because he couldn't reach the trigger. Bronco, you see, had lost significant portions of the fingers on his right hand. Was it cruel to make fun of him? Not at all – Bronco has a robust sense of humour and he was tough enough to take it. He was, and still is, one of the toughest, fittest men I have ever met, serving in the Regiment not only with portions of his fingers missing, but also with no toes. In Bronco's position, any ordinary worker in any ordinary job would have been ushered out of the door and packed off home fully deserving of a proper disability pension. Bronco was no ordinary worker, however. Bronco Lane is something special and the pride he took in everything he did with the Regiment demonstrates that he understood that being in the SAS was far from an ordinary job.

I had first-hand experience of how seriously Bronco took his work when I was teamed with him on a training jaunt in the late 1970s. We were in civilian clothing operating freely somewhere in the East Midlands of the UK, conducting a special exercise designed to test personnel from various units who had been selected for anti-terrorist training in surveillance and covert operations.

Bronco and I were given the task of walking around together in different town centres, visiting pubs and showing our faces in public buildings – all the time posing as terrorists. We were not to act deliberately suspiciously, but our activities were meant to arouse the suspicions of the students on the training course if they were properly observant. Their task was to identify us, then carry out surveillance on us without our knowledge. They then had to send a constant flow of intelligence on our movements and activities back to the operations centre.

Now, Bronco was a very laid-back, low-profile chap who could easily merge into the background or melt into a crowd. I, on the other hand, was quite the opposite. Whenever we entered any premises like pubs or restaurants, Bronco would be his normal quiet self, hardly noticeable, whereas I would be chatting with all and sundry and sharing a joke with anyone who would listen. I wasn't completely crazy. I knew that I was making an exhibition of myself – although no more so than any normal, gregarious sort of bloke like me does every day. My reasoning was that on an active operation nobody would suspect a person who so blatantly drew attention to himself. Poor Bronco winced at my antics and tried hard to dissociate himself from me.

At the end of the exercise, when we returned to base for a debriefing, Bronco ran straight into the ops room and, without waiting for the debriefing to begin, shouted, 'Scholey's mad! I'm never going out with him again!' A few days later, however, Bronco did concede that, 'Your way could work, Pete – but only if you were on your own!' He had obviously been thinking long and hard about how to improve operational effectiveness, both on his own and as part of a team. We certainly weren't best suited to work together on that sort of operation, but if I had to choose someone to stand by my side in a tight spot, a life-or-death situation, Bronco would be right up there at the top of the list. He has proved many times over that he has the courage and determination to overcome any challenge that is laid before him (except, perhaps, covertly touring pubs in the East Midlands with yours truly) and was awarded the MM in 1979 for his bravery while on active service in Northern Ireland.

The green, rolling countryside of Northern Ireland is a patchwork of wide fields bordered by miles of hedgerow and winding country lanes. The hedgerows, roadside ditches and stone walls combine to limit visibility when you are driving along one of the narrow roads. A foot patrol, mobile patrol or vehicle checkpoint on the road could have a severely restricted view of the surrounding terrain and, when stationary, soldiers had to use whatever vantage points there were to allow for good all-round observation. It could often be difficult to see what was coming towards you, a situation that created countless ideal ambush points and also made it easy for any quarry you were pursuing to vanish without trace.

The Regiment was officially deployed in the province in 1976, although it had previously been involved there with 14 Intelligence Company, the primary SAS roles being gathering intelligence and mounting surveillance operations. SAS personnel in Northern Ireland became very familiar with the ditches and hedgerows of the farming country, regularly secreting themselves for days on end in carefully concealed hides to keep watch on the homes of suspected terrorists or to monitor weapons caches that had been discovered buried in the countryside. Rather than risk keeping weapons, ammunition and explosives in their homes, where they would easily be found if the premises were raided by the police or the army, terrorists on both sides of the divide would weatherproof their guns and bombs before burying them out in the countryside. They would then retrieve whatever they needed prior to embarking on an attack. It was close to one such arms cache that an ordinary saloon car pulled off the main road late at night in the spring of 1979.

Although it was dark and the location was beyond the reach of any street lights, the car crept forward along the country lane with its headlights extinguished. It rolled to a halt and three men got out, leaving the driver behind the wheel. Dressed in dark anoraks, the men moved like shadows away from the car. One carried a spade and after a few paces he and one of the others moved ahead while the third man reached inside his coat to withdraw an automatic pistol. The gunman skipped up onto a low stone wall, scanning the darkened fields in the dim moonlight that filtered through a scattering of clouds. The two others walked briskly forward down into a dip, then pushed their way through a roadside hedge. The man with the spade dug into the soft earth, quickly hacking away until he uncovered a layer of black plastic. Together, he and his accomplice lifted a heavy, bulky package from the ground, carrying it through the hedge onto the road. The treasure trove containing the tools of the terrorist's trade was now in the hands of an IRA active service unit.

What the IRA men did not know was that this was not the first time that their arms cache had been unearthed. The hiding place had been discovered by Special Branch several days before, when the signs of recent excavation had been spotted. The weapons had been dug up by an SAS patrol and 'tagged' with a transmitter that sent out an alert the moment they were moved. Before the terrorists had even carried their haul back through the hedge, alarm bells were ringing at a nearby army base. First to respond when the call went out was Bronco Lane, patrolling the area with a partner in an unmarked car. They immediately raced to the scene, the engine screaming as the driver hurtled along the country roads, slamming the car through the gears.

The noise of the approaching car echoed through the still night air. The blaze of the headlights that cut up into the night sky as Bronco's car crested each small rise quickly let the IRA men know that someone was coming. While they couldn't be sure that they had been rumbled, they weren't taking any chances. They quickly loaded the weapons into the boot of their car then piled in, the car's wheels spinning as it took off, heading away from the oncoming vehicle. Just as the lights of Bronco's car had signalled his presence to the IRA gang, so too did their headlights help Bronco to pinpoint their vehicle. He could tell that he and his partner were gaining on their target and he soon spotted the red glow of its tail lights appearing and disappearing as the two cars slithered round corners among the hedgerows. Then the lights vanished completely and, rounding a bend, the SAS men spotted the IRA car sitting idle in the road up ahead, its lights off, its doors wide open, its occupants gone. The driver stood on the brakes and Bronco flung open his door, his Browning 9mm in his hand, leaping out before the vehicle had come to a complete stop.

The driver sent an urgent radio message requesting back-up from the army Quick Reaction Force (QRF), relaying their position. Bronco was already at the IRA car, giving it a cursory check to ensure that it was actually abandoned. He popped his head up above the hedgerow to try to spot the fleeing terrorists and was greeted with a fusillade of bullets. He ducked down, listening to the sound of running feet and the curses of the men stumbling across the muddy field in the dark. Judging that they were more occupied in trying to escape than looking out for him, Bronco picked out a gap in the hedge, squinted through it to try to spot any lurking gunmen and then pushed through, hurling himself to the ground. He could see four shadowy shapes making off across the field and opened fire, squeezing off half a dozen shots before rolling to his feet, charging forward and diving for cover again as a hail of fire from the IRA men sent spurts of mud and tufts of wet grass leaping into the air around him. He knew he was outnumbered and outgunned, but judged that his best course of action was simply to attack. Again he returned fire, emptying his magazine. Slapping another 13-round magazine into the grip of his Browning he sprinted forward, peering into the darkness then pausing to level another few shots at the figures up ahead. A barrage of fire came his way once more and he dived for cover.

Bronco could hear his partner coming up behind him, calling to identify himself. He yelled an acknowledgement then set off again, staying low, moving fast. But this time there was no sign of his elusive quarry. They had almost certainly split up, escaping through the hedgerows and across other fields or into the enveloping darkness of the nearby trees. The only consolation to temper Bronco's disappointment was that they were moving too fast to have taken the arms cache with them. That was still in the car. The job of scouring the area for the fugitives was now down to the army QRF.

Encounters such as the one just described, where quick thinking and lightning reactions are essential, were situations in which Bronco excelled. He was, by then, a highly experienced soldier, having been in the army since he was 16 years old. Bronco was born in south Manchester and enjoyed a fairly stable upbringing until he was eight, at which time his parents divorced. After that, young Bronco's home life fell apart and he went off the rails. He survived mainly on school dinners and made frequent visits to the Juvenile Court for a variety of misdemeanours. At the age of 16, however, he joined the Royal Artillery Junior Leaders, Mill Troop. Two years later he passed the entry course for the 7th Parachute Regiment, Royal Horse Artillery, and served with 1 Battery in Bahrain, attached to the

3rd Battalion, The Parachute Regiment. In 1966, Bronco went to Aden as part of 3 Para Battalion Group.

To understand why British Army forces, including the SAS, were in Aden at all, you need to know a little about the region's history. The port of Aden has been an important trading centre for about 3,000 years and was visited by both Marco Polo and the Arab explorer Ibn Batuta in the 11th and 12th centuries. The ancient natural harbour is protected by the crater of an extinct volcano, Jebel Shamsan, that lies at the end of the curving arm of a peninsula known as Khormaksar. The harbour is one of the largest natural anchorages in the world, with over 40 square miles (104 square km) of sheltered water. It is still very much in use today, with modern container-ship facilities having been built and a major oil refinery at Little Aden on the opposite side of the bay from the peninsula. The port became part of the British Empire in 1838 when one of the ruling sheikhs from the surrounding countryside ceded it to the Crown. Aden quickly grew to become a collection of small towns. Crater, nestling, as you might expect, in the crater of the Jebel Shamsan, is the old port town, having developed near to the harbour facilities that were originally established on the outer leg of the peninsula. On the inner bay are Tawahi at the end of the Khormaksar peninsula and Ma'alla, with Sheikh Othman round on the mainland. Little Aden stands on its own, a smaller peninsula, mirroring Khormaksar as a second arm to the pincer of Aden's anchorage.

The territory inland from the port and stretching along much of the southern coast of the Arabian peninsula became, through a series of agreements with different tribal leaders, the British Protectorate of Aden. The entire territory was roughly the size of England and Wales. One may well ask why the British should bother courting the friendship of sheikhs from far-flung desert tribes living in the mountains of a rather unlovely, inhospitable land strung out along a barren, sun-scorched coastline. Why did they see this area as being of value? The reason, as with almost any property, is its location. The port lies roughly halfway between the Suez Canal in Egypt and Bombay (now Mumbai) in India, making it an important stopping-off point where the old sailing ships could take on water and provisions. With the arrival of steam power, Aden took on extra significance as a coaling station too.

Aden was at first administered by the British East India Company, who sent in a detachment of Marines in 1838 in an attempt to eradicate the pirates preying on the company's ships from bases in the area. From then on, there was a permanent British military presence in the territory. The Royal Navy established a base there and, later, so too did the RAF, building a runway at Khormaksar. In the days before long-distance flights, when aircraft operated with limited range, Khormaksar served as a refuelling and transit point for military flights from the Far East bound to Africa and Europe.

When oil was discovered in Arabia, of course, Aden became even more important. The port became a British colony in 1937, the administrative links with India were finally severed, and British Petroleum (BP) completed the country's first large-scale oil refinery at Little Aden in 1954.

It was around this time that things began to go dramatically wrong for the British in Aden. The trouble could certainly be seen as a legacy of British misrule in the area, and the perception among the Arab population that Britain no longer had the political will to back what military strength she still retained only made things worse. Britain was seen as an ageing, toothless lion, unable to make a stand against the emerging might of Arab nationalism personified by Gamal Abdel Nasser of Egypt during what became known as 'the Suez crisis'.

The Suez Canal had been operating since 1869 and was run by the Suez Canal Company, which had negotiated a 99-year deal with the Egyptians to lease the land through which the canal was cut. Britain and France ultimately jointly owned the Suez Canal and, as the waterway became an ever more important lifeline between Britain and India, British troops were stationed in the vicinity of the canal, an area declared 'neutral' by international treaty, to protect British interests during localized disturbances.

In 1936, a treaty was signed between Britain and Egypt allowing Britain to consolidate its control of the canal zone, but a change in the Egyptian political leadership led to that agreement being rescinded in 1951. When Nasser seized power in Egypt in 1954, he negotiated a withdrawal of British forces from Egypt and Suez. Egypt's arms deals with the Soviet Bloc then led to a deterioration of relations with the Western powers, culminating in

Nasser nationalizing the Suez Canal in 1956. Britain and France responded by invading to regain control of the canal. They did not, however, have the support of America and when the Soviets demanded their withdrawal, they were forced to comply. There could be no Cold War stand-off without America's backing, so they were out of Egypt again within a week.

The impact of the Suez crisis, however, was felt throughout the Middle East. Emboldened by his Soviet-backed triumph, Nasser made inflammatory broadcasts on Radio Cairo calling for Arabs everywhere to rise up and cast off the yoke of colonialism. Lo and behold, Soviet-supplied weaponry began appearing to help the Arab brothers in their cause. Britain coerced the various factions within the Aden Protectorate (offering weapons and cash to win their cooperation) into forming the Federation of South Arabia (FSA) with its own Federal Regular Army (FRA) and armed police force. The FSA was promised full independence for the Protectorate and the colony and that, to ease the transition of power, British forces would remain stationed in Aden until after independence, which was scheduled for 1968. A strong British military presence was important to ensure that none of the rival groups attempted to flex their muscles and take sole control and that no other parties from outside the FSA could think about a military takeover during the shaky handover period. Britain, however, was to renege on its promise to stay, with disastrous consequences.

The Brits in Aden enjoyed a modern colonial lifestyle. Although the oppressive heat and barren countryside left Aden as a far-from-favourite posting, service personnel as well as BP employees and their families could enjoy swimming off beaches protected by shark nets, fishing for leopard ray or shark for those who ventured out in boats, and a sports stadium at Steamer Point. The ex-pats were also far from isolated as there was a great deal of interaction with the local populace. The military bases were required to employ a certain number of Arabs as part of the arrangement with the FSA. Locals brought all manner of goods on to the bases – from fresh fish to shaving soap – to sell to service personnel, and British families shopped in the markets, patronized local bars and restaurants and worked alongside the locals on a daily basis in the port or at the oil refinery. As relations between the British authorities and the FSA became ever more strained, however, the

British having decided to pull out of Aden earlier than promised, the colonials' relaxed lifestyle was to change. In the mountains of the Protectorate, disgruntled Queteibi tribesmen, who had long enjoyed a reputation for being violent and unpredictable, began launching attacks against troops of the FRA. Encouraged by communist propaganda and Nasser's fiery speeches, the tribesmen stepped up their activities when the ruler in Yemen was overthrown in an Egyptian-backed military coup in 1962. Communist insurgents began infiltrating south from Yemen into Aden, supplying weapons to those who now saw themselves as Adeni nationalists. The money and guns from the British had dried up, so the tribesmen turned to the communists.

The Yemenis viewed the colony of Aden and the lands of the FSA that lay between Yemen's southern border and the Gulf of Aden simply as being South Yemen. With their encouragement and support, two rival terrorist groups emerged in Aden, intent on destabilizing the region – the National Liberation Front (NLF) and the Front for the Liberation of Occupied South Yemen (FLOSY). It was these two groups who began fighting the British, the federal authorities and each other in the back streets of Aden. The situation reached crisis point in December 1963 at Khormaksar Civil Airport (the RAF base shared some of its facilities with commercial carriers), as a group of dignitaries waited to board a De Havilland Comet bound for London.

The group included the British High Commissioner of Aden, Sir Kennedy Trevaskis, and a delegation of representatives from the FSA, all heading for a summit on the future of the independent federation. Suddenly, a man appeared near the group in the crowded airport. In his hand he held a grenade. He hurled it at the high commissioner, and Sir Kennedy's assistant, George Henderson, threw himself in front of his boss. The grenade exploded in the middle of the group. Henderson was fatally wounded, dying several days later in hospital. One woman in the group was killed outright and 53 others, including Sir Kennedy, were injured by shrapnel. The British government then formally declared a state of emergency in Aden. Military patrols in urban areas were stepped up and more troops were sent out into the mountains to fight for control of the hinterland. In April 1964, the first elements of the SAS began to arrive in Aden. They were to take on specific tasks in the province, both up-country and in the urban areas.

As a Para, Bronco was a member of an artillery gun group, manning a 105mm field gun. His job was as that of a 'layer', which meant that he had to set the gun up correctly to send its shell off in the right direction at the right trajectory to drop on target. His commander on the gun was Sergeant Eric Gregory, a regimental heavyweight boxer who was a very professional soldier – there was no messing with him. The group were in a position in the line supporting 1 Troop, A Squadron, SAS.

The troop had located an enemy unit heading for a *bait* (Arab for village) and immediately called in an artillery strike on the enemy. Their command to the gun group was 'log tight', meaning quick action was needed. Gregory told Bronco not to rush, but to lay the gun correctly as 'This is for the lads that matter.' Gregory had the greatest respect for the SAS. At the age of 19, he had applied for, and passed, the SAS Selection course. At that time, however, the minimum age for entry into the Regiment was 21, so Gregory was sent back to his unit and told to come back when he was old enough. He never did go back, but continued to hold the Regiment in the highest esteem.

Bronco did as he was told, taking his time to lay the gun correctly. He fired an initial two rounds, intending them for 'adjustment' – the SAS spotter would report back how close they were to the target and Bronco could then reset the gun to hit the target with his next salvo. But there was no need. Bronco did his job so well the first time that his two rounds found their target straight away and the 1 Troop spotter radioed back to confirm that the enemy unit had been destroyed.

It was working with the SAS in Aden that persuaded Bronco to apply to join the Regiment. His battery sergeant-major 'persuaded' him to join the regimental boxing team to harden him up for the SAS Selection course. When the call finally came to go to Hereford for Selection, Bronco was told by the battery sergeant-major that if he came back having failed, he would let down his regiment and his life would not be worth living. This threat was made quite seriously and Bronco obviously took it to heart as he sailed through Selection.

Once he was 'badged', Bronco was posted to 1 Troop, A Squadron, the very outfit and troop that he'd supported with gunfire in Aden. His first operational tour was in the Musandam peninsula in Oman, on a 'search and destroy' operation against communist-backed insurgents during Operation *Storm* in 1970. In all, Bronco completed five operational tours in Oman, rising to become an operations sergeant.

One of these tours, in 1978, proved to be disturbingly eventful. He was part of a four-man 8mm mortar team that was moving across the *jebel* (mountain). The team comprised Bronco, Barry Jackson, Terry Jickells and the Regiment's then second-in-command, Major Henry Lee, a somewhat eccentric character. They were part of a large-scale operation involving two SAS squadrons, A and D, as well as a company of Beluchi soldiers of the Sultan's Armed Forces (SAF) and a company of Firquat. (In Arabic Firquat basically means 'military unit' and these were irregular troops, some former Adoo (Arabic for 'enemy') rebel fighters who had volunteered to serve the sultan and were being trained by the SAS.) Bronco's team set up a mortar position in support of the advancing troops. They found an ideal tactical fire base in a disused corral and set up the mortar. They now had to await the arrival of the mortar bombs, which were to be brought in by helicopter. They knew that they would come under attack from the enemy as soon as the helicopter landed, so they'd have to be very quick to unload it when it arrived.

When the helicopter arrived, however, they found to their dismay that it had brought them a cargo of water-filled jerry cans – but no mortar bombs. The helicopter made a swift exit. Almost immediately, just as expected, they came under intense fire from heavy machine-guns and small arms. The group hugged the ground, using every scrap of cover and returning fire as best they could with their rifles.

The attack went on for some time, with the four men clinging to the earth for protection. During a lull in the firing, the helicopter was able to land again, bringing in the urgently needed mortar bombs. The enemy attack resumed the moment the chopper was on the ground and, once again, it made a rapid exit. The mortar was soon brought into action and the team's retribution was swift and accurate. They dropped their bombs onto the enemy positions, wiping out one fire position after another, even after dark, when they targeted the muzzle flashes of the enemy weapons. The action lasted until 3.00am, when the enemy finally withdrew. Having originally arrived in the position in the early afternoon, the four men were by now thoroughly exhausted, but still could not relax as they had to take turns to stand watch on one-hour stints until first light.

While A Squadron's operational commitments kept Bronco extremely busy, he still managed to fit in a few little diversions. His troop, 1 Troop, was the squadron's Mountain Troop and, partly to keep himself up to scratch in mountaineering techniques, Bronco took part in three major British Army expeditions. The first was to the Axel Highberg in the Canadian Arctic, the second to the Indrasan Kula Kimal in India and the third, in 1975, was to scale a satellite peak to Everest in the Nepalese Himalayas. This was the prelude to a far more ambitious adventure in 1976 – an assault on Everest itself.

Bronco's climbing partner on the Everest expedition, where they were part of a military team of 28, was fellow SAS mountain expert John 'Brummie' Stokes. They had climbed together, professionally and for pleasure, for ten years and were determined to make their expedition the first to put British soldiers on the roof of the world.

Reaching the summit of Mount Everest is the ultimate goal for any mountaineer. The highest mountain in the world, Everest stands at just over 29,000ft (8,848m) and reaching the top poses a number of peculiar problems. The environment presents major medical hazards. The higher you go, the less oxygen there is in the air. At the summit of Mont Blanc in Europe, which stands at 15,774ft (4,808m), there is half the amount of oxygen most of us are used to, and at the top of Everest there is less than a third. Climbing at the highest altitudes, therefore, requires the use of oxygen masks and the carrying of heavy oxygen cylinders. Without this supplementary oxygen, the lungs cannot supply enough oxygen from the air to the blood to keep the muscles and organs functioning properly. The oxygen deprivation can result in the brain and lungs swelling in what is known as a high-altitude oedema and can also cause a thickening of the blood leading to burst blood vessels in the eyes and clots in the legs. At lower altitudes, these effects can be mitigated by acclimatization. Spending time at altitude allows the body to adjust to the strange environment, but at anything over 11,500ft (3,500m) it simply cannot cope. A skier stepping off a chair lift at that sort of elevation would feel no real ill-effects if he was then to start off down the mountain after a few minutes. If he hung around for a few days, however, his fitness levels would deteriorate, the muscles unable to achieve optimum performance. At altitudes above around 18,500ft (5,500m) the effects on the body are more dramatic. Starved of oxygen, the cells that go to make up everything in your body become damaged and if you hang around in that rarefied atmosphere for long enough, you will die.

Of course, it's also terrifyingly cold. The average temperature of dry air reduces by 3.6–5.4°F (2–3°C) for every 1,000ft (300m) you ascend. The temperature at the top of Everest can easily reach -40°F (-40°C). Such a cold environment works to reduce the body's core temperature. Proper protective clothing has to be worn to ward off hypothermia, which is a killer. With the sub-zero temperatures, of course, come unpredictable weather conditions, snow and ice. Traversing a glacier – a slowly moving frozen river of ice – is a very risky business. The glacial ice can be laced with cracks or crevasses concealed beneath snow 'bridges' that collapse when a climber sets foot on one. On 10 April 1976, a member of Bronco's expedition, Terry Thompson, a Royal Marines captain, was killed after falling into a crevasse.

Generally speaking, falling into a crevasse will not kill you. Many crevasses are relatively shallow, but the fall may well leave you injured and unable to climb up the icy walls to escape. Hypothermia will then take over in the extreme cold of the crevasse. The 1976 team, led by Lieutenant-Colonel Tony Streather of The Glosters (The Gloucestershire Regiment), planned their route via the Khumbu Ice Fall, the most dangerous part of the mountain. Notorious for avalanches and crevasses, more climbers have died at Khumbu than anywhere else on Everest. From there they would progress to the South Col, establishing six camps at ever-increasing altitudes en route to the summit. The South Col is a plateau at about 26,200ft (7,939m), beyond which the summit assault team faced the daunting ascent of a ridge to the South Summit at 28,750ft (8,712m). Beyond that lay their ultimate goal. Bronco and Brummie were selected as the first two to make the final assault.

On 14 May, Bronco and Brummie arrived at Camp Six at 27,600ft (8,363m). This was the final camp before the summit, but they were to be trapped there by atrocious weather, unable to leave their tent for 36 hours. By the morning of 16 May, the storm had broken and the two set off around 6.30am. Approaching the South Summit they encountered loose, powdery snow that slowed them up, a trek that they were expecting to take no more than 90 minutes stretching out to six hours. The delay meant that when they reached the South Summit, they had to assess their position. Common sense dictated that they should continue climbing until no later than 2.00pm, at which point they would have to turn back. Otherwise, they might reach the summit but would not make it back to the sanctuary of Camp Six before dark. They left two half-full oxygen bottles near the South Summit for use on their return journey, relying on one full bottle each to get them through the last few hundred feet of the climb.

By the time their self-imposed 2.00pm deadline arrived, Bronco and Brummie had just one hurdle standing between them and the summit. This was a sheer cliff of solid rock 30ft (9m) high. It took them 45 minutes to scale the cliff, at the top of which they faced the slope leading to the summit. A mound of snow ahead of them marked the highest point in the world. There are no words to describe their utter elation at reaching the summit of Mount Everest, but there was little time for celebration. Bronco and Brummie took a few photographs before beginning their long descent. They knew that they would have to move fast to reach Camp Six before dark. In order to speed their progress, Brummie took off his snow goggles to see better. What he saw filled him with dread. A dark bank of cloud was closing in, meaning bad weather was on the way.

More by luck than judgement, the two managed to locate the oxygen bottles they had left near the South Summit but, with a blizzard beginning to blow, they knew that they stood no chance of reaching the sanctuary of the tent at Camp Six before dark. They had no choice but to prepare for a night in the open. Utterly exhausted, they began digging a snow hole in which to spend the night. The likelihood of survival was slim, but both men knew that the hole was their only chance of staying alive. They had no radio to call for help and, even if they could have contacted the team lower down the mountain, no one could reach them until daylight, and then only if the morning brought fair weather. Crawling inside the snow hole, they huddled together to wait out the night and the storm.

As the weather worsened, snow began blowing into their refuge, threatening to bury them alive. They blocked the entrance with their rucksacks. By now Brummie was losing his sight. Removing his goggles had brought on 'snow blindness' and, although he knew that this was probably only a temporary condition, it made it all the more difficult for him to stay awake. If either of them drifted off to sleep, they would never wake up again. They smacked and punched each other to stay awake as the savage cold chilled them to the bone and the wind outside developed into a howling gale. Brummie eventually went completely blind and started having difficulty breathing. At that point Bronco removed one of his gloves to feed Brummie oxygen from his own bottle. In doing so he knew that he was exposing himself to the risk of frostbite and that he would probably lose the fingers of his right hand.

Through sheer determination, the two remained awake throughout the long hours of the night and were eventually discovered at around 9am by a team that had climbed up from Camp Five. The team, originally intent on reaching the summit themselves, now undertook the difficult and dangerous task of leading Bronco and Brummie down to safety. Every step was sheer agony for both of them, and Brummie, unable to see at all, had to rely on his rescuers to guide his boots into every foothold during the descent.

Both Bronco and Brummie lost all of their toes to frostbite, with Bronco ultimately having to have portions of the fingers on his right hand amputated as well. Remarkably, their ordeal didn't put them off climbing at all. They both returned to Everest in later years, including one expedition as part of an SAS team that was struck by tragedy when an avalanche wiped out their camp, causing serious injuries (Brummie suffered a broken neck) and killing Tony Swierzy of G Squadron.

Bronco has also been involved in expeditions to the North and South Poles and gives regular talks on mountaineering and polar exploration. On one of his early lecture tours, shortly after his return from the 1976 Everest climb, Bronco found himself in Glasgow, en route to an engagement in Ayr. One of the 'visual aids' he used during his lectures was a glass jar containing his amputated fingers and toes, carefully preserved. He was carrying the jar in his rucksack when he passed though a particularly rough area of Glasgow and started to worry about something that would surely never be a problem for anyone else. It was not unknown for the odd street fight to erupt in that area of the city and Bronco was wary of being caught anywhere near such a bust-up, knowing that the local constabulary was likely to round up everyone in sight, even innocent bystanders, and throw them into the cells. His great fear was that if he was arrested and searched, the fingers and toes in his rucksack would make the police think that they'd caught a serial killer complete with trophies from his 'victims'.

At one stage, the digits in question were in storage in the medical centre in the camp at Hereford, where I was assisting the medical officer in administering annual injections to the admin staff. Bronco was at home enjoying a few days' leave. As I decided we needed a little diversion, I phoned Bronco and told him he was urgently needed in the medical room. He instantly leapt on his bike and pedalled like fury to the camp. When he arrived, I handed him a pair of clippers and told him his toenails needed trimming. He saw the funny side and we both adjourned to the NAAFI (the Navy, Army and Air Force Institutes, the British armed forces' official trading organization) for a mug of tea.

Bronco now lives in Ledbury and remains very fit and active, having written several books and continuing to give talks about his adventures. He drives as little as possible, preferring to cycle wherever he can, including a twice-weekly visit to Hereford. He remains in close contact with his friend and co-climber Brummie Stokes, who now runs Taste for Adventure, an organization that arranges adventure activities for, among others, under-privileged youngsters.

Bronco may be best known for conquering Everest, but he ranks as one of my all-time heroes not only for his courage and endurance in the mountains, but also for his bravery and dedication as a truly professional soldier.

Chapter 4

WO2 SQUADRON SERGEANT-MAJOR DON 'LOFTY' LARGE

As we lay in our ambush position, the jungle floor beneath us was wet and soft, heavy with the damp smell of decay that had been all around us for days. We had nothing to do but wait for a target to appear on the river below us. Then it started to rain. The four of us exchanged glances as we heard the first rumbles of thunder echoing in the hills. The rain was both a good and a bad thing. At first, the drops were hitting the jungle canopy and the foliage of the old rubber plantation in which we were hiding made a gentle pattering sound. Soon, however, the downpour was crashing into the leaves and churning the surface of the river, creating a constant, unnerving hiss, like the sound from a badly tuned radio. The good thing was that the noise of the rain would mask any din we created when we struggled back along our escape route. On the other hand, the rising water level could also make the swamp through which we had originally come totally impassable. Our route could simply vanish, trapping us between the swamp and any pursuing enemy. For now, though, all we could do was wait.

During the last four days as we had observed the enemy river boats ploughing up and down the waterway laden with men and equipment, we had dutifully reported their movements by radio. Now our job was to hit one vessel, cause as much damage as possible and then pull out fast. We needed at least an hour of daylight in order to put as much distance as we could between us and anyone in pursuit before night fell – you can't make any headway in the jungle after dark. But, unlike the weather, it seemed like the enemy river traffic had dried up. So we waited.

It had been over a week since we had left the old mansion house that was D Squadron Headquarters just outside Kuching, the capital of Sarawak, in western Borneo. We were driven to an airfield where a Twin Pioneer light aircraft waited to take us on to Lundu. There, a chopper had been 'burning and turning' ready to lift us into the jungle right on the border between Sarawak and the Indonesian territory of Kalimantan. Today they are our friends, but back in 1965, under President Sukarno, the Indonesians were most definitely the enemy. (For more on the historical background of the Borneo conflict, see chapter 5.) Our patrol was one of many that had been sent into the jungle to cross into Indonesian Borneo to seek out the forward bases from which the 'Indos' launched their deadly cross-border raids. We had to identify the routes they used for infiltration and to find out how they supplied their jungle camps.

When we had been given our mission briefing, D Squadron had just three weeks left of our Borneo tour before being shipped home to the UK. This would be our last chance to locate the base that was thought to be on the Koemba River. Our approach to the river was through dense jungle in hilly terrain that fell away into swamps closer to the river. The smaller hills were not charted accurately on our maps and the extent of the swamps changed dramatically according to the amount of rainfall. Studying aerial photographs couldn't show you much of the lie of the land because of the jungle canopy, and once you were in among the canopy visibility was down to just a few yards in places because of the density of the vegetation. It was a confusing and frustrating landscape through which to try to navigate, but Kev (Kevin Walsh), Paddy (Colin 'Paddy' Millikin) and I had complete confidence in our patrol leader, Don 'Lofty' Large.

Lofty had been with the Regiment since 1957, and had hacked his way through the jungles of Malaya, hunting down Communist Terrorists (CTs) during the Malayan Emergency. He had 20 years' experience as a professional soldier and commanded a great deal of respect, not least because he was

6ft 6in (1.98m) tall (hence 'Lofty') and had fists like sacks of potatoes. In Oman in 1958 he once lost his temper with a donkey carrying supplies and felled it with a single punch. You rarely saw Lofty lose it like that, though. He was one of the most laid-back men in the British Army and it wasn't because of his physical stature that he had the respect of us all. We looked up to him because he was simply the finest soldier any of us had ever met. It was Lofty's navigation that took us through the hilly jungle towards the Koemba; it was Lofty who led us through the stinking, bug-infested swamps, wading waist-deep through water covered with green algae; it was Lofty who chose our lying-up position (LUP) just a few hundred yards from the elusive Indo base; and it was Lofty to whom we looked now as we waited impatiently for a target vessel to fall into our ambush.

Suddenly it appeared. The noise of the rain had almost drowned out the sound of its engines. Lofty had seen it first – as patrol leader, he had the best vantage point. It was his job to spring the ambush. Within a few seconds we all had a good view of it – a gleaming white 40ft (12.19m) motor launch flying the enemy flag and so many military pennants it almost made you want to stand to attention and salute it. On Lofty's signal, we would break cover, take up our fire positions and let loose. He held out his arm and we gripped our Self-Loading Rifles (SLRs), waiting for his 'thumbs up'. But the signal never came.

'What are we waiting for?' I heard a voice behind me mutter. 'The f***ing *Ark Royal*?'

As the motor launch disappeared round the bend in the river, Lofty squatted down beside us. 'Sorry, lads,' he said, making no pretence at a jungle whisper but speaking up above the sound of the downpour. 'There were women on that boat. Could have been kids as well.'

From Lofty's position, he had been able to see straight in through the glass surrounding the bridge of the motor launch. He had seen a man in a white naval uniform and another, obviously an officer, in army greens. The woman had been standing between them, dry as a bone under cover of the boat's bridge, and had any one of them chosen but to glance in Lofty's direction, they could not have failed to spot him. The line-of-sight distance between them was only about 10 yards (9m). Yet Lofty had stayed stock still, risked being spotted; risked being shot; risked his life because he had the impression that there were other women and children aboard the launch. There was no arguing with his decision. None of us would have wanted to shoot up a boat that had women and kids on board. So it was back to the waiting again.

Far from easing off, the rain grew even heavier. Thunder crashed and lightning lit up the mid-afternoon gloom of the jungle storm. Our time was running out. We were fast approaching the point where we had to choose whether to risk waiting until first light the next day, or whether to head for home without hitting a target. The decision was made for us when the unmistakable chugging sound of a diesel engine came thudding through the sloshing rain. When the boat nosed into view it was a long, wooden, barge-like river boat with a canvas roof that was rolled down at the sides. Lofty gave the 'thumbs up' and had placed three shots on target before I hit my firing position. His first shot took out a soldier who was facing in our direction, his second was for the man next to him and his third felled the soldier next nearest to us, thus eliminating the most immediate threats. We were each to expend 20 rounds on the target. The 7.62mm rounds from our SLRs, the standard British Army issue rifle of the day, were immensely powerful. They could pass through 2ft (0.6m) of timber, so even those soldiers on board the boat who tried to take cover would not have been safe from our shots penetrating the hull. We concentrated our fire on the rear of the boat, trying to disable the rudder, propeller or the engine and by the time Lofty called for us to stop, smoke was billowing out from under the canvas awning and flames flickered deep in the heart of the vessel. It was listing to one side and the engine had stopped, leaving the boat to drift back downstream, slowly sinking.

Kev and Paddy withdrew first, taking up positions to cover me and Lofty. Then we moved as quickly as possible along the route that would take us to the landing zone (LZ) where a chopper would lift us out of the jungle. With a few hiccups along the way, Lofty led us back, our route taking us close to the Indo base. Unlike other patrol leaders, who would march as second man, Lofty always took the lead scout role and led from the front. I was proud that he always wanted me as second man, trusting me to watch his back. The storm may have disguised the sound of the ambush and certainly disguised the noise we made crashing through the forest, but it wouldn't be long before the enemy was on our tail. We had seen numerous enemy tracks on our way in and had identified well-prepared, cleared paths that the Indos had probably used for rapid deployment from their camp, and even come across a few dozen Indonesian troops deep in the jungle. Fortunately, Lofty spotted them long before they even had the chance to realize that we were there. He led us on a long detour round them and was now running through all of the factors in his head, trying to avoid the pitfalls yet keeping us moving to cover as much ground as we could before nightfall.

He knew he could push us hard. He had no doubts about our fitness or energy levels. Having selected the observation post (OP) in the old rubber plantation and established that the Indo base was little more than a stone's throw away, he knew that we were pretty safe there. The Indos, fully aware that none of our patrols had ever found this particular base before, would never expect to find us right in their backyard. Lofty took advantage of that. Instead of following 'Hard Routine' jungle procedure with no hot drinks, no hot food, no talking and no smoking, he encouraged us to relax (within reason) while we observed the river. We smoked, brewed up tea or coffee every couple of hours and had a meal of curry and rice each evening. Instead of the gaunt, half-starved, wasted, ghost-like SAS creatures who normally emerged from a jungle operation, he wanted us to be on top form, strong and with good morale for what could be a difficult retreat to the LZ.

Once again, Lofty was right. By the time we stopped that night, backtracked and laid an ambush on the route we had just covered, we were all still in good shape. The next day, Lofty led us to the LZ, no mean feat in itself given that SAS LZs were deliberately located in areas that were particularly difficult to find, with no streams or regular tracks nearby. That made it less likely that the enemy would stumble across one of the prepared sites by chance. It was like finding one single football-pitch-sized clearing in an area of forest almost the size of the county of Kent, but Lofty got us there. We were back in Kuching before sunset that evening, looking forward to the long trip home. The Indos, on the other hand, were far from relaxed. Now they never quite knew when to expect another attack. Lofty's ambush on the Koemba forced them to commit hundreds of troops to defending their forward positions and eventually they pulled back from the border altogether.

So why does everything that you've just read make Lofty Large a hero? Just because he was exceptionally good at his job, and had mastered the skills of a soldier in a way that any of us would aspire to, doesn't make him that outstanding, does it? Perhaps not, but the fact that Lofty was still putting those skills to good use in Borneo, and beyond, is just one of the amazing things about this incredible man. Lofty, you see, should never have been with us in Borneo. Any betting shop would gladly have given you irresistible odds on Lofty never becoming part of the SAS. They'd have given you pretty good odds on Lofty never being able to make a career in the British Army. In fact, at one point they'd have happily taken your money if you'd offered a bet that young Donald Large would not live to see his 21st birthday.

Lofty had joined the army at the age of 15 in 1946 not because he couldn't get a job or because he was desperate to leave home – he simply wanted to be a soldier. He chose to become a 'band boy', even though he had little interest in playing or learning to play any musical instrument. He was a country boy, used to the outdoors and familiar with handling a firearm, albeit a shotgun, while stalking through the woods and hills around his family home in the Cotswolds. There were no vacancies for band boys in his county regiment, The Glosters, at the time, so he signed on with the Wiltshire Regiment. He then spent five years banging a drum on parade grounds in England and Germany before the Wiltshire Regiment was shipped out to Hong Kong. It was there that he requested a transfer to The Glosters and volunteered to go to Korea.

In between bouts of square- and drum-bashing, Lofty had been fairly well schooled in fieldcraft and weapons handling in the Wiltshire Regiment. Once he joined The Glosters, however, there was a whole new aspect to his training. Along with hundreds of other squaddies, he spent almost a week on a ship bound for Japan where they were re-equipped and put through a combat training course at the battle camp at Mara Hura. A few short weeks later, they were digging in on the frontline in Korea facing battle-hardened Chinese troops.

There had been fighting or civil unrest in Korea for as long as anyone living there could remember. The Japanese had been meddling in the country since before the end of the Russo-Japanese War in 1905, after which they placed the country under Japanese 'protection', and by 1910 they had effectively annexed the whole country, claiming it as a Japanese colony. They introduced a brutal, exploitative regime against which there was great political opposition within Korea as well as armed uprisings. The Japanese regime was rewriting Korean history, attempting to stamp out Korean culture and handing over great swathes of Korean farmland and forests to Japanese business interests. All opposition was ruthlessly crushed.

After World War II, when the Japanese were defeated, the Russians and Americans jointly occupied Korea, dividing their administration zones along the geographical line of the 38th parallel, which cut the country roughly in two. The Americans occupied the southern half, closest to Japan, with the Russians in the north where the country bordered China and, in the north-eastern coastal strip, the Soviet Union. This configuration was intended as a temporary arrangement until Korea could be stabilized under its own independent government. Unfortunately, Cold War politics prevented the establishment of a unified Korea. When the Russians and the Americans withdrew in 1948, they left behind the communist Democratic People's Republic of Korea (DPRK) in the north and the Republic of Korea (RoK) in the south. South Korea established military treaties with the United States and North Korea had military aid from the Soviets.

Each of the two new Korean states promised its people a united Korea and there were regular clashes along the 38th parallel border, culminating in North Korean forces launching an invasion of the south in June 1950. The South Koreans were quickly overwhelmed by the massive onslaught, the north being supremely well equipped with Soviet-supplied tanks and aircraft. South Korea appealed to the United States and the United Nations (UN) for help, but there were no US combat units left in Korea. American forces were dispatched from Japan, but by August the communists had the South Koreans and Americans contained in a small pocket of south-eastern Korea around the city of Pusan. Retaining a foothold on the Korean peninsula allowed the Americans to build up their resources and use their air power to deny the communists a complete takeover of the south. They disrupted the North Korean supply lines and eventually forced the communists to retreat back beyond the 38th parallel. UN forces working with the Americans and the South Koreans included troops from Britain, Canada, Australia, The Philippines, Turkey, The Netherlands, France, New Zealand, Thailand, Ethiopia, Greece, Colombia, Belgium, South Africa, and even Luxembourg.

As the UN drove north into the DPRK, the communist government in China began to worry that the Western powers might not stop at the Chinese border. In any case, they did not want a new pro-American, anti-communist state to be created on their border, so they threw the might of the Chinese People's Volunteer Army (PVA) behind the North Koreans. The UN forces were pushed back south beyond the 38th parallel, but as the battle lines ebbed and flowed across the countryside the UN troops soon reclaimed some territory in the north.

It was into this catastrophic Cold War confrontation that Lofty was inserted in late March 1951. Eventually, after a long series of train and truck journeys, he and 30 other new Glosters were delivered to B Company's positions in the low hills above the Imjin River. The Glosters' job, as part of the 29th Brigade, was to defend the routes through the valleys that the Chinese could use if they launched an offensive south towards the South Korean capital, Seoul. At the time when Lofty arrived, no such offensive was expected. A few days later, on 22 April, that changed. Chinese troops were spotted in the hills on the far north bank of the river and that night there were exchanges of mortar and machine-gun fire, with Chinese patrols probing forward towards the Glosters' positions, lobbing grenades and generally making a nuisance of themselves.

The next day, the battle of Imjin River started in earnest. The Chinese had been making ground during the night and B Company was withdrawn to new positions, clearing the enemy from a rocky hilltop in a short firefight. Lofty had no chance of digging a trench on this new hill as the ground was so hard, but he scraped away what soil there was and prepared his fire position alongside two other men to cover the slope below them. Chinese soldiers were spotted in the surrounding hills and Lofty's section came under sporadic sniper fire throughout the day. They could hear the thunder of artillery and air strikes as distant battles raged to the north and west, but there was nothing close enough to cause them any immediate problems.

That night, Lofty huddled down in his fire position behind the low wall of dirt and rubble they had scraped together and slept. He was rudely awoken sometime before dawn by the crash of a mortar shell falling nearby. Wide awake in an instant, he could hear the whistle of more incoming shells and an eruption of explosions that were soon joined by the agonized screams of the wounded and the clatter of machine-gun fire. Propping himself up behind the protection of the breastwork, through the dust and smoke he could see scores of men scrambling up the hill towards them in the moonlight. They were firing a hail of bullets from their SMGs (submachine-guns) that sent grit and rock splinters spouting into the air all over the hilltop. Although each section of Glosters had its own Bren light machine-gun, individual soldiers were armed with the Lee-Enfield No.4 bolt action rifle. It was an accurate weapon at long range, but could never match the rate of fire of the Chinese troops' automatics. Nevertheless, Lofty and his mates worked the bolts, squeezed the triggers and emptied their ten-round magazines as fast as they could, firing at fleeting targets or the muzzle flashes of enemy weapons. The voices of officers and NCOs calling orders or identifying targets cut through the clamour of the battle, drowned out only when mortar shells exploded nearby, the blast waves squeezing the breath out of the lucky ones, tearing the limbs from the less fortunate. The occasional lull in the mortar barrage brought with it no respite: it simply meant that the enemy assault troops were once again high on the slope, close to overrunning The Glosters.

During the night of 23 April, the men of The Glosters fought off seven major assaults. When dawn came in the Land of the Morning Calm (as Korea was named over 4,000 years ago) the battle raged on. They fought with bayonets and bare hands when the Chinese threatened to overwhelm them and, when the units on their flanks were pushed back, the Glosters were cut off, surrounded on their hilltop by Chinese infantry. Lofty and the others did not know it at the time, but fewer than 800 Glosters had held up the advance of three Chinese divisions totalling around 27,000 men. On the morning of 24 April, however, with ammunition running low, their situation was utterly desperate. All efforts by American and UN forces to break through to the besieged Glosters had failed. The bigger picture, however, was not Lofty's immediate concern. There were now just two of them firing from behind the low wall. Peppered with shrapnel and rock splinters, they were filthy and exhausted. With the morning sunshine cutting through the battle's haze, Lofty flung a hand grenade over the wall, squeezed off a couple of shots at two Chinese sneaking round their flank, then popped his head up to pick off anyone below him who had survived the grenade. Suddenly, Lofty's rifle was blasted to pieces in his hands and he was hurled backwards. He had been caught with a burst of machine-gun fire and two rounds had torn into his left shoulder. As he lay on his back, unable to move, the next thing he expected to see was a Chinese gun barrel. But it never came. A mortar bombardment right in front of Lofty's position forced the Chinese back, although the hilltop continued to be raked by machine-gun fire.

Lofty was dragged out of the firing line, his wound was dressed and he soon found that he was able to stand and to walk. In great pain and with the two rounds still inside his shoulder, he joined a party of walking wounded trying to find a way through the Chinese lines to the south. The Glosters were ultimately forced to surrender. They had suffered appalling casualties and B Company had been reduced to just 15 men, but they had held up the Chinese long enough for the UN forces to regroup and halt the Chinese advance. Even had they known this, it would have been little consolation for the men who were taken prisoner, as Lofty's ragged bunch of walking wounded was. They were forced to march north for ten days, with no food at all for the first week, and then only a handful of rice when food did finally arrive. At some point Lofty's wounds were cleaned and re-dressed by Chinese medics, but that was the last medical attention he was to receive for the next two years. His paralyzed left arm caused constant pain that was matched only by the ache from his side where one of the machine-gun bullets had ricocheted off a bone in his shoulder and ploughed downwards, breaking a couple of ribs. The long march was almost intolerable, but Lofty survived. There were many wounded in the column of 200–300 prisoners who did not.

Their final destination was a prison camp just outside the town of Chongsung in North Korea. There were no walls or fences surrounding the camp, just a guard positioned here and there around the perimeter. The prisoners were crowded ten to a room in basic huts and slept on the floor. There was little food and dysentery was rife, as was malaria. In the winter they huddled together under their blankets to keep warm. The Chinese troops fared little better. Some of them froze to death at their guard posts. It was in this camp that Lofty celebrated his 21st birthday.

Lofty lived with the pain in his side until March 1953 when he was operated on in the camp hospital by a Chinese doctor who removed a tracer round from his ribs. In fact, they were 'tidying him up' prior to releasing him as part of a prisoner exchange. By the time he was back in the hands of the British Army, he had regained a little movement in his arm and hand but still had no real control. The doctors told him that had he not been captured by the Chinese he might well have had his arm amputated by the British!

When he arrived back home, Lofty was expected to leave the army. He was offered a discharge on medical grounds but refused. He wanted to remain a soldier. He worked on his fitness and on rehabilitating his arm. It was to take him years before the army eventually declared him fully fit again. In the meantime, he had a stint in The Glosters' regimental police, worked as an instructor and in the quartermaster's stores. He also married Ann, the girl he had met when he stopped over in the UK before leaving for Hong Kong. She had written to him constantly when he was in the prisoner of war (POW) camp, and they became utterly devoted to one another, inseparable except for those times when Lofty was posted overseas. In 1957, you see, having fought his way back to fitness, Lofty volunteered for the SAS.

Lofty wanted to have a crack at real soldiering once again. He went on the SAS Selection course and passed, only to crash his motorbike immediately afterwards. His ankle was badly injured and he spent several weeks trying to put it right before he had to take the course all over again. In fact, his ankle was so swollen and painful on his second course that he had to wear a boot one size too big to fit over the bandages. Not only did he pass Selection twice, but he did so the second time in odd boots.

I first met Lofty shortly after I joined the Regiment. I had been posted to D Squadron's Boat Troop, but was quickly transferred to the Rover Troop where the legendary Lofty Large was the troop sergeant. Having been in

Malaya and on operation in Oman in 1958/59, Lofty had recently returned from a stint as an instructor with 23 SAS, part of the TA. Now he was raring to go, anxious to get back to soldiering again. He didn't have long to wait. Following training exercises in the UK and in Aden, we were shipped out to Borneo. When our tour finished there, we were back in Hereford again before a desert training course in Libya and deployment to Aden.

All in all, I spent some of the wettest and driest days of my life with Lofty. I learned a great deal from him about being a soldier, and also discovered one of his greatest fears – he suffered from vertigo. A fear of heights is a difficult thing when part of your job is to jump out of aeroplanes, but then Lofty never pretended that parachuting was one of his favourite things. Who could blame him? The old 'X-type' parachute that we all first learned to jump with was standard issue in the British Army from World War II right up to the early 1960s. The only trouble with it was that it didn't have a very big canopy – a diameter of just under 24ft (7.3m) – pretty poor compared to the huge sports parachutes that are available today. The theory was that a large canopy would slow the descent of a soldier in combat too much, leaving him liable to drift with the wind and miss his DZ, or leaving him hanging in the air too long, presenting an easy target for any enemy on the ground. In practice, the size of the X-type meant that a little skinny bloke could float down like a leaf on the breeze and barely break a blade of grass when he hit the ground. Your average squaddy laden with kit, on the other hand, would make a far more robust descent. Lofty, tipping the scales at over 17 stone (108kg) before you added on the massive amount of kit we had to jump with and the extra rations he always carried to feed his enormous appetite, dropped out of the sky like a house.

His first ever training jump with full equipment, which included an equipment container strapped to his right leg, was almost his last. Being 6ft 6in (1.98m) tall, Lofty was obliged to nod his head forward to duck under the lip of the aircraft's fuselage door. Nodding his head forward like that, combined with the unbalancing weight of the equipment container, made him perform a beautiful forward roll on exiting the plane. Although he didn't realize it at first, this meant that his legs became entangled in the rigging lines. When he looked in the direction he thought was 'up' to check his canopy, what he actually saw was a white circle with a red cross on it – the roof of the medical team's ambulance that was waiting for him on the ground! He managed to kick one of his legs free and released the equipment container, which was designed to dangle on a cord as the paratrooper descended. This action pulled him half-way vertical – he still had one leg stuck in the rigging and was now heading for a landing flat on his back. Kicking the rigging lines off his entangled leg with his free boot, his feet swung into the vertical just in time to touch the ground. He reckoned it was the best landing he'd ever made.

Lofty's parachute experience goes to show that nobody's perfect – you can't be the best at everything. But I would defy most trainee paratroopers to keep their heads while plummeting earthwards and extricate themselves from that upside-down drop in the way that Lofty did. His clear thinking and calm demeanour, no matter how panicked he may have been feeling inside at times, was an inspiration to those around him. He was the epitome of a professional soldier, with an admirable sense of fair play and compassion. Once when we were in Aden in 1964, we found ourselves stuck on a hilltop, too far from the exchange of fire that we could see to be able to make any real impression except with the Bren gun that I was carrying. Lofty told me to give the group of rebel gunmen that we could see a few bursts, knowing that this would drive them into cover and give our lads, at whom they had been firing, less of a problem. Sure enough, the rebels tucked themselves away behind some rocks. An expert in directing mortar and artillery fire, Lofty then called in a mortar bombardment of the rebels' position among the rocks, bringing in such accurate fire that the rebels took a real pasting. When the smoke cleared, we were amazed to see one of them stumble out into the open, clearly disorientated but otherwise unharmed. I made to get him in the sights of my Bren gun but Lofty, perhaps remembering being on the receiving end of a bombardment in Korea, simply said, 'If he can survive that lot he deserves a break. Let him go.'

About a year after we came back from Aden, Lofty left the troop to spend the rest of his service as an instructor with the reservists in 23 SAS. I never felt the same after he had left. In fact, I transferred to a different troop, joining the free-fall mob in 16 Troop. The SAS had become my home, but without Lofty there it seemed about the right time for a change of room.

Chapter 5

SERGEANT IAIN 'JOCK' THOMSON

Iain 'Jock' Thomson was one of the most dedicated, natural soldiers I have ever met. He was a superb weapons handler and the star of the battalion shooting team when we served together in 2 Para, competing against other British forces teams at the annual shooting event at Bisley. The squad from 2 Para regularly won the team award and Iain generally swept the board in the individual events. Yet there was nothing grand or arrogant about our Jock. He was always willing to help out weaker shots, working with some of the lads on the rifle range when it came time for our annual range classifications. Failing to classify meant the loss of your trade pay, so obviously everyone wanted to pass. Being able to shoot straight, of course, might also save your life and let you enjoy spending your pay.

Jock was a great help to me and Reg 'Brummie' Hassall when we applied for SAS Selection in 1963. Brum, Jock and I had been firm friends and drinking buddies ever since I was first posted to Cyprus with 2 Para in 1959. Jock and Brum were then just 20 and I was 22. We had some riotous times together, sharing the same sense of humour and having the same 'devil-may-care' attitude that goes with the seeming invincibility of youth. Jock left 2 Para to join the SAS about a year before Brum and I did, but he kept in touch with us, telling us how much he loved soldiering with the SAS and passing on a lot of useful tips about how to get through the Selection course when our turn came. Without Jock's advice we would both have found Selection a lot tougher ... and it was tough enough as it was. Only nine out of the 120 candidates on our course passed, but once Brum and I were in we were posted to D Squadron and eventually reunited with Jock. He may have been wearing the beige beret of the SAS instead of the maroon of the Paras (The Parachute Regiment), but apart from that he hadn't changed a bit. A short, stocky, tough Scotsman, Jock had what I call a 'no-neck' physique and a jaw like a cash register. If you hadn't known he had once been a miner, you could probably have guessed. He had, in fact, lost his father in a mining accident, which is as good an incentive as any to get out of that dangerous occupation. Why then opt for the Paras and the SAS? A case of out of the frying pan into the firing line, maybe, but Jock genuinely loved being in the army. From the very first day we met in Cyprus, Jock showed me, by example, how to be a serious soldier ... and how to have a seriously good time. It was in Cyprus that Jock demonstrated a little-known Scottish martial art during one hair-raising night out in Limassol.

The *Ethniki Organosis Kyprion Agoniston* (EOKA; National Organization of Cypriot Fighters) emergency and the fighting between the Greek-Cypriot terrorists, the Turks and the British was all but over by the time I arrived in Cyprus, but it was still not advisable for British service personnel to leave the camp in groups of fewer than four. Cyprus was a British Crown Colony from 1924 up to the time it was granted independence in 1960 and EOKA was a terrorist organization bent on bringing about a Cypriot union with Greece, causing no end of problems for the British administration and the military in much the same way that terrorists did in Northern Ireland. You might say that the EOKA in Cyprus was like the IRA in Ulster, only with sunshine. There were numerous attacks on police stations and military bases as well as on service personnel and their families. Around three-quarters of the Cypriot population were of Greek origin, the rest mainly of Turkish ancestry, although it was not until 1974 that Turkey invaded Cyprus, occupying about a third of the island, ostensibly to protect the Turkish community and dividing Cyprus into northern Turkish- and southern Greek-aligned states. Then, as now, the British maintained extensive military bases in the east between Larnaca and Famagusta and in the west near Limassol.

One night in 1960, Jock, Brum Halsall, Pete 'Lippy' Lipman and I set off for an evening's bar-crawling in Limassol, intending to meet up with a few other mates in the main square. By the end of the night, Jock and I had become separated from the rest and were heading back to camp on our own in a Greek-Cypriot taxi around 2.00am, full of laughs, chat and Bacardi and Coke. After about 15 minutes touring the backstreets we started to realize that we were not taking the most direct route back to camp. The laughing and chatting stopped. The driver ignored us when we challenged him, claiming not to speak any English. Now we were seriously worried that we were being kidnapped to face a fate worse than death at the hands of murderous EOKA terrorists. Somehow we had to get out of the speeding taxi. Jock then had a Caledonian brainwave. Being a proud Scot, it was his habit to wear his kilt when we went out on the town, so he stood up in the back of the cab as best he could, leant forward, lifted his kilt and dropped it over the driver's head. There was a horrified shriek from the taxi driver and he slammed on the brakes. The car slewed round in a skid, then rolled gently over onto its side. We clambered out, unhurt, and as we ran off down the road, Jock yelled to the taxi driver that he should remember that both Scotsmen and Arabs wore skirts but '... the difference is that Arabs wear underpants as well!'

Jock was also wearing his kilt the day he spotted a massive Claymore-like (medieval Scottish) sword in a shop window. He couldn't resist it and bought it there and then, shoving it into his belt and walking out into the street with the tip dragging along the pavement, trailing sparks. It was a brave policeman who stopped him and told him to get it under wraps, despite Jock arguing that the sword was part of his ceremonial dress. That night in the mess, when he was asked what he wanted to eat, he jumped on the table, waving the sword around his head and yelling, 'Civilians!'

Jock's sense of fun was legendary, but aside from the laughs and the good times we shared, Jock took his soldiering very seriously. His skills in the field were second to none and he was to need all of his expertise, his determination and his courage when we were sent into the jungles of Borneo in 1965.

You can't run in a jungle. Forget anything you've seen in the movies – Rambo charging through the jungle in his vest and headband or even Tarzan swinging through the trees. These are things that only happen in Hollywood jungles. There are several different types of jungle, but in none of them can you thunder around like a rugby player or swing on vines like an Olympic gymnast. Jungles are hostile environments through which you must pick your way with great care. In a tropical rainforest, which is what most people imagine when they think of a jungle, the entire area is covered by several layers of canopy formed by the interlocking branches and broad leaves of the trees. At the tops of the tallest trees, the canopy will be over 200ft (60m) high, and below this, smaller trees will spread their branches at various levels down to around 33ft (10m). This blocks out almost all direct sunshine, creating a gloomy half-light on the jungle floor and making undergrowth fairly limited, although the forest floor is still a treacherous maze of tangled roots, fallen leaves and rotting logs. The poor light also combines with webs of vines and lianas, some festooned with razor-sharp spines, and the sheer density of tree growth to reduce visibility to less than 165ft (50m). Tarzan wouldn't be able to swing very far before he smashed into a tree trunk and Rambo would have his bare arms and shoulders ripped to shreds by the lower vegetation, providing he didn't break his ankle on a tree root first.

Below any breaks in the canopy, on the fringes of the forest by the banks of rivers or where land may have been cleared for cultivation, the primary jungle gives way to secondary jungle. With access to sunlight, plants such as grasses, thorny shrubs, ferns and bamboo grow in profusion, creating walls of vegetation through which you can only progress by hacking or slashing with a *panga* or jungle knife. The temperature climbs to over 86°F (30°C) during the day, with strength-sapping humidity levels that leave your clothes constantly soaked with sweat, if they're not already wet through with rain water. After a time, whatever you are wearing will start to rot and disintegrate. Your skin chafes on the damp clothing and your feet rot inside your damp boots. You are under persistent attack from all manner of biting or stinging insects and leeches (another good reason for wearing a shirt with a collar and long sleeves) that inhabit the jungle floor as well as live on the vegetation, although larger jungle animals such as snakes, wild pigs and jungle predators are quite shy and will generally try to avoid you. Progress through a jungle is slow, arduous and exhausting. After about 5.00pm you have to stop completely to make camp before the sun goes down, after which it's pitch black, making any kind of movement completely impossible. Even under ideal daylight conditions, you can't really expect to walk more than about 1,100 yards (1,000m) in an hour.

Now imagine that you are not walking, but dragging yourself arm over arm across the tangle of roots on the forest floor. Imagine that you can't stand because you're in so much pain from a broken leg – not just a simple snapped bone from an unlucky fall, but a thigh shattered by an enemy bullet. Imagine that you are losing blood from a gaping wound that you've had to pack with a field dressing. Then imagine that you are being hunted by the enemy and that capture means torture and almost certain death. Now fire your rifle in the air. You know that this will help them to keep stalking you, hunting you, but you also know that it will help to lead them away from a wounded comrade who is even worse off than yourself. That's what Jock Thomson did, and it's just one of the reasons why he is one of my heroes.

In December 1962, several months before I was accepted into the SAS, it was decided that the Regiment should be sent into Brunei in Borneo where an uprising against the ruling sultan had taken place. All SAS troopers had to attend weekly briefings that gave fairly detailed updates on what was happening in trouble spots around the world, so that we would have a reasonably good knowledge of where we were going and what to expect if we were suddenly shipped out somewhere. By the time we were due to go to Borneo, we'd had lots of 'classroom' time on the situation in Brunei.

Borneo was, and still is, an island divided into four separate states: Sabah (formerly North Borneo) and Sarawak, which were previously under British rule but became independent states as part of the Federation of Malaysia in 1963; Brunei, which was a British protectorate; and the Indonesian province of Kalimantan, which occupies around two-thirds of the island. In the early 1960s, Indonesia's President Sukarno declared his intention of creating a united South-East Asia, seeing himself as the head of an eastern superpower that would be rich in oil, rubber, minerals and other natural resources. Not all of his neighbours, however, were quite so keen to submit to Sukarno's rule and when the idea of the Federation of Malaysia was proposed, Sukarno saw it as a clear threat to his long-term ambitions. In an effort to destabilize those nations intent on combining under the Malaysian banner, he encouraged internal subversion through a group known as the Clandestine Communist Organization (CCO). He also instigated a propaganda campaign aimed at creating fear and mistrust among the population in the region and bringing about the closure of British military bases. Brunei's oil wealth and close links to Britain made the sultan a prime target to be overthrown as Sukarno escalated his campaign from one of subversion to outright insurrection. Although he categorically denied any involvement at the time, Sukarno's armed forces secretly trained and equipped the North Kalimantan National Army (NKNA) which sponsored the revolt in Brunei. It would not have suited Sukarno's plans for him to be seen openly supporting a revolution in a neighbouring state. For him to take his place at the head of the United States of South-East Asia, his image had to be that of a respectable politician and international statesman, not a warmonger.

The Sultan of Brunei requested military assistance from Britain to help quell the rebellion and a detachment comprised of Gurkhas, Queen's Own Highlanders and 42 Royal Marine Commando was dispatched from Singapore. Within a week, the revolution was over, although troops were still rooting out rebels in the Brunei jungles for many months. Sukarno, however, had not yet exhausted his clandestine military options. Sabah and Sarawak had already been infiltrated by Indonesian-backed insurgents, as had Brunei itself. They saw the isolated border police facilities as easy targets and on 12 April 1963 a force of around 35 rebels struck at the police post in the town of Tebedu. Of the few officers on duty at the time, one was killed and two wounded before the rebels looted the local market and fled across the border into Sarawak, whose territory surrounds Brunei. Prior to withdrawing from Tebedu ahead of the arrival of a force of Royal Marines, the rebels scattered propaganda leaflets claiming that the attack was the work of the NKNA, but it was strongly suspected that regular Indonesian soldiers were responsible.

It had been hoped that Sarawak's dense jungle terrain, lying as it does between Brunei and Kalimantan, might help to shield the sultanate from direct attacks. Instead, it gave the Indonesians all the cover they needed to launch incursions across the border into Brunei and the vast jungle proved almost impossible to police. Lieutenant-Colonel John Woodhouse, commanding the SAS squadron sent to Brunei, could clearly see how the experience developed by the Regiment in Malaya in the 1950s could be put to good use in this conflict. Major-General Walter Walker, commander of British Forces Borneo Territories (BFBT), was delighted to have the SAS unit at his disposal, initially believing that, with our helicopters and parachute 'tree-jumping' techniques, we could be used as a mobile strike force. What he didn't know was that none of us was happy about tree-jumping, not even Jock. We had to do at least two ordinary jumps every year to qualify for parachute pay and whenever the RAF instructor turned up to round us up for a day at Shobdon Airport, a few miles from our Hereford base, Jock was always first in the queue to volunteer to jump, he loved it so much. Tree-jumping, however, was another matter. The idea was that when you jumped into the jungle, your parachute would become entangled in the branches of the tallest trees and you would then cut yourself free and abseil down out of the tree. In practice, however, the parachute didn't always become securely entangled, leaving you in a very precarious situation 200ft (61m) up a tree. There were many casualties sustained during tree-jumping escapades, with guys breaking their arms or legs when they hit the branches, so the practice was phased out almost as quickly as it had been dreamt up. Fortunately for us, Lieutenant-Colonel Woodhouse soon persuaded Walker that we would be far more valuable if deployed in a more subtle way. With only around 100 men at his disposal, including headquarters and logistical support, Woodhouse's plan was to send out four-man teams to work with local tribesmen to monitor the known tracks and most likely routes the enemy would use to cross the border. With over 900 miles (1,448km) of border to cover, they would need all the help they could get and they would use the 'hearts and minds' policy that had worked to such great effect in Malaya to win the support of the locals.

In the first instance, the SAS patrol would set up a hide near a village, or *kampong*, and watch the activities in the village for a few days without being seen. Once they had established that there were no Indonesians in the kampong, they would introduce themselves to the headman or elder, showing that they had no hostile intent. In many cases, the SAS unit would contain the first white men the villagers had ever seen, so the soldiers would take care to observe protocol, respect local customs and act with utmost tact and courtesy. They would visit the village each day and retire to their own camp each night, covering their tracks as best they could. By offering gifts and basic medical aid, conversing in a mixture of Malay and sign language, they would befriend the villagers, warning that evil men lived across the mountains. These men would come one day and if they were ever seen, the villagers were encouraged to let the SAS know about it. Eventually, the SAS team would set up camp on the edge of the village, embarking on patrols of the local area that might last several days, looking for evidence of any Indonesian activity in the area. If they found a fresh enemy trail, the team would radio HQ, using Morse transceivers, for support to set up an ambush. This system proved to be an effective tactic. Movement in the jungle was tediously slow for everyone but by using helicopters, an ambush team could be inserted further down the trail to lie in wait for the enemy.

Using the network of kampongs in their 'patch' as their eyes and ears, the SAS teams were able to make it far more difficult for the Indonesians to infiltrate the border area undetected, but on 28 September 1963 the British suffered a major setback when a group of Gurkhas and Border Scouts (locals armed by the SAS and trained by the Gurkhas) was attacked at a post they had established in the village of Long Jawi in Sarawak. The 30 men defending the village had little chance against the force of around 200 Indonesian soldiers and were unable to radio for help due to poor atmospheric conditions. Only two Gurkhas and one Border Scout survived, escaping through the jungle to make a four-day trek to the Gurkha HQ. Gurkha ambush squads were immediately dispatched by helicopter to lie in wait along the Indonesians' anticipated routes of retreat and when their escape craft were discovered on a river bank, the Gurkhas destroyed them, leaving the raiders to face a series of jungle ambushes in which many were killed. More were hunted down in small groups over the following month before they could reach the safety of their own border.

Further raids were mounted by the Indonesians throughout the year, until there came a major turning-point in the campaign in December 1963. A force of more than 120 guerrillas launched an attack against the village of Kalabakan in eastern Sabah, killing eight and wounding 19 members of the Royal Malay Regiment. As the raiders withdrew towards the Kalimantan border, they were ambushed by Gurkhas who killed or captured most of their number. At least 21 of these so-called 'guerrillas' were identified as regular Indonesian marines, confirming the long-held suspicions about Sukarno's direct involvement in the conflict. In January 1964, further evidence, if any were needed, came to light when British troops discovered an enemy camp on the Sabah/Sarawak border. The camp was attacked and seven Indonesians were killed before the others fled into the jungle. Documentation found at the scene provided irrefutable proof of Indonesian Army involvement in recent attacks and when Sukarno was confronted with this evidence, he called a ceasefire, asking for negotiations to end the hostilities.

The ceasefire lasted only a few weeks, however, before the Indonesians abandoned the talks and recommenced military action against the British and Malay forces, making no attempt now to disguise the fact that their regular army, rather than an independent guerrilla force, was involved. By March 1964 they were once again employing their usual hit-and-run tactics, attacking small, vulnerable garrisons before disappearing back over their own border, happy in the knowledge that British forces were forbidden to pursue them into Kalimantan territory. They believed they could launch their attacks from forward bases in Kalimantan and enjoy complete safety once they withdrew back to those bases. Their complacency was about to be shattered.

In the spring of 1964, the SAS began covert cross-border patrols into Indonesian territory in Kalimantan. Their aim was to seek out the Indonesian forward bases, identify routes used by the enemy to approach the border and create detailed maps of both. If compromised by the Indonesians, the SAS patrols knew that they would be on their own. Reinforcements could not be called in when the patrols were operating in enemy territory, as the British government would immediately be accused of invading Indonesia. The patrols wore regular British Army uniforms and carried standard-issue SLR rifles so that, should any of them be killed or captured, the British could claim that they were ordinary soldiers who had become disorientated in the jungle and strayed across the border by accident. Such an excuse would hold little water if the men were identified as being SAS. The reconnaissance patrols were limited to a maximum of three weeks, after which the patrol members would often emerge from the jungle looking like zombies. Their clothes would be in rags, they would be exhausted and half-starved, having survived on rations that provided only about 3,500 calories a day compared to the recommended 5,000 calories – nobody ever put on any weight during a jungle patrol. Good results were obtained, however, allowing British forces to become more pro-active, intercepting the Indonesians as they launched an incursion rather than simply waiting to react to the latest cross-border attack.

As operations intensified, the Indonesians began to move their forward bases back from the immediate border areas. This meant that patrols had to penetrate deeper into enemy territory. Previously limited to infiltrations of only 3 miles (5km), they were now permitted to extend this to 12 miles (20km). There was now no point in attempting to use the 'map-reading error' excuse and the SAS patrols began to use more unconventional weapons, including hunting shotguns and the American Armalite rifle, both ideal for jungle operations. It was around this time, too, that what were known as 'Claret' operations were sanctioned. The object of these sorties was to seek out Indonesian special forces bases and pre-empt any build-up prior to an Indonesian attack, harassing the Indonesians through ambushes and attacks on their supply routes within their own territory. These operations were deemed top secret as, technically, Britain was not at war with Indonesia. The Indonesians, however, were soon on their guard.

This was the situation, then, in February 1965 when Jock, as lead scout, found himself at the head of a five-man patrol just inside the Kalimantan border, tasked with seeking out an Indonesian special forces unit thought to be operating in the area. With the patrol commander, Geordie Lillico, following a short distance behind him, Jock led the group down from a jungle ridge onto a rough, narrow track that wound its way through thick bamboo towards a clearing where an old Indonesian camp had been spotted the day before. It was thought that the camp had been abandoned some six months previously, but as Jock pushed aside a curtain of bamboo across their path, a flicker of movement to his right caught his eye. Raising his head after ducking under the bamboo, he spotted an Indonesian soldier less than 20ft (6m) away. The soldier opened fire, hitting Jock in the upper thigh and knocking him off the track. Jock let out a few bursts from his Armalite as he went down and landed in the bamboo just a few feet away from another Indonesian. As the enemy soldier moved to bring his weapon to bear, Jock shot him.

Meanwhile, Geordie Lillico, who had rushed forward immediately on hearing the gunfire, had also been hit. He had taken a bullet in the hip that had blown a big hole in his back as it exited. Geordie collapsed on the track. He couldn't move his legs, but he could still use his rifle and returned the enemy fire. Jock hopped over in Geordie's direction to join in the firefight but Geordie, having seen Jock apparently on his feet, yelled at him to make his way back to the rest of the patrol. He didn't realize that Jock's femur had been smashed and that Jock was little better off than himself. If they stayed together, however, each of them knew that they were both going to be found and killed. Jock reluctantly did as he was told and crawled away.

The remainder of the patrol, unable to see exactly what was going on, decided that rather than charge forward into what appeared to be a well-prepared Indonesian ambush, they would follow the standard 'shoot-and-scoot' policy and withdraw to a pre-designated rendezvous (RV) point. They knew that they were certainly outgunned, the Indonesians operating in far larger numbers than the SAS, but fired their weapons in the air, making plenty of noise to give the enemy the impression that there were dozens of British troops somewhere on the ridge. Hopefully, this might persuade the enemy fighters to keep their heads down in their ambush position instead of venturing out to hunt down their prey. Had Geordie and Jock not been wounded, that might have bought them enough time to get away.

By now Jock was beginning to realize just how seriously he had been wounded. There was no way he could get to his feet, or use his wounded leg, so he dragged himself back up the track to the ridge where he fired several bursts from his weapon in the general direction of the enemy fighters, hoping either to lead them away from Lillico or to persuade them to withdraw altogether as British reinforcements were arriving. He continued to fire two rounds every 15 minutes, the standard recognition signal for any search party out looking for him to home in on. This also, of course, meant giving away his position to any Indonesians close enough to identify where the shots were coming from. He was losing a lot of blood, so applied a tourniquet to his thigh and bandaged the wound as best he could with a field dressing. Using a tourniquet, however, is a dangerous procedure and it must be released from time to time to prevent gangrene, among other complications. Then he had no choice but to continue towards the border, clawing his way hand-over-hand along the fetid jungle floor. Every few minutes, every few feet, he had to stop and partly unwind the tourniquet. He injected himself with morphine to help him cope with the excruciating pain and during one short break even managed to write a brief report of the engagement on part of his blood-stained map. The maps we used in Borneo had large areas where the grid squares had been left blank, signifying only that no accurate survey of that part of the jungle had been completed. In one of the blank sections of grid Jock wrote: 'As far as I could see there was only a patrol. They heard us coming through the bamboo. I killed their leading scout. Just in case I don't make it. They had a tiger flash. Jock.'

This was potentially important information, Jock's observations suggesting that the Indonesians might be sending out patrols similar in size to our own, possibly even to look for us. Certainly the 'tiger flash' shoulder patch Jock saw them wearing suggested that this was an Indonesian special forces patrol. Naturally, all the time, Jock was wondering about Geordie. The gunfire had petered out about ten minutes after the initial contact. That either meant that the Indonesians had backed off, as was normal in jungle skirmishes, or that Geordie had been captured or killed.

As darkness fell, Jock slumped in a muddy hollow to wait out the night. He drifted in and out of consciousness until, at first light, he forced himself to start moving again. His painful progress saw him cover about 0.6 miles (1km) during the course of the day, about half the distance to the Gurkha border post for which he was heading. As he lay in a stream bed around 6.00pm, contemplating another night out in the open, he was found by a rescue party.

When Jock and Geordie had failed to make the rendezvous, the rest of his patrol, knowing that they stood little chance of finding them on their own and every chance of walking into another ambush, had moved quickly back to the Gurkha post, collected reinforcements and immediately formed a search party. At the time I was out with another patrol, led by Lofty Large, so the first I heard that Jock had been hit was when we stepped off the helicopter, having just been lifted out of the jungle. Major Woodiwiss, our squadron commander, was there to meet us and told us what had happened. We still had a full day's rations, the chopper was still 'burning and turning' and Lofty immediately volunteered us to go back into the jungle and help the search teams. We were all up for it, but the major said the situation was under control and we were sent off for debriefing. In fact, by then Jock had already been found. His own patrol, with the help of their Gurkha back-up, had heard his two-shot recognition signal and zeroed in on him. Ginge Tyler (see Chapter 7) was part of Jock's patrol and was the one who tended to his wounds in the stream bed. He later recalled:

> The maggots in the wound were not a pleasant sight, but I knew they were cleaning the wound. I then administered morphine and penicillin and strapped his legs to his Armalite as the injured one was twisted and could not be manipulated.
>
> I then put him in the most comfortable position (so he said), gave him a cup of tea and then a chopper came overhead and tried to drop the winch and stretcher. The trees were too tall – the stretcher was within 10 feet and we could do nothing about it.

As it was getting dark, the chopper had to return to base. Ginge detailed four Gurkhas of roughly the same height to carry Jock's stretcher, reasoning that four of the same size could take a corner each and keep Jock level and as comfortable as possible. Conditions were as slippery and treacherous as anywhere else in the jungle and the four sure-footed Gurkhas were the best bet to get Jock out without causing him any further injury. They made for an RV where there were shorter trees and Ginge tended to Jock through the night until another helicopter arrived in the morning to take them both to Kuching hospital. When they were there, Ginge was told that another SAS soldier had been brought in. It was Geordie. He had taken morphine and passed out in a clump of bamboo after the firefight, then, although unable to walk, managed to evade the Indonesian troops and drag himself 440 yards (400m) up the ridge. He eventually used a search and rescue beacon to signal a helicopter (having let several flights pass by because he knew the enemy was too close), which winched him aboard.

Sergeant Lillico was awarded the MM for his actions that day and Jock was mentioned in dispatches. This was by no means the end of Jock's career with the Regiment, though. I didn't get the chance to visit him in the hospital in Kuching as we were kept pretty busy between patrols. There was no time for hospital visits, so the next time I saw Jock was when we were all back in the UK. I went to see him in hospital the first chance I got. The surgeons had done a wonderful job on his leg, but he was hating every second of his time as an invalid. Jock simply wasn't the type to be content with loafing around all day waiting to get better.

No one was surprised, then, when he came hobbling into the base in Hereford on two walking sticks. It was only nine or ten months since he had been shot in the jungle and sustained the wounds that would probably have finished off a lesser man, but here he was, upright, mobile and demanding to know who was coming out on the town with him for a booze-up! It wasn't long before he discarded the sticks altogether and he worked with his usual determination to get himself fully fit again. Unfortunately, despite the reconstructive surgery, he suffered permanent damage to his wounded leg, which ended up marginally shorter than his good leg, and even Jock eventually had to admit that he'd never be operational with a Sabre Squadron (operational fighting squadron) again. He was adamant, though, that this wouldn't be the end of his career with the SAS. It was quite unusual for anyone to transfer from a Sabre Squadron to the SAS signals unit, but Jock taught himself all there was to know about radios and the communications networks on which we relied, becoming as skilled in the technical aspects of signalling as he was with the weapons and equipment we used in the field. When we went out to the Middle East, Jock came too, setting up radio relay stations and doing every bit as proficient and reliable a job with the signals boys as he had done when on operations.

Jock even went back to parachuting again after arguing relentlessly that he was fit enough to jump. The jump master used to joke that he'd try to land

Jock by a hole in the drop zone to make up for his short leg. Eventually, Jock returned to The Parachute Regiment, from where we had both come, then had a stint with a Scottish regiment and served as an instructor with a TA light infantry unit before flying out to Beirut to work as a security consultant. He worked with both the Polish and the Americans in Beirut, receiving the *Zloty Krzyz Zaslugi* (the Gold Cross of Honour) from the Polish government in 1985 for his distinguished service with them, and a similar award from the Americans.

Yet if this short appraisal of Jock's career should make him appear to be a completely carefree adventurer, it should also be remembered that, like most of us 'lifers', he was married and had a family life at home. Even battle-hardened veterans like Jock need to feel the comfort of knowing, when crouched in a shell-hole thousands of miles from home with bullets zipping over your head, that there is someone at home waiting, hoping, praying that you will come back unharmed. Jock's compassionate nature and generosity extended even beyond his own family. He 'sponsored' a young girl in West Africa, donating a little from his earnings each month to help pay for her schooling and to try to help give her a good start in life. This may not sound like much, but Jock's attitude was that if everyone like him who could afford to do so gave just a little, we would all be giving a whole lot to help those less fortunate than ourselves.

Sadly, Jock died in 2004. He is sorely missed by all who knew him and will forever remain one of my greatest heroes.

Chapter 6

WO2 SQUADRON SERGEANT-MAJOR KEVIN WALSH

The sun struggled to penetrate the dense jungle canopy, creating a gloomy half-light, eerie and unsettling for those unused to such conditions but familiar surroundings to the men of the D Squadron patrol, who lay under the cover of fallen timbers or crouched at the foot of the massive Shorea hardwood trees. In the few places where the sun's rays burst through the foliage, beaming down towards the forest floor, the ever-present jungle dampness was transformed into a steamy mist, drifting lazily up through the shafts of light.

Kevin Walsh stared intently through the drooping leaves and creepers, looking past the great tree trunks, slowly scanning the sector of forest in front of him, alert for any sign of movement, any hint of a form, shape or shadow flitting through his limited field of vision. Like the others, he had 'tuned out' the constant rustling of the foliage, the sounds of the insects and distant animal calls. He had no interest in the background noise, but any unusual sounds – a twig breaking underfoot or the distinctly unnatural click of a weapon being cocked – would reach his ears like a bugle call. Like the rest of the patrol, he was now a veteran of the campaign in Borneo. He knew the enemy Indos were up ahead and exchanged the occasional glance with the others, although they all remained totally silent.

Suddenly a thunderous crash split the air, flooding the surrounding hills with the boom of a mighty explosion. Then the unmistakable howl of a second incoming artillery round heralded another massive blast, then another and another. The high-explosive shells smashed through the upper canopy, sending great eruptions of composted earth, wood fragments and other debris from the forest floor shooting skywards. Where they detonated on contact with the trunks or thicker limbs of the hardwood trees, the shells sent wood splinters as lethal as any shrapnel hurtling through the air, slicing through lesser foliage and embedding themselves in tree trunks, roots or anything solid enough to stop them. Kevin scrabbled to bury himself deeper in cover as shrapnel and shards of wood buzzed past him like deadly insects. Huge branches came crashing down and among the explosions he could hear the screeching of trees being torn apart.

But this wasn't meant to be happening – not to them. It was the Indos who were now meant to be engulfed in this hell. The barrage was meant for them. Kevin didn't look up, didn't dare risk a glance at the patrol's radio man, but he knew he would now be frantically tapping out a message in Morse to have the barrage lifted. If the gunners didn't let up quickly, the patrol was going to be torn to pieces.

Then, just as suddenly as it started, the barrage stopped. The echoes from the explosions rolled around the hills, then faded away. Falling debris from damaged trees was still tumbling down as Kevin popped his head out to take a look. The others were doing the same, checking that everyone was okay. By some miracle, no one was hurt. They rose as one and moved out as fast as they could. Someone had cocked up big time, but at that moment no one cared about apportioning blame. They were all just glad to be alive and heading for their helicopter rendezvous. They would all be back at base before nightfall.

Poor old Kevin didn't have much luck in the jungle. Beginning with his very first experience with the Regiment in the tropics, it seemed like the rainforests had it in for him. Kevin was a fine soldier, one of the best, and went through Selection on the course before mine, but then suffered a slight delay before joining his squadron. He had been sent out to the Far East to finish his Continuation Training on a jungle exercise before going to

Borneo. Towards the end of the exercise, he and his squad were clearing vegetation from the jungle floor to create a helicopter LZ. They were using the *parang*, a kind of machete knife with a blade that is over a foot long. The blade is curved to deliver the maximum cutting force from its extremely sharp edge when used for chopping away anything from light undergrowth and bamboo to small trees. It is heavy enough even to be used like an axe for cutting down really big trees. Different parts of the blade, in the hands of an expert, can be used for skinning game or even carving. Unfortunately, Kevin was not yet an expert. While taking a huge swipe at a large branch, he got the angle of attack wrong and quickly found that he had his stance all wrong, too. The parang glanced off the branch and buried itself in his leg. I was not, of course, there at the time but I don't have to try very hard to hear exactly what he said in that instant after the blade sliced through his flesh and just before the real pain hit home. It would be unprintable.

Kevin was hospitalized and spent some time recovering from the wound, but fought his way back to fitness in time to join D Squadron in Borneo. His luck in the jungle, however, was not to change. Kevin was part of the Geordie Lillicoe patrol that was ambushed by the Indonesians. Unlike Geordie Lillicoe and Jock Thompson, Kevin was not in the line of fire and was not wounded – but he suffered the agony of guilt at having to follow Standard Operating Procedures (SOPs) and withdraw from the ambush to the predesignated RV, not knowing whether the two lead members of the patrol were alive or dead. No one ever wants to be in the position of having to leave friends behind, but it wasn't until Jock and Geordie failed to make the rendezvous that Kevin and the rest of the patrol knew for certain that something had happened to them. When they went out later with a search party, Kevin was the one who found Jock, badly wounded, lying in a stream bed. They couldn't get Jock out by helicopter that night, but Kevin was the one who held him all night, keeping him warm, helping the medic Ginge Tyler to keep him alive until the casevac chopper could reach them at first light.

By the time I first met Kevin in 1965, when he was posted to 18 Troop and joined the patrol that consisted of me, Paddy Millikin and patrol commander Lofty Large, Kevin was regarded as something of a Jungle Jonah. Would you want to set off into an extremely hostile environment with someone who was known to have almost chopped off his own leg, was ambushed on his first patrol and was subsequently nearly blown to bits by our own artillery? You can understand that we were slightly wary that he might be some kind of jinx. Little did I know then what a good friend he was to become.

It turned out that we had quite a lot in common. Like me, Kevin had come to the Regiment from the Paras, having served with Support Company, 1st Battalion, The Parachute Regiment. Like me, he had also seen active service against the EOKA terrorists in Cyprus and like me, he had a sense of humour that was not always appreciated by our esteemed officers. During one classroom theory session, an officer had put it to him that while being pursued by a superior enemy force, Kevin had fallen and broken his leg. The officer proposed the hypothetical situation that the patrol was in a bad way, short of food and ammo, and would not be able to make their escape while carrying the burden of a lame trooper. He suggested that he would leave Kevin with enough food and water for 48 hours and two rounds for his rifle and asked him what he would do. Without hesitation, Kevin replied, 'As you walked away, Sir, I'd put both rounds right between your f***ing shoulder blades!'

Having Kevin as part of our patrol turned out to be a real boon, but he was not the most impressive of soldiers at first sight. He was just over 5ft (1.5m) of bull-strong Yorkshireman with a face like a crumpled dishcloth (he was nicknamed 'the airborne wart') and a voice that sounded like a frog in a biscuit tin gargling with pebbles. Once, while back home in Hereford between ops, my wife Lyn and I went to the cinema to see *Snow White* – not really the kind of guts-and-glory action film you might expect an SAS soldier to want to see, but sometimes you need a complete break from all that. When one of Snow White's dwarves, 'Grumpy', appeared on the screen, I nudged Lyn and said in a voice that was a little too loud, 'He's just like Kevin!' The frog voice rumbled out of the darkness from somewhere behind me, 'Shut it, Scholey...' Kevin was there, too, and, from the sniggering that then erupted all over the cinema, it was obvious that most of the audience was composed of members of Her Majesty's elite fighting force, all out for the evening to watch a Disney movie.

In Borneo, Kevin soon proved his mettle on countless operational patrols, but we never got over the fact that the jungle seemed to be out to get him. He was with us when we penetrated deep into Indonesian territory to find the Indos' Koemba River supply route, the operation that is described in detail in chapter 4. The enemy believed the jungle would be impenetrable due to the flooding of the swamps caused by the monsoon rains. They thought that they were safe to use the river to transport men and supplies to their positions without fear of being detected or ambushed. They were almost right. Wading through swamps and crossing swollen rivers is dangerous, exhausting work. Even when we took to the higher ground to try to avoid the swamps, we had to cross hill streams that had turned into raging torrents.

Crossing one such stream, a parade-ground punishment may well have saved Kevin's bacon. How many times have you seen an archetypal sergeant-major on TV bellowing at a raw recruit, 'You 'orrible little man. Down! Twenty press-ups! Now!'? We hadn't ventured very far into Indonesian territory when we had to cross a fast-flowing stream that was about 18in (46cm) deep and about 6ft (1.8m) wide. Lofty leapt it easily. Paddy and I followed suit but Kevin, bringing up the rear, made a complete hash of it. Lofty and I had moved well forward from the stream by the time we realized that the others were no longer following on. When we returned to the stream, we found Paddy weak with laughter. Beyond him was Kevin, his boots tangled in a tree root just below the surface and the rest of him stretched flat out across the stream. He hadn't made it. Not only that, his feet were so entangled that he couldn't move and was doing press ups in the slimy mud to push his face out of the water so that he could breathe.

After a long, arduous journey we finally reached the Koemba River, the first patrol to have done so, and were able to send back information detailing all of the enemy's river traffic. Before withdrawing, we also managed to destroy one of the enemy's supply launches. We watched the traffic for some time before deciding which boat to attack. Eventually one was chosen but, before we could fire on it, Lofty stopped us. He'd spotted a woman with a high-ranking officer on the deck of this particular launch and thought there might also be children aboard. We allowed it to pass unharmed. We later learned that the first launch had been carrying Colonel Mordano, one of the enemy's top brass. Twelve years after that ambush, the then brigadier of the Regiment, General John Watts, was walking the corridors of power in Whitehall when he met Colonel Mordano, by then a politician in the Indonesian government. During their conversation, they talked about the Regiment's operations in Borneo and the incident on the Koemba cropped up. Colonel Mordano mentioned the ambush that had sunk the launch behind his. When told that two members of the patrol involved were still serving in the Regiment, he asked if he could meet them.

Kevin and I were summoned to the office of the then commanding officer (CO), Colonel Wilkes. We were instructed to dress smartly in blazers as we would be going to London to meet Mordano. On the appointed day, we were flown in the CO's helicopter, accompanied by him, to SAS Group HQ in London where we introduced to Colonel Mordano. He greeted us warmly and congratulated us on a brilliant tactical operation. He was about the same height as Kevin and seemed quite a cheerful sort. His last words to us, having chatted for some time, were 'Thank you for letting me live.'

As we walked out of the office, Kevin wrung his hands in a strangling motion and said to the brigadier in a loud voice, 'Can we finish him off now, Sir?' He took one look at us and snapped, 'Get out of here now!' But he did have a smile on his face.

On our return to the UK from Borneo, the squadron was put on alert for a quick move to Aden. The codeword was 'Free Beer'. Wherever we were when we received the message, we all had to return to base immediately and prepare for departure. Within a couple of hours of the codeword being sent, we would be on an RAF aircraft en route to Aden, where we were to be deployed against the 'Red Wolves of Radfan', as the communist-backed hill fighters had been dubbed by the press. It was supposed to be a highly secret move. We were all in operational gear, with no obvious signs or badges that would identify us as SAS, ready to move immediately into enemy-held territory in the mountains. On landing in Aden, the squadron was led to the arrivals lounge at Khormaksar. Having been told time and time again that our deployment was a sensitive issue to be kept totally secret, you can imagine our surprise at being met by an HQ captain and his aides in 'full Monty' SAS uniforms – beige berets, winged daggers, the lot. To cap it all a loud greeting boomed out over the tannoy – 'Welcome to the SAS!' Kevin's response was, 'So much for top secret. I bet we've even got a welcome card from the Red Wolves.'

Kevin had an eventful tour in Aden. He was sent up-country with the troop officer to a village where they were to act as liaison reps. He thought this was quite a cushy job, but it was a strange one for Kevin. Being nice to the locals while in the company of an officer could never be described as something at which he would excel. He was no diplomat, after all. He had, however, been on a language course and could speak Arabic, the main reason why he was sent. Everything seemed to be going well. The mountain village was hot and dusty, but still cooler than being down in Aden town, and strolling along the street in the sunshine certainly beat humping a full load of kit up a mountain track. Then it all went wrong. The crack of a rifle discharge was followed by the sound of a round smacking into the mud wall of the building they were passing. Kev and the officer dived for cover as more rounds bit into the dusty path where they had been standing. Not all of the villagers, it seemed, were pleased to see them. They were pinned down under heavy fire for 15 long minutes until the volleys of rifle fire from the distant hillside and not-so-distant rooftops eventually subsided. Kevin was glad to abandon his 'cushy' job and spend the rest of his tour in Aden within the bosom of 18 Troop.

I got to know Kevin quite well during our time together in D Squadron, and when we were back in the UK between jobs, before either of us was married, he used to come home with me to Brighton on our weekends off. Sadly, those days when we could let our hair down without a care never lasted as long as we would have liked. As if growing up and starting families didn't bring enough pressures of its own, the Regiment was fast becoming busier than ever. When we were not on operations, there were constant rounds of courses and refresher training. One of these courses was the annual escape and evasion exercise. This involved being parachuted into 'enemy' territory, evading the hunter forces, resisting interrogation if captured and making every effort to escape. It was a very important part of our training and was run very professionally and realistically. On one occasion, we were dropped into the Pyrenees mountains on the French/Spanish border, and had to evade capture by the French Paras.

Eventually, Kevin and I were both run to ground, captured and escorted to the interrogation centre, where we were immediately stripped down to our underpants and made to stand facing a wall in an old, disused barn. We stood at arms' length from the wall, with our arms outstretched, leaning forwards so that we balanced with our hands against the brickwork. Hoods covered our heads so that we could see nothing. We were left standing there, shivering, for hours on end with nothing to eat or drink. Occasionally we were taken and interrogated by a British unit called the Joint Services Interrogation Unit (JSIU), highly skilled soldiers of the Intelligence Corps. They were very experienced interrogators whose methods ranged from the soft, persuasive, almost friendly approach to outright aggression.

Having got nothing out of Kevin using the aggressive treatment, they took him into a cold, bare room containing only a small table and one chair. The interrogator was a sergeant-major of the Intelligence Corps. He sat behind the table while Kevin was left standing about a foot in front of it. The guards waited just outside the locked door.

The interrogation started with about ten minutes of soft talking; no information given. Kevin stood there looking knackered and ill, just as we had been taught as a delaying ploy on our SAS 'resistance to interrogation' training (not too much acting required). Knowing that Kevin had had nothing to eat or drink for hours, the interrogator thought he could break him. He took a large bar of chocolate out of the table drawer, snapped a piece off and asked Kevin if he would like it. Kev just gave the reply we'd been instructed to give, 'I'm sorry, Sir, I cannot answer that question.' The officer put the piece of chocolate into his own mouth and made a show of savouring the taste. With his mouth full, he said to Kevin, 'Just tell me your regiment, and you can have some.'

Still no response from Kevin.

The interrogator continued to break off one piece of chocolate after another, slowly chewing as he chatted away. To Kevin it seemed like the entire room was now filled with the scent of chocolate. Parched though he was, he could feel himself salivating; the smell of the chocolate was so strong that he could almost taste the stuff. The interrogator continued to chat casually, slowly trying to persuade Kevin that talking to him really was his best option. Leaving the rest of the chocolate on the table, he rose to stroll around the room, teasing Kevin as he burbled on through a mouthful of chocolate. Then, just for a moment, he turned his back on Kevin and the table. Big mistake! Kevin lunged at the table and snatched up the chocolate. By the time the interrogator realized what was happening, Kevin had the remains of the chocolate in both hands and was stuffing it into his mouth as fast as he could, drooling down his chin with a big smirk on his face.

The interrogator stood stock still, spluttering with shock. Then he completely lost all control and shouted, 'Guards! Take this man away!' Kevin had actually broken the interrogator.

It was easy to underestimate Kevin. He gave the impression of being a really grumpy old sod, but it was difficult not to laugh when he was around. His appearance, combined with a deep Yorkshire drawl, sardonic sense of humour and straight-from-the-shoulder attitude made him a great morale booster. Yet, Kevin's appearance and demeanour belied a highly intelligent and competent soldier. He was particularly skilled at running a mortar line; a young officer once commented that he was like 'fire control without a map'. Because of this he really came into his own in the desert and mountains of southern Oman.

During the Regiment's 'secret war' in the Dhofar region of southern Oman in the early 1970s, Kevin was with B Squadron and was heavily involved in many fierce actions against the Adoo who had infiltrated from South Yemen. On one occasion, when a patrol was in real trouble on open ground and under heavy fire, the patrol commander badly needed mortar support. The patrol was unable to pinpoint the enemy's exact position, so was unable to bring fire to bear. Kevin, being a qualified mortar instructor so skilled that he could fire the weapon accurately using only a helmet as a base plate if need be, was able to put down a bomb safely in a position that was quite close to the friendly patrol. From the enemy's return fire, the patrol commander managed to locate them and direct accurate mortar fire on to them.

Yet Kevin managed all of this while sharing a common affliction with me – he was hopeless in the classroom. Put Kevin behind a desk and he went to pieces. Having been wasters at school, we both needed help when it came to sitting the written exams we had to do as part of our army education. You had to be able to pass the exams to get any kind of real promotion. Kevin's comment on this was, 'Don't know why you need sums to kill people'. Fortunately, we both had help from the best teacher I know – my wife Lyn. She took us through the basics of percentages, fractions and general mathematics, setting exercises and tests for us at home in our front room. Lyn got us to a standard where we both passed our exams, but I was always more worried about myself than Kevin. All Kevin really needed was a change of attitude to get him through the abstract paperwork. He could never really see why such tests were at all relevant to his work, but I already knew that he could handle all sorts of calculations if he thought they had a practical purpose; he had proved that when we were training in the Libyan Desert.

In the featureless desert, where shifting sand dunes can create hills where there were none before or completely disguise features that may be marked on a map, the most accurate form of navigation before the high-tech days of the Global Positioning System (GPS) was to do things the way that David Stirling's desert raiders had done during World War II. You had to navigate using the sun and the stars. Astral navigation involves using almanacs and calculation tables that are thoroughly bamboozling until you have a sound understanding of the subject and have mastered the use of these 'tools of the trade'. Just as he had a flair for range and bearing as a mortarman, Kevin quickly grasped the fundamentals of astral navigation ... long before Lyn began coaching us in maths. Not only that, but he then devoted a great deal of time and uncharacteristic patience to leading me through the subject one step at a time. I will be forever grateful to him for that.

The grumpy sod in Kevin, however, was never far from the surface, always there to bolster the bolshy attitude that so exasperated his superiors. When Kevin was with B Squadron, approaching the end of a gruelling five-month tour in Oman, he was looking forward to a well-deserved break back home in Hereford, with G Squadron already on the ground as B Squadron's replacements. However, as he prepared to leave, Kevin was summoned by the squadron commander and told that his tour was to be extended by two weeks. During the early deployment of the Regiment in the 'secret war', a squadron would set up temporary defensive positions in certain areas of the jebel. According to the tactics decided upon and manpower available, some of these positions would become permanent while others were abandoned, to be re-occupied if it became necessary at a later date. One such position was in an area called Tawe a Tair. This was a very high-risk position to try to re-occupy, as the Adoo were known to have drifted back into the area and would put up very fierce resistance.

Because Kevin had previously spent several weeks at Tawe a Tair, his familiarity with the position made him the ideal choice to lead a troop of G Squadron to re-take it, reinforced with elements of the sultan's Baluchi troops and local Firquas (surrendered enemy soldiers retrained by the SAS to fight against the units they'd left). Kevin had no problem with the two-week extension of his tour; the problem arose when he was told that he'd have two Firquas with him.

'Is that two platoons, Sir, or two companies?' he asked.

'Neither,' replied the squadron commander. 'You'll have two leading scouts from the Firquas!'

'Two blokes?' Kevin went berserk. 'What do you mean, two blokes? No way! I wouldn't want to lead on that position with two brigades.'

Yet just as I suspect the squadron commander knew he would, Kevin did lead on the position. Along with his two Firquas, Kevin made his way up onto the jebel under cover of darkness. They climbed in silence towards the eastern sector of the jebel where Tawe a Tair lay, with loose kit, water bottles, their radio and spare magazines well strapped down to avoid any embarrassing clanking. Any noise would carry through the still night air in the mountains like a foghorn, announcing their presence to any sentries who might be lurking on the hillside. Every footstep was placed with care to avoid sending a scattering of pebbles or crumbling rock clattering down the slope.

They were within striking distance of Tawe a Tair before dawn and settled into cover among the rocks. As the sky grew lighter, Kevin surveyed the rough collection of sangars (a sangar is a small fortified position with breastwork of stone or sandbags). There was no sign of movement, no lights, no tell-tale wisps of smoke or glowing camp fires. The place looked deserted. Moving cautiously, making use of every boulder and rocky outcrop for cover, they approached the position, straining to hear the dreaded sound of a weapon being cocked or, worse still, the bark of a rifle. The three lonely figures sneaking forward in the spreading dawn would stand little chance against any enemy hidden in the protection of the stone sangars. It was with immense relief that they eventually confirmed that the position was unoccupied – for now.

Kevin's next task was to explore the various sangars. As a demolitions expert, he was expected to check for any parting gifts that might have been left by the Adoo. Booby traps could lurk beneath any seemingly discarded piece of equipment (although it was unlike the Adoo to leave anything like that behind), among a pile of rocks or in a fire position, waiting only for an unwary trooper to trip a wire or kick a stone to set off a grenade. Kevin and the two Firquas carefully swept the area, then set up the radio to signal that it was safe for G Squadron to join them.

Arriving at Tawe a Tair in strength, and with a helicopter dropping off an 81mm mortar to advertise the fact, it wasn't long before unseen eyes on the surrounding mountains spotted that G Squadron had moved in. The Adoo were quick to respond. The men of G Squadron were settling in, ever alert for an attack, when the familiar whistle and crump of an incoming mortar round sent them scurrying for cover. A wave of Adoo mortar bombs was accompanied by rocket fire that sent shrapnel and rock splinters zinging through the air. The explosions lifted great clouds of dust that drifted across their positions but, peering out from behind their sangar walls, G Squadron soon located the Adoo. Kevin took command of the mortar and, yelling fire instructions and adjustments, he directed a rain of deadly accurate high explosives on his opposite number. The exchange continued until the Adoo were seen to be withdrawing, carrying with them a number of wounded. G Squadron retained possession of Tawe a Tair.

During Kevin's fourth tour in Oman in October 1971, he was involved in Operation *Jaguar* and badly wounded. By that time I was with B Squadron and both B and G Squadrons, along with a large force of Firquas and a battalion of the sultan's troops, were deployed in an ambitious operation to seize a large mountain area around an Adoo stronghold in the village of Jibjat.

For Kevin and the rest of us in B Squadron, Operation *Jaguar* began with a long night march that Pete Winner (see Chapter 13) refers to as 'the death march'. We were all carrying obscenely heavy loads, but the idea was to take advantage of the hours of darkness when we could move into the jebel without fear of being targeted by snipers and without suffering in the heat of the day. There were no roads for vehicles and no paths suitable for mules in the darkness, so everything that we needed had to be carried on our backs. Our first objective was to secure a plateau where there was an old air strip. Helicopters could then resupply us with water, ammunition and reinforcements.

Old hands like Kevin simply resigned themselves to the fact that they were in for a long slog and kept plodding on up the ever steeper, rocky path. The darkness kept us safe from enemy snipers, but the night brought no respite from the strength-sapping heat. There was little or no sign of the dramatic temperature drop you can experience in the desert at night. The heat made the air feel heavy and dead when you sucked it into your lungs, as though the mountains were punishing us with a torture of suffocation for desecrating their slopes with every infidel footstep. We stopped for a water break every hour or so and a proper rest after six hours. Pulling yourself back on your feet after a short break, when every muscle in your body is screaming at you to lie down and rest, takes every ounce of willpower you can muster. Ginge Rees, who was carrying three radio sets, simply didn't move after one break. He was lying flat on his back and, when he was checked for pulse and breathing, appeared simply to have dropped dead. Mouth-to-mouth, CPR (cardiopulmonary resuscitation) and pints of precious cooling water eventually brought him round. His kit was distributed among the rest of us and Ginge, showing a real fighting spirit, came back from the dead to carry on with the march.

We made it to the landing site and secured the area by dawn the next morning. A couple of guys were evacuated with heat exhaustion when the choppers came in, another with an injured knee. After we'd been fed and rested, we were split into battle groups that were further divided into smaller patrols to start probing towards the enemy. Kevin's group was involved in a diversionary manoeuvre to the east of our position and came under heavy fire on several occasions. It occupied a small hill and drew accurate machine-gun and mortar fire from the Adoo who were determined to oust them from the position. In the past, when the sultan's forces had made forays into the jebel, territory that the Adoo and hill tribes most definitely regarded as 'theirs', concerted attacks had sent the government troops scurrying back down the mountain again. The SAS-led forces now on the hill, however, were made of sterner stuff.

They dug themselves in and built stone sangars from which they returned the enemy fire. During four days of intense fighting on what the SAS came to refer to as 'Pork Chop Hill' (after the two fierce battles of the same name between Chinese and American troops in the Korean War), Strikemaster aircraft were called in seven times to plaster the Adoo positions with their rockets, devastate them on bombing runs and rake them with machine-gun fire. Eventually, the Adoo got the message – this group was not going to be chased out of the mountains. Operation *Jaguar* was to continue for three weeks, with B and G Squadrons gradually expanding their area of operations until the Adoo had been driven from the area. Heavy casualties were suffered on both sides. One of those was Kevin.

Kevin's group was settling into a new position, going about the business of setting up its base camp, when suddenly the rocks and dust around their feet were spat into the air as the position was raked with machine-gun fire. The men dived for the cover of their sangars, getting their heads down and shouting to each other to establish from where the incoming rounds were being fired. Where were the Adoo? Kevin had a more immediate problem than finding out where the Adoo were. He needed to get himself under cover. He was nowhere near a sangar (although he later always maintained that he couldn't get into one because they were all full of officers), so dived behind a stack of jerry cans. Cover from view, however, as any infantryman will tell you, is not cover from fire. A jerry can full of water might be enough to stop a bullet. Unfortunately, the jerry cans Kevin was hiding behind were all empty. He was hit in the arse.

As soon as other soldiers were able to get to him, Kevin was carried to a casevac helicopter, complaining bitterly not about his wound, but about the idiot medic who had left a morphine syringe sticking in his bum. He was flown to Salalah where his wound was tended to by the surgical team and he soon found himself lying face down on the clean white sheets of a hospital bed. Word quickly got around that the airborne wart had been wounded and exactly where that wound was situated. Kevin was far from pleased about that. When one ranking officer paid a visit to the hospital he commiserated Kevin about having been shot in the arse. Kevin could stand it no more. 'Listen, Sir,' he hissed. 'I've told everyone else and now I'm telling you – it's not my arse it's my upper thigh!' An SAS NCO who was on hand quickly stepped in to explain: 'What you have to understand, Sir, is that Kevin's arse starts at the back of his neck and goes all the way down to his ankles...'

The wound was actually no laughing matter. It was serious enough to lay Kevin low for a while, but eventually he couldn't stand the hospital routine any longer and discharged himself. He was back on operations before long and served with the Regiment on active service in a number of different theatres, including Northern Ireland. Having been with both D and B Squadrons in 22 SAS, Kevin went on to join the permanent staff of C Squadron 21 SAS (TA), where he rose to the rank of squadron sergeant-major. When he retired from the British Army, Kevin went back to Oman to work with the sultan's Special Forces.

Kevin was an exceptional SAS soldier, with a terrific sense of humour, one of the Regiment's immortal characters and a great friend.

Chapter 7

SERGEANT MICK 'GINGE' TYLER

Mick Tyler was the very first SAS soldier I met, although I didn't know it at the time. When I first came to Hereford to attempt Selection at the tail end of 1963, I arrived by train with about ten others from an assortment of units, all feeling a bit nervous, all pretty unsure of what to expect. When we got outside the railway station we were all a bit surprised to find that there was no reception committee. For us, all of whom had been part of the British Army in the 1950s or gone through National Service, it was a strange sensation to turn up as 'new boys' at what felt like a new posting or training course and not have a sergeant or corporal there to meet you, bristling with menace, razor-sharp creases in the battledress (BD) trousers, impossible shine on the boots and a voice like a foghorn.

We looked around, but saw no such thing. Eventually, we noticed a green-coloured 3-ton Bedford RL truck, but no driver in evidence. We wondered at first if it was some sort of initiative test. Maybe we had to drive ourselves to the camp. Maybe there was a map or some kind of instructions in the truck cab? Before we could decide what to do, a scruffy-looking soldier approached us with a *Daily Mirror* under his arm and a half-eaten bacon sandwich in his hand. What was he then? The base dogsbody sent to collect the next lot of hopefuls in between taking out the garbage and polishing the real SAS soldiers' medals? No, this was 'Ginge' Tyler, a fully badged, fully qualified SAS trooper. He'd been killing time while waiting for us by having a brew (mug of tea) in the refreshment room on the platform. This, then, was our introduction to the SAS.

Already a seasoned soldier by then, Ginge came from a military background, although he'd be the first to admit that it wasn't exactly the same sort of pedigree as the SAS's Colonel Viscount John Douglas Slim or General Sir Peter Edgar de la Couer de la Billière. Ginge's military heritage comes courtesy of his father, who was serving in the army when Ginge was born in 1939, and his four brothers, all of whom joined the army. Ginge didn't see a great deal of his father when he was growing up during the war as he was away so often, but when the war was over that situation didn't change much. His dad deserted them and sold the small house that they lived in, leaving them without even a roof over their heads.

Ginge always said that he never saw this as a real problem because they had become real survivors during the austere period of the war years. In fact, during the war he reckoned they had been better off than a lot of others who suffered badly with food shortages. Living in the countryside in the Weald of Kent, they knew how to live off the land and rarely lacked for fresh food. They could find rabbits, moorhen's eggs, duck eggs (and ducks) as well as plenty of fruit that they foraged from the hedgerows and vegetables either grown by themselves, found wild or 'acquired' from a field. This was all experience that would be put to good use by Ginge in later years. Surviving off the land is a skill that some struggle to master. To Ginge it was second nature.

When Ginge's brothers all disappeared off to the army, he was left behind with his mum, leaving school at the age of 14 to work on farms. Lifting 2cwt (224lb/102kg) bags of corn certainly helped to build up his physique and as soon as he was 15 he enlisted as a boy soldier at the Canterbury Recruiting Office. Joining the Royal Artillery, he was actually stationed at Bradbury Lines in Hereford long before it became the home of the SAS. Strong and athletic, he won the half-mile race at Aldershot Stadium in 1956 as well as running and throwing the javelin for the county of Hereford. He was quickly promoted to boy sergeant in charge of Ironside Troop before he moved on to an Advanced Training Camp at Oswestry in 1957.

In 1958 he progressed from the boys' service to the regular army and passed his parachute course to join the 33rd Para Light Regiment, Royal Artillery. He was soon off to Cyprus on active service during the EOKA emergency and was subsequently posted to Jordan, where Egyptian Arab nationalist Gamal Abdel Nasser was threatening King Hussein's regime. After a spell camping out in the Jordanian desert to deter the rampant Nasser, Ginge was posted to the 29th Field Regiment, Royal Artillery, at the Citadel in Plymouth, but scarcely had time to get his feet under the table before he was shipped back out to the desert, this time to Kuwait where, surprise, surprise, the Iraqis were threatening to invade.

While he was out in Kuwait he took the opportunity to impress everyone, probably even the Iraqis, by running up and down huge sand dunes in the desert heat while carrying a Bergen (rucksack) weighed down with kit and sand. They must all have thought he'd gone nuts, except, perhaps, for those who knew that he had applied for SAS Selection. He was in the process of being transferred to a commando gunnery unit, and had even been flown out to Aden to work with the commandos on the Yemeni border, when his papers came through for the SAS. He went through Selection in the winter of 1962, the year before I did, and was one of only seven out of 150 who passed. On the route marches across the Brecon Beacons, Ginge was first to arrive at every RV throughout the whole course.

By the time he was enjoying a bacon sandwich at Hereford station waiting for me to show up, Ginge had completed a year's Continuation and Skills training to become a fully-fledged member of D Squadron's Mountain Troop and, while I was just about to begin my training, Ginge was off to Borneo and Aden.

Ginge had some strange experiences in Borneo. He was a trained medic and a vital part of the 'hearts and minds' operation. He spent a great deal of time with the Dayak people, stitching machete cuts, curing fevers and treating skin rashes. In return, they showed him some of their jungle survival skills: the right type of vines to cut for fresh water; where to find the sorts of insects and generally unpalatable small creatures and grubs that passed for fast food in those parts. They were headhunters, of course, but as far as I know that's not a habit they passed on to Ginge. Gathered around a river bank one day, Ginge and the Dayak crouched in the cover of the thickest tree trunks they could find. A few beams of sunlight penetrated the jungle canopy to play on the surface in the middle of the narrow river and the sound of moving water accompanied the usual rustling, buzzing, screeching cacophony that so often formed the background music to life in the jungle. For Ginge it was the perfect ambush set-up. He hefted the weight of the grenade in his hand – less than 2lb (0.9kg) but it had all the destructive power he needed. He slipped a finger through the ring of the safety pin and yanked it out then released his grip to allow the spring-loaded lever to pop free. With only a four-second fuse, there was no point in hanging on to it.

He bowled the grenade underarm the few short yards into the river. There was a splosh as it hit the water then a muted bang as the grenade detonated below the surface. A fountain of water shot skywards and birds shrieked in alarm, taking to the safety of the skies. Ginge popped his head out from behind the tree and grinned at his Dayak companions. Floating on the water were enough fish, killed stone dead by the blast wave from the grenade, to feed the whole village. Tonight there would be a feast.

But it wasn't all fun and games with the Dayak. During one patrol with a pal named Spence, whom Ginge had known since he went through his Selection course, they were moving through the kampong of Padawan in Sabah, where Ginge had worked as a medic with the Dayak. He had come to know the tribespeople so well that their children played with him as though he were some kind of strange, pale-skinned uncle. He had learned a little of the language when working in the region and that was about to come in handy.

Being able to talk to some of the locals, Ginge learned that they were being bullied by a band of insurgents who were crossing the border and terrorizing the villagers. Intelligence came back that the men were probably couriers of some sort, rogue bandits who lived off the land and members of the Clandestine Communist Organization (CCO). The SAS was ordered to bring in a prisoner, so an ambush was organized, with a detachment of Scots Guards as back-up. Guided by locals who knew where the terrorists came from, the four-man SAS patrol was to move out to where a river lay across the border. They would then cross the river and the border, and approach the terrorist settlement. At their first opportunity, they would snatch a prisoner and quickly retreat back across the border and through the Guards' ambush position, the Guards taking care of anyone who was following on behind them.

Leaving the Guards in position, Ginge and the patrol trekked through the jungle to the border river crossing, led by their guides, and waded through the water into enemy territory. Once they had crossed the river, with the light fading, they smeared themselves with mud to cover their white skin and settled down to wait until first light. They came under constant assault from sand flies during the long night, lying still as corpses and making not a sound. Then, when the darkness finally gave way to a watery dawn, the guides led them forward to a point where they could clearly identify the hut used by the terrorists. Ginge now motioned the locals to stay well clear and the men melted away into the jungle.

A track ran out of the denser part of the forest through the lesser vegetation at the edge of the village clearing, leading straight to the terrorists' billet. A clumsy booby trap constructed from a large stone, a mortar bomb and a piece of string lay across the path. Carefully Ginge and Spence dismantled it while the other two members of the patrol circled round the back of the hut. There was now some movement at the hut itself. Two men were in view, but more could be heard inside. One of the men sat on the veranda with a Bren gun close at hand. They exchanged a few words and the younger of the two moved off in Ginge's direction. It seemed clear that he was intending to disable the booby trap that Ginge and Spence had just taken apart. The man took a few paces and then could not help but see Ginge and Spence lying near the track. With eyes like saucers, he uttered a strangled cry and scurried into the bush. Ginge sent a few shots after him, firing blind through the foliage. The man on the veranda jumped to his feet and reached for the Bren. It was the last move he ever made. He was cut down by the two SAS men, as were all of the others who emerged from the hut, weapons at the ready. Caught in a murderous crossfire from both sides of their hut, they didn't stand a chance. There were no prisoners to take back, but the patrol did recover a substantial quantity of weapons and a mound of documents that was to provide further useful intelligence.

I caught up with Ginge eventually when I was posted to D Squadron and we ended up in Borneo together. Usually, a tour on ops in Borneo involved being away for about five months; working in groups of four, we would carry out cross-border patrols lasting about 14 days or so, depending on the task. Then we would be back at base for three to four days before re-entering the jungle. The first day out would be spent on a debrief and cleaning weapons and kit; then a good sleep, a good feed and a day and night on the beer! The third day was weapon testing and preparing to go back in the following day.

Our base was in the city of Kuching. Due to the lack of availability of military accommodation, we were billeted wherever space could be found. If we were lucky we could end up in the Palm Grove Hotel. It was nothing very special but it had air-conditioning and a nightclub. We let off a lot of steam there. Having worked not only with the Dayak headhunters but also with the Iban tribe, Ginge had a unique party piece. The Ibans were a very kind, gentle people who greatly appreciated all that Ginge did for them. They had nothing to give him, no gift that they felt would amount to an adequate reward for all his skill and hard work. Instead, they taught him one of their ceremonial dances. This dance later became Ginge's 'party piece' on the dancefloor in the Palm Grove Nightclub. He would bounce around all over the place with incredible energy and agility. The dance would go on for ages with Ginge's moves getting wilder and wilder. I was never entirely sure that the crazy gyrations were exactly the same every time, but Ginge swore that was the way he been taught by the Iban. I could never hope to keep up with Ginge's Iban dance, but he always enjoyed watching me eating a glass or squeezing petrol into my mouth from a small rubber capsule of lighter fuel (don't swallow!). This I would then blow back out again in a fine spray and light with a match, sending a ball of flame rolling across the room. We always went down well with the locals – I think they looked forward to D Squadron's days off.

On one patrol into the jungle, Ginge was lead scout, picking his way through the vegetation as they left their drop-off point and foraging slightly ahead of the rest of the six-man column. He led them uphill towards the ridge that marked the border, where they rested, deciding to make this spot their emergency RV. The patrol commander and one other crossed over into Indonesian territory on a short reconnaissance. Not too far from the patrol's position, they found what appeared to be a disused Indo camp. Noting its position, they returned to the RV and informed the others. They would rest at the border RV for the night and take a proper look at the camp again in the morning.

The next day, the entire patrol headed down from the ridge in the direction of the Indo camp. They were passing through thick vegetation and spread out so that each man could see only the man directly in front of him. Ginge was no longer acting as lead scout. The man the patrol commander had taken with him the previous afternoon knew where they were heading, so took over the job of leading them in. That was Jock Thomson, and the patrol commander following him down the hill was Geordie Lillicoe.

When the rest of the patrol heard the firefight from up ahead where Jock and Geordie had been bounced by the Indos, they followed standard procedure: fired into the air and made as much noise as they could to make it sound like there were far more than just four of them. Then they moved back to the RV. When Jock and Geordie did not join them there, the patrol set off to bring in reinforcements. They returned with a Gurkha detachment the next day and conducted a sweep of the area, searching for their missing friends. Ginge led one of the search parties, as he was roughly familiar with the ground they had covered. It was his party that found Jock Thomson. Ginge treated Jock's wounds and had him loaded onto a makeshift stretcher to get him to a helicopter RV, detailing four of the Gurkhas to carry the injured Scotsman. He then tended to Jock's wounds, keeping him going through the night with the help of Kevin Walsh, who lay beside his injured friend, keeping him warm and chatting to him. In the morning a chopper was guided in to evacuate Jock, and Ginge accompanied his patient all the way to the hospital in Kuching. Ginge had handled himself in a thoroughly professional manner throughout, belying the fact that the ambush had been his first contact with the enemy in the jungle.

Ginge and I became firm friends, which was just as well because we ended up spending a lot of our working time together, both on operations and on various training courses, escape and evasion exercises or hospital attachments all over the world. He was an easy chap to get along with, and had a great sense of humour. He and I, along with four others, once did a four-week stint at St Mary's Hospital in Paddington. We took it very seriously and learned a huge amount in that short period. Working under the direction of the highly efficient senior sister of the casualty department, we were expected to assist with the vast variety of cases that passed through her department. We learned how to insert sutures, apply plaster casts and give injections. We even had to learn the rudiments of obstetrics and dentistry.

As well as training together as medics, Ginge and I also served at the same time in Aden. Unlike in the jungle, in Aden we would mount patrols that lasted only a week as we had to carry with us all of the water that we would need. We also moved at night to avoid being spotted, and the patrols would fall into a regular routine of observation and ambush. More often than not, when you set an ambush, you'd lie there for hours in your fire position waiting for an enemy that never turned up.

Ginge well remembers one patrol that set out from the Habilayn camp at the main forward base near the village of Thumier. The patrol moved out after dark and made its way up into the mountains, heading for a cliff ledge that had previously been identified as a suitable OP. The overhang gave them an excellent view of the entrance to a mountain village suspected to be a base for a well-armed band of terrorists. The SAS soldiers arrived in darkness and settled into their position, hunkered down behind rocks and boulders that would shield them from any prying eyes in the valley when the sun came up.

At first light, they saw a line of men marching along a valley trail in the direction of the village. They were in Arab dress and carrying weapons that identified them as a raiding force that had clearly been taking pot shots and lobbing a few mortars at the camp down at Thumier, which was a regular target for harassing fire from such guerrillas. The men were too far distant for the patrol to engage them effectively, so they called in an air strike. After a few terse radio messages, they finally persuaded the 'head shed', Major

Roger Woodiwiss, D Squadron commander, at the other end that they had identified a valid target.

Two Hawker Hunters eventually came screaming up the valley in time to strafe the group with cannon fire before they reached the sanctuary of the village. Gravel and boulders around the men exploded in showers of flying rock fragments and ricochets. The men scurried for cover while the jets circled to line up for another attack. From the safety of their cliff-top eyrie, the patrol had what amounted to ringside seats – at a suitably safe distance – for the spectacle being played out below them. The jets swooped in again and blasted the rocks and gulleys where the insurgents cowered, desperately trying to find shelter from the aerial bombardment. When the Hunters finally soared off into the sky, heading back to base, the remnants of the terrorist band, shell-shocked and bedraggled, scurried on towards the village, leaving their dead behind while they carried or helped the wounded towards the relative safety of the village.

Ginge and the rest of the patrol decided not to let the terrorists off that easily. They had enjoyed the prelude to this show so much that they reckoned it was time to bring on the main act. They radioed back to base to let them know that the terrorists were now taking refuge in the motley scattering of tumble-down huts and, before long, an attack force was delivered by helicopter down on the valley floor, the men spilling out of the choppers and scattering to their defensive positions before executing a classic 'advance-to-contact' manoeuvre. The attack on the village continued all day, creating what Ginge described as looking like a cross between the set of an action film and a non-stop fireworks display. When the mopping-up operation was complete, the patrol retired to their own predesignated LZ, where they were lifted out by helicopter before last light for an easy ride back to base.

Of course, not all ambush operations in Aden went quite so smoothly. Ginge and I were on one op that didn't go at all as planned. We were ferried to our drop-off point in a convoy of Stalwart amphibious trucks. There wasn't really much requirement for their swimming abilities in the mountain desert region, but their six-wheel-drive capability made them ideal transport over rough ground, although the 4.5 miles (7.2km) to the gallon they achieved made the journey to the operation area an expensive trip. Jumping down from the Stalwarts' tailgates, we formed up and moved out, heading up a wadi to our ambush position. We trudged carefully up the wadi over the familiar terrain of gravel patches, scree, boulders and loose rocks which, when they rolled sideways underfoot, could easily bring you down. It wasn't difficult to lose balance on a narrow track in the dark when we were so overloaded with kit.

The plan was to divide the force into two groups. The group I was with took up positions on higher ground, above a ridge, while Ginge and 19 Troop were down below on flatter ground, closer to the track through the wadi that was to be our killing zone. In pitch darkness, Ginge and the others settled down to wait, lying still and quiet. Suddenly, the sound of rifle fire cut through the silence, echoing round the mountains.

It was all over as suddenly as it began and it became clear that 19 Troop had a man down. It was Yogi Hollingsworth. One of the troop's medics, Ray Hallam, reached him first but one look at the huge exit wounds on his torso was enough to make it abundantly clear that Yogi was not going to make it. He was barely conscious and in incredible pain. He was given two doses of morphine, even though morphine should not be used for wounds to the head or chest as it inhibits breathing. The morphine was administered to help ease Yogi's passage and he died in Ray's arms about 20 minutes later. Ginge helped carry him on a makeshift stretcher all the way to the emergency RV. From there, they were lifted out by helicopter at first light and flown back to the forward base.

Following that Aden tour, Ginge applied for a transfer and eventually moved to the Regiment's Training Wing. After a while, Ginge went back to his roots with the Royal Artillery at the Citadel in Plymouth. This was a commando unit and they sent him to Lympstone on the Commando Course. He passed the course, winning the Commando Medal, the award that is given to the student who comes top. He spent the next year training would-be commandos who were about to take the course, then had to make a decision about whether to return to the Regiment or take a posting to Singapore, where he could move with his family for a year. He chose Singapore.

With his vast experience of operating in so many different environments, and his patient, methodical, understanding nature, Ginge was a natural instructor. He had been a patrol medic, parachute and survival instructor with expertise in desert, jungle and Arctic tactics, as well as a mountain leadership instructor. He was an easy choice when a job came up in the UK organizing the training of young soldiers at the Royal Artillery Adventure Training Centre in Snowdonia. As well as his military expertise, the skills and knowledge Ginge had acquired as a child in Kent could now be passed on to young men who had not enjoyed such an enlightened upbringing. He not only trained the soldiers, but also encouraged them in the tough sport of fell running, competing in most of the fell runs across the country himself. Many of the soldiers he trained went on to serve with the Regiment, including Mick Clifford, who became regimental sergeant-major (RSM) of 22 SAS.

When he left the Army in 1982, Ginge, by then recognized as one of the foremost survival experts in the country, ran survival courses for an outfit called Survival Aids in Cumbria before setting up his own successful adventure training and survival school. His Breakaway Survival School courses are based around the places he knows so well, like the Brecon Beacons and the mountains of North Wales. In fact, the last place I saw him perform his Iban dance was on the lower slopes of Snowdonia in 2005.

Chapter 8

STAFF SERGEANT JOHN PARTRIDGE

What on earth was he doing trudging around in snow? It was only a month or so ago that he had been drenched in sweat and tropical rain, hacking his way along a jungle path in Malaya. If you'd told him then that he would be up to his knees in snow in a few weeks' time, he would have thought you were nuts. If you'd told him the same thing a few days ago, when he was looking for his hat to protect his head in an area where he barely cast a shadow (he was pretty much on the equator and the sun was right above him), he'd have thought it was you who'd been out in the sun too long.

John Partridge put his hands on his hips and drank in the spectacular view. Standing on the Gregory Glacier on Mount Kenya, he could see the rocky, scree-covered slopes climbing away from him to one side, with the glacier's wide expanse of snow and ice stretching up into the distance, combining with the Lewis Glacier as it reached up to the east almost as high as Point Lenana at over 16,000ft (4,876m). He squinted in the bright sunshine, its dazzling effect exacerbated by the reflection from the pure white surface of the glacier, and then stared back down in the direction from which he had come. Down there beyond the jagged rocks, beyond the ancient lava flows that were crumbling under the onslaught of centuries of freezing ice at night and relentless daytime sunshine, was Shipton's

Cave, named after Eric Shipton, the first man to climb Mount Kenya's Nelion Peak in 1929. He could still make out the forms of the buzzards wheeling in the clear blue sky above the area of the cave and Shipton's Camp. He crunched his feet in the snow, shifting his weight and that of the rucksack on his back. He wondered if they were Shipton's crampons he was now driving into the snow of the glacier under his boots. The gear he was using was certainly old enough to have belonged to the first man to have made the climb.

He smiled. What a crazy idea. They had come here to do advanced jungle training and practise the new close-quarters battle (CQB) techniques, not climb the second highest mountain in Africa. Unfortunately, John Slim's CBQ camp at Nanyuki, almost 90 miles (145km) north of Nairobi on the other side of the Aberdaire mountains, was at the foot of Mount Kenya. Kirinyaga was what the local Kikuyu people called it. They believed that their supreme god, Ngai, lived somewhere among the peaks of the extinct volcano. Now, of course, they had a different kind of leader to worship. The Kikuyu were Jomo Kenyatta's people and he seemed set to become the leader of the shining new, independent Kenya.

John heaved at the straps of his rucksack again, shifting the load ever so slightly on his shoulders. They had thought they might have come up against the Mau Mau terrorists when they first came out to Kenya for this three-month training stint, but the serious trouble had pretty much died down by the time they arrived in 1960. Not that they would have been much help anyway. There had been a flu epidemic raging back home when they left and a couple of the lads were suffering when they boarded the plane back in England. By the time they landed in Kenya, most of the rest of them had it too, having been shut up in an enclosed environment with those already suffering for hours. For the first ten days or so at Nanyuki, the squadron had been pretty much bedridden.

Once they were all fit enough, they were flung into an intensive training regime. When they weren't learning the new CQB drills on the strange little trenches hacked out of the side of a crater on one of the lower slopes of Kirinyaga, or disturbing Ngai's peace and quiet by charging through the sandbag corridors and rooms of the makeshift 'killing house', blasting away at cardboard targets, they were out patrolling through the mountain forests. The African forest wasn't as dense as the jungles of Malaya, nor as humid, but it gave them the chance to try out a few different patrol manoeuvres, and operating in the forest was given a special edge by the knowledge that a few of the most notorious Mau Mau terrorists were still on the loose, hiding out somewhere in the Aberdaire region. They never came across any of them, though. Pity. With all that target practice under their belts, they were itching to go operational again.

John found the experience of patrolling through the Aberdaire forests fascinating nonetheless. It was hard going, but John soon found that the higher they climbed the more the nature of the forest changed. Lower down it could be dense and distinctly tropical, but then they would ascend into an area where the trees were smaller and spaced much further apart. The canopy was less dense and, during the day, more sunlight streamed through, illuminating the different coloured mosses or 'goat's beard' lichens clinging to the tree bark. Then they would come into areas that were tangled with blackberry bushes or dotted with giant lobelia and higher still, above around 11,000ft (3,352m), the trees disappeared altogether, the landscape changing to moorland cloaked in giant heather.

The forest also changed entirely after sunset, just as it did in Malaya, with no twilight but immediate pitch darkness. In Malaya, they generally set up their *basha* (Malay for 'hut' or 'shelter') and camped where they were when the light faded. Here, they crept through the darkness, hearing the occasional crash and thump of heavy animals moving around. John had kept telling himself that the jungle creatures were more scared of him than he was of them, that they would hear the clumsy soldiers coming long before the patrol got close. All the same, he had been glad to be carrying the Bren. He wasn't sure if it would actually stop a charging bull elephant, but he would have given it a go if he'd had to.

John remembered when he had first gone into the jungle. The SAS had offered him a Sterling SMG. The weapon had been in service for around five years at the time and had a reasonably good reputation for reliability. It fired a 9mm round from a 34-round magazine and, in the right hands, was accurate up to as much as 100 yards (91m). He turned it down, however, for he knew all about the Sterling. John may only have been 19, but he had been in the army for more than four years. He had enlisted straight from school in Leicester and joined the Boys' Regiment, Royal Artillery, based at Bradbury Lines in Hereford. There he'd received a proper, old-fashioned grounding as a soldier.

The boy soldiers had a particularly tough disciplinary regime. They had 19-year-old bombadiers, the same age as he was when he joined the SAS, screeching at them on the parade ground, bullying them with both verbal and, from time to time, physical abuse. If you weren't already tough enough to take it, you had to toughen up fast. The uniform at the time was World War I-issue service dress with plenty of brass buttons that had to be polished thoroughly every day. Boots had to be finished to an immaculate, deep, mirror shine. For the boy soldiers the Hereford bull was all in the barracks, not in the farmer's field. They were schooled in infantry tactics and given intensive training on the 25pdr field gun.

Three years later, when his boys' service ended and John progressed into the regular army, he was sent on the Advanced Leadership Course for former boy soldiers at the 64th Training Regiment at Oswestry. John came top of the course and was presented with the RSM's Cane of Honour. He then volunteered for and passed P Company selection for the 16th Independent Parachute Brigade. He was posted to the 33rd Parachute Light Regiment, Royal Artillery. He was now an airborne gunner and completed his parachute course in 1956. Following that, he was trained as part of a mortar crew to give close fire support to the 1st Battalion, The Parachute Regiment.

In that time, with all that experience under his belt, John had come to know a thing or two about the Sterling. The weapon weighed just 6lb (2.7kg) and had a high rate of fire, but he'd heard it didn't pack much of a punch. He'd heard that in Malaya when patrols had come up against CTs high on 'waccy baccy' (smoked narcotics) or some kind of 'loony juice' (intoxicating spirits), some of those jungle maniacs had taken multiple rounds from the Sterling and still kept coming. He'd heard that Surrendered Enemy Personnel (SEP) had been brought in with eight rounds from a Sterling lodged in their bodies and still survived. So, given the choice, John had opted for the 7.62mm Bren gun. That had real stopping power. Eight rounds from a Bren would just about cut a man in half. No amount of artificial courage would hold up an enemy after he'd been hit by eight rounds from a Bren. All the king's horses and all the king's men, as the old nursery rhyme 'Humpty Dumpty' goes, wouldn't do him any good at all.

John also knew that the Bren weighed more than three times as much as the Sterling. He'd have to carry at least ten magazines loaded with 28 rounds in each. There would be no shoulder strap. The SAS did not carry weapons on straps or slung over their shoulders. The weapon would have to be in his hands, ready for use at all times when on patrol. You don't have time to unsling your weapon in the jungle when an enemy soldier pops up in front of you just a few yards away. In any case, slings and straps get caught up on jungle vegetation, making a noise when you least want it or whipping the weapon out of your hands at just the wrong moment. No, John would have to carry the Bren unaided. It was a lot of weight for a 19-year-old to lug over long distances in the exhausting heat and humidity of the jungle, but he knew he'd made the right decision whenever they got a sniff of a contact. If the patrol was approaching an area where they thought there might be a chance of coming up against the CTs, or they came across an enemy camp showing signs of recent occupation, one or two members of the patrol would inevitably offer to carry the Bren. Just to take the weight off him for a while, they would swap him for a Sterling SMG. Needless to say, John just smiled and declined the kind offers. So it was a Bren that he carried on the forested slopes of Mount Kenya.

It was patrolling the lower reaches of Mount Kenya that probably sparked the idea of climbing the entire mountain. Surely the resourceful, highly trained, superfit SAS squadron could reach the top? All they had to decide was which of the mountain's peaks to aim for, as Kirinyaga was like a whole range, its three highest peaks being Lenana at 16,450ft (5,014m) and Nelion and Batian, both soaring up to well over 17,000ft (5,181ft). The peaks had been climbed several times, the first recorded ascent over 60 years before. If some amateur could make it up there at the turn of the century, then surely the modern SAS could handle it, too? The trouble was, they were kitted out for operations in the tropics and, even from way down in the foothills, you could see the glaring white frosting of snow up high.

Cold-weather clothes they could probably rustle up, but they would be mad to attempt it without the proper gear for climbing on snow.

John and the rest of the squadron mulled the problem over for a few days, discussing it around the camp from time to time until a local farmer turned up one day with a large wooden box. He had come to hear that the SAS was considering climbing the mountain and wondered if he might be able to help. In the box was all the equipment they could have wished for – crampons, ice axes, the lot – all beautifully made by local craftsmen for a small team of mountaineers who had climbed Kirinyaga as long ago as 1929. That may well have been the team that included Eric Shipton. The gear was gratefully accepted and 19 Troop, the Mountain Troop, came into being.

John turned again to look up the mountain towards their destination. Climbing through snow, in Africa, practically right on the equator, who'd have thought it? Even as they had planned their expedition, aiming to follow what was said to be an established route up the mountain, he could hardly believe that they were actually going to do it. Even when they had made their way to their start point some 15 miles (24km) east of Nanyuki, where the trucks had dropped them off, it had seemed like a madcap scheme. But once they were plodding up the mountain slopes, weighed down with enough high-energy rations and water to last them several days, John really started to enjoy the trek. It certainly made a change being out in a foreign country in patrol strength without having to worry about someone taking pot shots at you.

Following a rest stop, a brief call of 'Let's go' spurred all of the small team into action. They lifted their now wearying legs and planted one foot in front of the other to continue their methodical ascent. This wasn't the first mountain John had climbed with the Regiment, nor would it be the last, but it was the highest. That John and the rest of the team succeeded in such a demanding climb using antiquated equipment is a tribute to their courage and endurance, but they achieved much more than just the ascent of an icy glacier. They established that the SAS was capable of operating not only in environments as diverse as the desert and the jungle, but that it could cope with the unforgiving, rarefied atmosphere at high altitude with minimal acclimatization. They had effectively established Mountain Troop and the SAS would return to the heights of Kirinyaga many times over the following years, evaluating and training with the most advanced mountain equipment available, forever in debt to John and the other trailblazers.

If John thought that the peaks of Mount Kenya were the highest outdoor experience he would ever enjoy, he was wrong. Within a few short years he would be much higher still, and plummeting to earth at over 120mph (293km/h). Having operated with Mobility, Amphibious and, of course, Mountain Troops, John had opted for a change to put his parachute experience to good use and joined B Squadron's Air Troop. He was one of the first to train for High-Altitude Low-Opening (HALO) parachute jumps with the SAS.

Cyprus, 1970s. The cavernous interior of a C-130 Hercules becomes surprisingly overcrowded when a detachment of free-fall SAS paras and all their kit is crammed in. John looked around at the men standing in the aircraft, anonymous behind their oxygen masks, goggles and jump helmets. You were supposed to be able to get over 60 paratroops in one of these, over 90 regular passengers. He couldn't see how. A thunder of windrush topped off by the roar of the four Allison engines dragged his attention back to the task in hand. The tailgate was now almost fully lowered and the black of the night made the blacked-out interior of the aircraft seem positively bright. His hands wandered over his equipment as he felt his way through one final check. Even if he had still had enough light, the mask and goggles would not have made it easy for him to make a visual check of all of the kit that was now strapped to his body. Over his jump boots he wore gaiters that zipped up the front and enclosed his legs almost up to the knee. They would help to keep him warm when he exited into the sub-zero temperatures outside the Hercules, but they also stopped the legs of his jump suit flapping around as he dropped – any loose piece of kit could potentially throw him off balance in the air and that was to be avoided at all costs. When you were jumping from over 25,000ft (7,620m) – almost 5 miles (8km) high – you didn't take any unnecessary risks.

His gloved fingers gripped webbing and harness straps, tugging to ensure a snug fit. He nestled his M16 rifle in a little tighter to his body. The butt was in his shoulder, the barrel pointing at the floor. It was secure. His hands,

Memorial plaque in the Regiment's Garden of Remembrance at St Martin's Church, Hereford.

Lt Col Blair ('Paddy') Mayne, the most decorated British serviceman of World War II.

Len Owens, proudly wearing his own and his father's medals.

Members of B Squadron, with a detachment of American special forces, testing a vehicle for mobility troop, 1960s. Standing 1st left, Dave Abbot; seated 3rd from left, Mike Kealy; 4th from left, Steve Callan; 5th from left, Kevin Walsh; extreme right, Roger Cole.

Don 'Lofty' Large (foreground) serving in the Sultan of Oman's forces after leaving the Regiment.

Iain 'Jock' Thomson, 1963.

The Jebel Akhdar, Muscat, northern Oman.

Camel training in the Middle East.

Bronco Lane whilst conquering Everest in 1976.

Ginge Tyler.

Kevin Walsh, 'the airborne wart', enjoys a five-minute break while running an 81mm mortar course.

John Partridge in the Far East, 1950s.

Bob Podesta with a slippery friend on survival training in the Far East.

Bob Podesta having his parachute equipment adjusted before a jump.

Alfie Tasker (right) awaiting extraction after a patrol in the Radfan mountains, 16 June 1966.

Bob Podesta served all over the world with the Regiment including Northern Ireland.

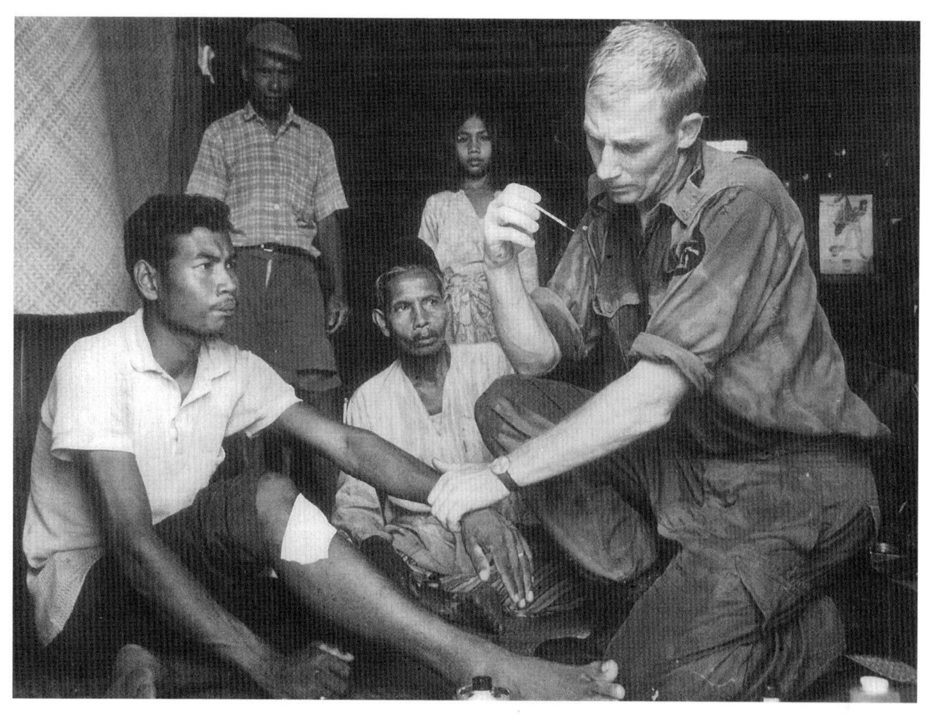

Mick 'Ginge' Tyler at work in Borneo, winning hearts and minds through his medical training. In return for his help, the natives gave Ginge many survival tips which he would later put to good use.

Talaiasi Labalaba on operations, southern Oman, 1971.

Talaiasi Labalaba in an observation post position, Aden, 1960s.

A two-man team setting up and testing a Claymore mine in the Middle East.

Colin Wallace plants two British Legion crosses at the spot where Tommy Tobin and Laba were fatally wounded in front of Mirbat fort.

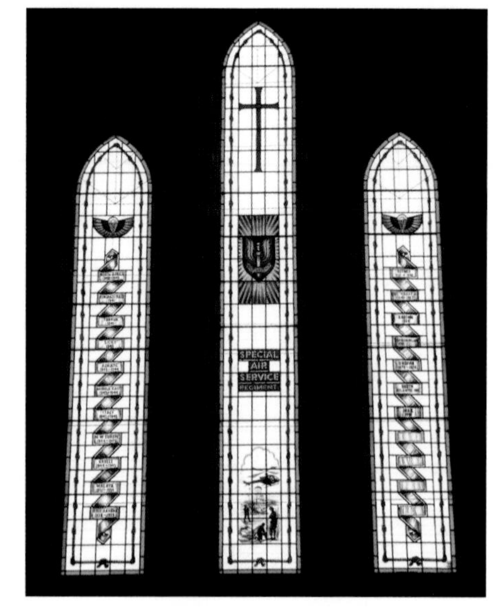

ABOVE *Regimental memorial window at St Martin's Church, Hereford.*

LEFT *Talaiasi Labalaba's grave at St Martin's Church, Hereford, with the badge of The Royal Irish Rangers and the winged dagger of the SAS.*

with an altimeter fastened to each wrist, came to rest on the oxygen bottle strapped to his belly. They had been on pure oxygen for almost 45 minutes to expel any nitrogen from their bloodstreams before they switched from the aircraft's supply to their own bottles. You had to be careful on the switch. There wasn't much air to breathe in the aircraft flying at that height, but there was enough to boost the nitrogen almost back up to normal if you took just one whiff. You had to make the switch smoothly and calmly while holding your breath. Nitrogen in the bloodstream could induce hypoxia that would lead to a blackout when you were in mid-air. You couldn't enjoy your jump if you were unconscious – and you certainly wouldn't enjoy the landing.

The oxygen was, of course, essential. John remembered training in a decompression chamber where six of them had sat opposite each other, all wearing oxygen masks. The air pressure in the chamber was then reduced until the oxygen level was equivalent to that at around 26,000ft (7,924m). John watched as those sitting opposite him were ordered to remove their masks. They then had to carry out some simple instructions, counting backwards in fives from 100 and writing the sequence on a pad in front of them. They also had to draw a house. John and the others observed so that that they could recognize the effects of oxygen deprivation. The lips and fingertips of those opposite started to turn faintly blue. Their counting became progressively confused and their draughtsmanship would have embarrassed the average five-year-old. He recalled being exactly the same when he took his turn, and also noticed that he started to develop tunnel vision, a peculiarity that was reversed as soon as he went back on the oxygen.

You needed a cool head and nerves of steel to tackle HALO jumping in full kit. So many things could so easily go wrong. John shifted his legs forward slightly and felt the weight of the Bergen on the back of his thighs. The rucksack was slung upside down below his parachute and was carefully packed with all the kit he would need for a normal patrol. Altogether he was carrying kit that tipped the scales at well over 100lb (45kg). Once his canopy opened, he would unclip the Bergen to let it dangle below him on a length of line. It would hit the ground before he did, leaving him free of its encumbrance when he landed. For the time being, it was secure and felt well balanced. If it wasn't, it would spell disaster. John knew full well that the Bergen was probably what did for poor old Rip Reddy.

When G Squadron was sent into northern Oman in 1970 looking for terrorists, who very sensibly then made it their business to be elsewhere, one of the places where the SAS was charged with attempting to track down the elusive foe was in the Wadi Rawdah. The wadi was an enormous bowl or crater scooped out of the mountains. Its ragged cliff walls soared a thousand feet high and the only way in or out was through a narrow cleft in the rock wall facing the sea. Approaching the area on foot, you had to pass through this narrow rock corridor before it opened out onto the vast expanse of the valley floor. This place was home to an isolated tribe called the Bani Shihoo. They lived in houses built with carved blocks of solid stone and constructed great rock cisterns to catch and store water. They were rumoured to be a bloodthirsty lot who had few firearms but made up for that through their prowess with their traditional battle axes. They were also rumoured to be harbouring a heavily armed bunch of terrorist guerrillas. As with so many rumours, both would turn out to be nonsense. The Bani Shihoo were not deadly cut-throats, but perfectly friendly and there were no terrorists in the wadi.

The men of G Squadron, however, were not to know that. The intelligence was that the insurgents were there and the SAS was tasked with going in after them. The plan was for a pathfinder group, including Paul 'Rip' Reddy, to free-fall into the wadi at night to secure a landing area for the helicopters that would bring in the rest of the squadron. They would also secure the exit from the wadi to make sure that none of the terrorists escaped. The free-fall group jumped from 11,000ft (3,352m), plummeting down past mountain peaks 4,000ft (1,219m) high before their parachutes deployed above the Wadi Rawdah. No one will ever really know what went wrong as Rip fell through the darkness. The best guess was that the Bergen moved and he had lost stability in the air. When his parachute deployed it may have become tangled on some other part of his kit. What is certain is that it did not fully deploy until it was too late. The rest of the pathfinder force located each other using their Surface to Air Rescue Beacon (SARBE) radios, but Rip never checked in. They found his body the next day on a low rocky slope at the edge of the wadi.

It didn't do to dwell on memories like that. Sure, these jumps were dangerous, but John accepted that they still had a part to play in the way the Regiment operated. The advantages of HALO insertion were that a team could be delivered quickly, accurately and covertly to its destination. A man falling through the air at free-fall speeds would be almost undetectable on enemy radar, whereas a chopper would have to fly in low and drop off its passengers some distance from the intended target in order to avoid being picked up on radar and alerting the enemy to the team's presence. In some situations, a HALO team could be dropped in to secure landing and drop zones ahead of the main force.

HALO was dangerous and there had been accidents, but since that very first free-fall operational jump in Oman, the Regiment had trained dozens of free-fall artists and John had done scores of these jumps. He'd completed two RAF HALO courses and jumped in training exercises at home in England, at the French parachute school at Pau in the Pyrenees, and in the mountains of Norway, too. During one troop training jaunt to Cyprus they had jumped from 30,000ft (9,144m), close to the service ceiling of the C-130.

The RAF loadmaster signalled for John to move forward. He was first in the stick, with no one to shield him from the blackness of the night, no one to follow blindly out of the tailgate. The loadmaster straightened the strap of the harness that secured him to a safety point on the aircraft's inner fuselage, all the while looking up at the red light that glowed above him. The instant it turned to green, he yelled 'Go!' and waved John out. Even if John could have heard him above the howling windroar from the gaping tailgate, he would not have waited for the sound of the command. He wouldn't hold up the rest of the stick. He stepped forward off the end of the tailgate and dropped out into the night.

The slipstream from the Hercules buffeted him for a moment, flinging his body out behind the aircraft as he twisted himself into the face-down, starfish position for free-fall, balancing his body with his solar plexus as his centre of gravity. This part was the real thrill, the part any speed freak would sell his granny for. This was when he accelerated towards the ground, Mother Earth dragging him back to her bosom, gravity snatching him out of the sky. From leaving the C-130 it took him just 12 seconds to drop 1,500ft (457m) as he accelerated to his terminal velocity of just over 120mph (293km/h). The windrush tore at his clothing and kit, setting up a whistling that sounded like an express train hurtling past his ears. He could see the shape of the night far better now that he was out there and part of it. He could see a layer of cloud rushing up towards him. If he adjusted his posture slightly, he could track across the sky towards a gap in cloud and drop through the clear air. On the other hand, he knew that the cloudbank was not very thick and attempting any kind of manoeuvre when overloaded with kit was not advisable.

People who jump free-fall for sport can pull off all sorts of acrobatic tricks in the air – 'fly' across the sky, 'surf', somersault or spin like an aerial gymnast. They don't have all that combat kit to contend with. Weighed down by that load, you have to think twice about any kind of movement. The sport parachutists will pull their own ripcords to deploy their chutes. They can move one arm to the pull ring and reach forward with the other to maintain stability. That is not to be tried except in an emergency when you are jumping laden with SAS gear. To avoid having to make that move, SAS free-fall teams use a device that opens the parachute pack automatically when the jumper has descended to a predetermined altitude.

John's goggles started to ice over. He knew that it must be cold but he wasn't feeling it at all. The adrenalin rush, as much as his jump suit, was keeping out the frosty air. He didn't want to be falling blind with his goggles iced up, but he'd let it go for a few seconds more. If he was going to clear them, he only wanted to have to do it once. He couldn't just drag the back of his hand across the goggles to banish the ice. He had to keep his outline symmetrical to maintain stability. He couldn't afford to start tumbling through the sky. Once he reached the altitude where the parachute would deploy, he had to be in perfect control otherwise he would end up with his canopy wrapped around him. Then it would cease to function as a parachute and serve only as his shroud. Carefully, the movements simultaneous, confident and deliberate, he brought both gloved hands in to rub the ice from his goggles. This pitched him into a 'head-down' attitude where he was diving through the air, picking up even more speed, but as he extended his arms again he brought himself back into the perfect posture.

The night disappeared in a soup of mist as John hurtled down through the thin cloud, then, around 2 minutes and 30 seconds after exiting the Hercules, John felt the tug of the small pilot chute as it cleared the pack and caught in his slipstream, popping open the parachute bag and dragging his canopy out behind it. Then came the reassuring snap of the canopy filling with air and the jolt as it pulled him into an upright position and began to slow his descent. He looked up and checked the chute as best he could in the dark. It all seemed fine. Another free-fall jump was all over bar the landing. It was one of more than 100 HALO free-fall parachute descents John was to undertake in training during a career with the SAS that spanned over 20 years.

From his first taste of SAS active service as a teenager in Malaya, where he participated in deep-penetration patrols that lasted up to three months with air drops for re-supply only every 14 days, John proved that he had what it takes to make an outstanding SAS soldier. After Malaya, he went to Oman, where he and his comrades faced entirely different, but equally harsh, conditions. They spent months probing with reconnaissance patrols to find a way to seize the 12,000ft (3,658m) high plateau on the Jebel Akhdar from communist-backed insurgents. They eventually made it to the top on Christmas Day. They had routed the enemy by March of 1959, but John had not seen the last of Oman. He was back there in 1970 during Operation *Storm*.

I was a corporal with D Squadron by the time the unit went to Borneo in 1963, and it was on operations in the jungle that I first came to know John. He often found himself acting as a patrol commander and regularly deputized for the troop commander during the exhausting operations against the Indonesian border raiders. Between tours in Borneo, John was also active during the campaign in Aden. John threw himself wholeheartedly into every job he was asked to undertake, whether it was the classroom training with which some of us struggled so hard, or setting out in the middle of winter with a shovel to clear the snow off the local railway line. He would join the lads in the pub for a drink, but would sit quietly by if things ever started to get a bit out of hand. He was never one to lose control. John's normally even temper and good nature made him an excellent instructor, too. He had a spell with the Training Wing as a demolitions instructor, ran a course to train Malay Police and Special Branch officers in Ipoh, Malaysia, and even became a 'spook' when he was seconded as an instructor to MI6 for two years.

Having completed 22 years' service in the army, John left the Regiment in 1978 with the rank of staff sergeant. He then spent some time in Florida providing close protection for a VIP before moving back to Europe to work as a bodyguard to a Dutch industrialist. He stayed in that job for 12 years before finally hanging up his shoulder holster to enjoy a well-deserved retirement.

John was one of the most professional soldiers I ever met and his incredibly positive attitude under in any circumstances, under any amount of pressure, was matched only by his unstinting courage. I remain proud to have served with him.

Chapter 9

WO2 SQUADRON SERGEANT-MAJOR ALFIE TASKER

The Hawker Hunter was one of the most beautiful jet aircraft ever conceived. With its swept wings and graceful lines it looked incredibly elegant in flight and was swift enough to go supersonic in a shallow dive, yet it was also a purposeful and deadly machine. The Hunter did not officially enter service with the RAF until 1954, but Squadron Leader Neville Duke piloted one to a new world air speed record of 727.63mph (1,170.97km/h) in 1953, proving that in those days the Hunter was one of the finest fighter aircraft around. Faster planes quickly came along, such was the pace at which technology was advancing in the 1950s and 1960s, and the Hunter was soon to find itself outperformed as a pure fighter. But the Hunter was such a stable weapons platform that it readily switched to the ground-attack role, and by the mid-1960s, when the SAS was embroiled in Aden, it was a more than welcome sight in the sky over the mountains. Today, every SAS soldier is trained to call in air strikes, but then it was a less common skill and some were far better at communicating with aircraft than others. One of the best was Alfie Tasker.

In 1966 I was part of a D Squadron patrol, led by Alfie, in the Radfan Mountains of Aden, heading towards suspected enemy positions. The only way to get anywhere on foot in the mountains of the Aden Protectorate was to use the wadis. The mountains themselves are steep, rocky and barren, except when they level out onto plateaus which are equally flat, rocky and barren. Trying to make progress on the high ground is a slow and exhausting business, constantly scrabbling for grip on the loose, sun-baked rocks that litter the ground. Needless to say, you are also fairly exposed up there, allowing the enemy to spot your approach from miles away. In low visibility at night, traversing the mountain tops is so dangerous that it is virtually impossible.

The dry river beds of the wadis, on the other hand, provide excellent cover for night movement and climb far more gently into the mountains than the scree-strewn slopes of the peaks themselves. The wadis can be anything from a few feet wide to a couple of miles across. Some have undulating floors of scree, sand and giant boulders. Some are carpeted with camel thorn bushes, or bordered by walls that are sheer cliff faces. Turn a corner in some wadis and you could come across a flat area of open ground that stretched for hundreds of yards – an ideal killing ground for anyone lying in ambush. There is generally plenty of cover in a wadi, good if you are under attack, better if you have laid an ambush. Many of the wadis are linked by small gulleys or hill paths, making them the mountain motorway system – as long as you are slogging through them on foot, of course.

The tactics we used when patrolling in the desert mountains in Aden were broadly similar to those we used in the jungle mountains of Borneo, except that we could usually travel more effectively at night and the lead scout could generally forage farther ahead of the rest of the patrol. On the patrol that was led by Alfie, we were out in the mountains in broad daylight and as we approached the enemy positions, the mountain tribesmen, who knew every bush and boulder of their territory, easily spotted us coming and couldn't resist taking a few pot shots at us. Over long distance in the desert, the rounds from a machine-gun or a rifle will be with you an instant before you actually hear them being fired, so the first indication that you are under fire might be the sound of a ricochet sending boulder splinters flying, or the snap of a camel thorn stalk as a bullet rips through it. Any soldier who aspires one day to collect his army pension will then take cover, fast.

The enemy tribesmen had good cover on higher ground and their shots were coming close enough to give cause for concern, but Alfie knew that we had to get ourselves into a better position to be able to return accurate fire effectively. He led us forward, each of us scurrying from one cover position to the next as the others gave covering fire. All the time the enemy rounds were spitting up dust from the wadi floor or bouncing off the rocky cliff walls. Once Alfie was in a good enough position to see exactly where the enemy tribesmen were, it became clear that no amount of fire from the light weapons carried by the patrol was going to dislodge them, so he got on the radio and sent a coded message to our base at Thumier to ask for air support.

The codeword sent by Alfie set a chain of events in motion that culminated in two Hawker Hunter jets screaming down the runway on the coast at RAF Khormaksar. The Hunters were over our position within minutes, thundering across the mountains then standing on one wing-tip to wheel round and survey the situation on the ground. Alfie was in direct radio contact with the Hunter pilots. By great good fortune we had trained in the desert in Libya with the same Hunter squadrons, calling in mock attacks from the same pilots with whom we later worked in Aden. Calling in an air strike is the equivalent of directing aerial artillery. Alfie was able to give them exact map coordinates of the enemy position and chat to the pilots to make sure that they knew exactly what they were aiming at – i.e. not us. The little people on the ground all look much the same from a few hundred feet up.

The Hunters then lined up for their first attack run. They would be coming in directly over our positions, blasting the enemy with the four 30mm Aden cannon mounted in the Hunter's nose. The Aden (named after the Armament Development Establishment at Enfield, not the place where we were making targets of ourselves) had a rate of fire in excess of 1,200 rounds per minute, so the four in the Hunter's nose could make a real mess of any enemy defences. As the first jet swooped in, we all craned our necks as far out of cover as we dared in order to watch the action. Alfie, on the other hand, crept aside into deeper cover below an overhanging cliff face, advising us to do the same. 'Get yourselves under cover now,' he said, 'or you'll learn the hard way.'

We quickly found out exactly what he meant. Just below its 'shoulders', where the leading edge of the wings meets the fuselage, the Hunter had two large bulges called Sabrinas. (They were named after a popular actress of the time who also had two large bulges just below her shoulders.) The Sabrinas were there to accommodate the empty links from the 30mm ammunition belts that fed the Aden cannon. Simply letting the link belts shoot out of a slot behind the aircraft's nose might have allowed the belts to foul the aircraft's control surfaces. There were no such fears, however, about the spent shell cases. They were ejected from two holes immediately above each Sabrina – and even a quick three-second burst meant that at least 240 30mm brass shell cases came tumbling down. If just one of those caught you on the head it would be enough to lay you out. As soon as the brass rain started, we were under cover with Alfie quicker than you could say 'concussion'. While he advised us not to 'learn the hard way', that's pretty much how Alfie had learned. He'd needed the help of the Hunter pilots in Aden before, not simply to attack an enemy position, but to keep himself and his mates alive.

Alfie was most definitely 'old school' SAS, with almost ten years' service in the Regiment under his belt before I ever arrived. He was a big man with a shock of undisciplined hair and a way of glowering at you from beneath his brow that let you know he was being serious and you'd better bloody well listen. He gave me that look when he handed me the shear pin for an outboard motor as our troop loaded two assault boats at a beautiful beach on the island of Santubong in Sarawak, Borneo. We had just enjoyed a period of 'light training', but the outboard motors' shear pins were forever breaking. The shear pin is a slim rod that slots into a hole and holds the engine's propeller in place. It is designed to break if the prop hits something hard, the theory being that the prop will then spin free and avoid damaging itself or any other vital parts of the engine.

We had two boats ready to depart the island for the trip back to Kuching, but only one shear pin. Alfie entrusted me with the vital item. It was safe in my hands – for about two seconds. Sometimes inanimate objects can just take on a life of their own. I think that the shear pin must have been some kind of sea serpent in a previous life, because it seemed to wriggle and slither in my fingers before it dived into the sea and made its way straight to the bottom, never to be seen again. Alfie grabbed a handful of my shirt front and growled, 'Scholey, as soon as we get back, you are dead. You understand that, don't you?' That wasn't much of an incentive for me to put my back into it on the two-hour row along the coast and upriver to Kuching. Still, I knew that Alfie wouldn't stay angry with me for long. He was a good-hearted, fun-loving guy, really. He would see the funny side of it eventually. Probably when the rowing blisters on his hands cleared up ...

Those outboard engines were the bane of Alfie's life in Borneo. We had been sent down to Santubong in 1967 to take some well-deserved rest and to give our political masters a new card to play at the negotiating table where they were attempting to come to a peaceful settlement with the Indonesians (now our friends) who had been causing all the trouble. Withdrawing the SAS was deemed to be a show of goodwill. Alfie and the rest of us certainly appreciated it, although I think Alfie would ultimately rather have been shooting at Indos than tangling with those outboard motors.

We set up a camp on the beach, relaxed for a while, then, after a few days, our troop sergeant, Willie Mundell, decided to give us some instruction in the fine art of amphibious assaults. Two of the 40hp (30kW) outboard motors were attached to one assault boat with Alfie at the helm. The plan was that Alfie would take the boat out far enough to give us a long run in to the beach. Then we would hurtle in with the engines on full power before cutting the motors short of the beach and gliding in to ground on the sand, so that we could all then storm ashore. Those not involved lay around sunbathing or pottered around in the water to watch the fun. All went well at first. Alfie took us out, he lined the boat up and then gunned the engines. We took off for the shore like a bat out of hell, but when the signal was given to cut the engines, we just kept going. Alfie cursed and thumped the switches but the engines simply would not stop.

The aquatic spectators broke Olympic swimming records to get out of our way. Dodgy shear pins or not, no one wants to get chewed up by a runaway outboard motor. In the boat, with Alfie roaring almost as loud as the engines, we all exchanged glances. No one had to say anything. No one fancied baling out at high speed. We'd just have to brace ourselves for the crunch on the beach. We didn't have to wait long. I was thrown out into the water by the impact and surfaced pretty much unscathed in time to see the others scrabbling away from the boat as it tried to grind its way up the beach. Alfie leapt clear into what he thought was shallow water. He disappeared from sight completely. It took him so long to resurface we thought he was going to be posted Absent Without Leave (AWOL).

You have to give Alfie credit for his sheer determination in persevering with those boats, though. He was at the helm again when one bunch decided to try a spot of fishing. Ordinary fishing, however, can be a boring and time-consuming business. Their idea was to catch enough fish in one fell swoop to see us through a few days once the fish had been dried or smoked over our camp fires – or at least enough for a major barbecue. How do you catch that many fish? Not with a rod, line, hook and worm, that's for sure. You need a net and a trawler. We didn't have that. What we did have was enough explosives to rekindle the volcano Krakatoa. Everyone knows that if you drop a hand grenade in a river or pond, every fish in the area will end up floating on the surface, just about ready to be served up with a few chips. In the sea, we reckoned it would be slightly different. Rivers and ponds are enclosed spaces. In the sea, the blast would dissipate as it spread over a far wider area. The answer was to use more than just a grenade and, since we had been doing some demolition training, more was available. Alfie and the intrepid fishermen set off in a boat for their fishing ground armed with an ammunition box packed with plastic explosive.

When Alfie had positioned them over what they thought was just the right spot, they set the timer and lowered their bomb over the side of the boat. We watched from the shore as Alfie gunned the engine to take them clear of the blast. The engine tone rose sharply, then cut out altogether. The engine had died. With the bomb ticking away below them, there followed a great deal of frantic gesturing and several panicked attempts to restart the engine. One of the fish bombers, having clearly decided that the boat was going nowhere (except perhaps to kingdom come), dived over the side and started swimming for the shore where most of us spectators were falling about laughing. With one last desperate attempt, Alfie got the engine running and the boat took off for the beach, full steam ahead, slowing only slightly to pluck the swimmer out of the water. They hadn't gone very far when their home-made depth charge detonated, sending a massive fountain of water shooting skyward. The boat was flipped over and they were all dumped in the water. They had to swim back clinging on to the upturned boat. And there was not a fish to be seen.

Alfie couldn't be blamed for the unreliability of our outboard motors, of course. In any case, he was a soldier, not a sailor, despite having been born in the harbour town of Seaham in County Durham. Alfie, known to most as 'Geordie', worked down the local coal mines when he left school, but by the time he reached his early twenties he had decided that he needed to get out of the pits and so joined the army. On completion of his basic training, he was posted to Germany with the Royal Lincolnshire Regiment. By late 1952, he was part of the re-emerging SAS Regiment in Malaya.

Following jungle training and his parachute course, Alfie joined 8 Troop, B Squadron, and became an expert jungle operator, eventually receiving a well-earned promotion. Over the next five years, he took part in all of B Squadron's operations against the CTs and was also involved in the resettlement of villagers who had been living under the tyranny of the terrorist groups. Working in the jungle for up to 120 days at a stretch was hugely taxing both mentally and physically and the few days' leave Alfie and the rest of B Squadron enjoyed between tours was spent in the bars of Singapore. When Alfie finally managed to have some real time at home in the UK once the Malayan Emergency was over, he was based at the Regiment's headquarters in Malvern, Worcestershire. While in Malvern, Alfie met his wife-to-be, a young Welsh girl called Margaret.

As with all SAS marriages, Alfie and Margaret had to endure some lengthy separations when he was away on operations. In 1960, he became part of A Squadron when the Regiment moved to its new home at Bradbury Lines in Hereford and by 1963 Alfie was back in the jungle, this time in Borneo. In April the following year, the squadron was sent into Aden and Alfie got his first taste of the Radfan Mountains. He was to come to know the mountain conditions well, slipping into the area on covert patrols to set up secret observation posts overlooking the wadis. From their lofty vantage points, Alfie and his cohorts could spot terrorist groups in the wadis, sneaking into Aden from Yemen with supplies of guns and grenades for the terrorists. They would then direct artillery fire onto the enemy with such accuracy that the superstitious hill tribesmen began to talk of a new magical weapon controlled by the British – a weapon that could seek out the tribesmen wherever they were.

A Squadron's arrival in Aden was, however, something of a baptism of fire. The normal period for acclimatization to any region is around two weeks. In Aden, where the temperatures can easily top 120°F (49°C) during the day but drop to almost freezing in the mountains at night, men who had only recently spent five months in the humidity of the jungle in Borneo might reasonably have been given a while longer to get used to the intense dry heat. In fact, immediately after landing at RAF Khormaksar, they transferred to what would be their operational base at Thumier, 60 miles (97km) north of the port of Aden and less than 30 miles (48km) from the Yemeni border. They were out on patrol in the mountains that very night. They had no time for a relaxed settling-in period. Within two weeks they were to participate in Operation *Cap Badge*. The object was to infiltrate an area of the Radfan Mountains known as 'Cap Badge' in order to secure and mark DZs for a much larger airborne force that was to occupy Cap Badge and another area, Rice Bowl. These two areas of high ground dominated the ancient trade routes from Yemen that were being used to smuggle men and weapons into Aden. Whoever controlled these sites effectively controlled the old camel routes.

Alfie was one of two senior sergeants on the operation, the rest of the men being highly experienced veterans of Malaya and Borneo. The two exceptions were their troop commander, Captain Robin Edwards, and their signaller, Trooper Warburton. Edwards was fairly new to the Regiment, having come from the Somerset & Cornwall Light Infantry, but had established himself as a capable and reliable young officer. Warburton was a tough and wiry former sapper.

It was early evening on 29 April 1964 when the patrol left the Regiment's base at Thumier in a small convoy of armoured cars, setting off down the Dhala Road towards the Wadi Rabwa. There the convoy turned off the road and began making its way up the wadi. The armoured cars had bounced and swayed over the rough track for only a few minutes before they came under rifle and machine-gun fire from concealed positions high up in the cliffs above the wadi. By now it was dark enough for Alfie and the others to slip away from the convoy as the gunners in the armoured cars engaged the enemy positions with their machine-guns. Their departure went unnoticed by the tribesmen in their rocky sangars, the fortified bunkers that blended so well with the surrounding landscape. They were more intent on driving back what they obviously thought was an armoured patrol probing their positions.

Captain Edwards' plan was to continue up the Wadi Rabwa, then gain some height by traversing the slopes of the 3,900ft (1,188m) Jebel Ashqab, then descend towards the Cap Badge objective and be in position before dawn. They would then lie up during the day, ready to mark the DZ for the Paras the following night. The crucial thing was to reach their LUPs before first light, as they would be easily spotted on the mountainside in the daylight. They had only a few miles to cover, but it was rough going over steep, rocky terrain. Each man carried a 60lb (27kg) pack, four magazines loaded with 80 rounds total for his SLR, 200 rounds of 7.62mm ammo in a bandolier and 200 rounds of .303 ammo for the patrol's Bren gun, which was carried by Alfie. The Bren weighed more than twice as much as the 10lb (4.5kg) SLR. In addition, each man carried at least four water bottles and there was supplementary kit, including torches and an Aldis lamp to mark the DZ the following night. Altogether each man's kit amounted to quite a load. Warburton did not carry as much ammo as the rest because he had a 45lb (20kg) radio to lug up the mountain. He was also hampered by a problem about which nobody knew until it was too late.

No soldier likes to duck out of a patrol just because he's feeling a bit off colour. You take a day off primary school if you have an upset tummy, but no one would ever want to be seen to duck out of an SAS operation for that. Apart from anything else, stepping down means that someone else has to go in your place, and if anything happens to him you've got that on your conscience. All of that, of course, amounts to nothing if you think you're going to be a liability to the patrol. Warburton was having stomach cramps pretty much from the moment the patrol left Thumier. No doubt he thought it was nerves. If he'd mentioned it to Alfie, things might have turned out differently. Alfie had the experience to judge whether the lad was fit to go out with the patrol. Warburton, however, didn't want to let anyone down and thought he could tough it out. But as they laboured silently up the mountain in the moonlight, he began lagging further and further behind. He had some kind of food poisoning, one of the myriad of bugs that can lay you low in places like Aden. Alfie and the other patrol sergeant decided that Warburton had to march in the centre of the column to ensure that he wouldn't fall behind and get lost. They redistributed the kit everyone was carrying so that Warburton's load was shared by the rest of the patrol and someone else could take on the burden of the radio. Inevitably, the patrol had to reduce its pace so that the signaller could keep plodding on.

By 2.00am it was starting to look like they were not going to reach their objective before dawn. They were still more than 3 miles (4.8km) from Cap Badge over rough country and sunrise was less than three-and-a-half hours away. They couldn't risk being caught out in the open, but Captain Edwards had spotted a couple of stone sangars that looked like they were abandoned. This could be the ideal place to take cover. When they checked out the sangars it was obvious that they had not been used for some time. Now they could all wait out the daylight hours and hopefully Warburton would recover enough to make the final push to Cap Badge as darkness fell.

Edwards radioed the squadron commander back at Thumier to advise him of the situation. The patrol members were still confident that they could fulfil their mission. They were in a good position just below a ridge that led to the summit of Jebel Ashqab. They had decent cover in the sangars which, having been built by the locals, would not attract any undue attention. (Rearranging any part of the local landscape in an attempt to conceal nine men would have been spotted the instant any nearby villagers rubbed the sleep from their eyes.) Behind the low stone walls of the sangars, the patrol would even have some shade from the sun during the day. They had little choice but to stay put in any case. Move on to Cap Badge and they would be out in the open in daylight. Abandon the operation and head back towards the Dhala Road and they would also be out in the open in daylight. Sitting tight was their only real option – and they almost got away with it.

When the sun came up, Alfie and the rest of the patrol were dismayed to find that they were only about 1,000 yards (914m) from the mountain village of Shab Taym, known to be an enemy stronghold. Sure enough, at first light local sentries were seen leaving the village, carrying their rifles to their lookout posts and sniper positions above the approaches to the village. None came in the direction of the hidden patrol. By 11.00am it was starting to look like the patrol was going to survive a quiet and uneventful day on the mountainside. Then they heard the jangling bells and scrabbling hoofs of a herd of goats approaching up a small wadi close by the sangars. The herd was accompanied by a man and a woman, the man shouting loudly to the woman as they made their way up the wadi. The men in the sangars hardly dared breathe. The goats were now only a few feet away. Unless the herder walked by facing completely the wrong direction, he was almost sure to spot them. But would he? The answer came an instant later. A cry of alarm from the herdsman told them that the game was up. The man set off for the village, yelling for help. A single round from an SLR cut him down. The sound of the shot echoed through the mountains, bringing an immediate reaction in the village below. The herdsman's death would buy the patrol some time to prepare themselves, perhaps giving them a slight edge for the first few minutes of the firefight that was about to commence.

The woman and the herd of goats vanished as though they had never existed. They were no longer important. The focus of Alfie's attention was now the growing band of armed tribesmen making their way slowly, curiously in the direction of the sangars. They may have thought that the rifle shot was from one of their own sentries, firing either by accident or as a signal. They were certainly taking no pains to conceal themselves as they made their way up the slope. When he thought they had come close enough, Edwards gave the order to open fire. Several of the tribesmen went down, the others dived for cover. Alfie held his fire with the Bren, searching for a viable target, as the tribesmen wallowed in confusion. They were still uncertain about the source of the gunfire, but it didn't take them long to work out what their next move should be.

Captain Edwards already knew. Had he been the one taking fire from the sangars, he would certainly have tried to move round the flanks and take up a position on the ridge above. That is exactly what the tribesmen did. It took them two hours to place men on the ridge and, just as the first shots from the snipers cracked into the stonework, Alfie watched Edwards' response come into play. Edwards was on the radio to Thumier, where his instructions were being relayed to an RAF Air Support Officer who radioed them directly to the pilots of four Hawker Hunters that dropped out of the sky to blast the ridge with their cannon. After the first pass, with the spent brass cannon shell cases still tinkling into the hillside, the enemy tribesmen abandoned their exposed positions on the ridge. They would not be able to dominate the sangars from the heights, but their sniper fire was to be merciless and continuous. In return, the Hunters circled above, swooping down to blast the enemy positions whenever there were signs of movement. The patrol was also able to call in artillery barrages to keep the tribesmen at bay. The result was a stalemate. The Hunters and the artillery stopped the enemy from overrunning the sangars, but the patrol couldn't leave the sangars without being cut to pieces by the deadly accurate sniper fire. Even the slightest movement in the sangar attracted a fusillade of well-aimed shots. Ricochets and razor-sharp stone chips flying through the air meant that everyone picked up a few scratches, although some were less lucky.

Just over five hours after the first shot of the conflict had been fired, Paddy Baker, another member of the troop, huddled in the same sangar as Alfie, was hit twice in the left leg. A moment later another of the patrol had a bullet crease his back. Alfie kept watch as Paddy did his best to dress the wounds, then another bullet grazed Paddy's right leg. Perhaps sensing that they had caught the men in this sangar off guard, two of the enemy broke cover and dashed forwards. They threw themselves at the sangar wall, in an attempt to push the loose stone barricade over on top of those inside. Alfie and Paddy popped up above the parapet, Alfie with the Bren and Paddy with his SLR. Alfie dispatched the attackers before Paddy had time to squeeze his trigger.

The Hunters had been working in relays all afternoon, maintaining an almost constant presence over the battlefield. Now, as Alfie watched them wheeling round over the peaks, he could see that the rocks were turning pink. The undersides of the Hunters, too, glowed pink as they caught the last rays of the setting sun. The shadows among the rocks on the ground were growing longer, making it far more difficult for the pilots to pick out targets. As darkness approached, Alfie knew that the aircraft would, in any case, have to return to Khormaksar. Without air cover, the patrol would not be able to hold off the enemy who had grown in strength during the course of the day, with more and more men arriving from neighbouring villages. SAS reinforcements had attempted to fly in by helicopter, but the aircraft had been badly shot up on the way in and had to turn back. The patrol's only hope now was that they could vacate the sangars under cover of darkness before the enemy had a chance to storm the positions.

They were to make a run for it carrying only their weapons, water and emergency rations. Everything else was destroyed in the sangars including, following a final message to base, the radio. Alfie and the four others in the larger sangar, who included Captain Edwards and Warburton, gave covering fire as the four from the other sangar made a break for the cover of some rocks. Then it was the turn of Alfie and his group. As the four in the rocks poured fire in the direction of the enemy, Alfie jumped to his feet and bounded downhill to the left, heading for cover. Firing the Bren from the hip as he ran, he blasted away at two boulders to his right, behind which he knew there were tribesmen sheltering. Collapsing behind the cover of a rocky outcrop, Alfie could see Warburton still in the sangar. He had been hit several times and was clearly dead. Captain Edwards had made it only a few yards before he too had been hit. The enemy snipers were now targeting his body, just to make sure. The other two were safe. The three of them were in positions 10–15 yards (9–14m) ahead of the first group, and Alfie called on the other four to get ready to move. The sangars were still the main focus of the enemy fire, the tribesmen having no idea how many more soldiers might still be lurking inside.

Alfie and the surviving six members of the patrol were able to use the cover on the mountainside and the gathering darkness to stay on high ground, heading back round the mountain to the slopes above the Wadi Rabwa and the route back to the Dhala Road. Confusion reigned around the sangars. Two groups of the enemy had closed on the positions from opposite directions and had started shooting at each other. The activity around the sangars ended when they were carpeted by a pre-arranged artillery barrage, called in by Captain Edwards and Warburton with their final radio message. By then, however, the tribesmen had also vacated the sangars, taking with them the bodies of Edwards and Warburton.

Alfie and the others were now in the unenviable position of traversing the high ground above the wadi in the dark. Inevitably, the two most badly wounded lagged behind the rest. This did give the others the advantage of having back markers, though. Twice the wounded men heard footsteps approaching and laid an ambush. Twice they eliminated the tribesmen stalking them. Alfie then sent a few bursts from the Bren back into the darkness along the trail to make anyone else think twice about creeping up behind them. The whole patrol made increasingly frequent stops to close ranks and for the medic to check the wounded. They were all running low on water. They were also utterly exhausted, having been out in the mountains for more than 24 hours, fighting for their lives for almost half that time. Some were further weakened from loss of blood, making the demanding climb down through the rocky gulleys to the main wadi even more treacherous. By the time they all slumped down by the muddy water of a stream on the bed of the Wadi Rabwa, Alfie knew that they were only a short march from safety. Nevertheless, the sensible thing to do was to stay put until morning. The last thing they wanted to do now was to run into a trigger-happy patrol of local federal troops who were likely to open fire on anything that came towards them out of the darkness. In daylight, they would be able to identify themselves and avoid being shot by their own side.

The next morning they began the last leg of their long journey. After only about 30 minutes, Alfie heard a familiar and comforting sound – the rumble of an armoured car engine. Out of the dust on the road loomed the unmistakable shape of a Saladin. The two worst wounded rode the rest of the way to Thumier in the Saladin. Alfie and the others made it under their own steam. They had survived but, for Alfie and the others, one of the worst shocks of the mission was yet to come. News filtered through that a Yemeni radio broadcast that claimed that the heads of two British soldiers had been put on display on stakes in the main square in the city of Taiz. A patrol would later find the decapitated bodies of Edwards and Warburton buried in shallow graves near the sangars.

Alfie went on to enjoy a long career with the Regiment. I served with him in D Squadron in Borneo and Aden as well as on exercises in Germany, Norway and Canada. In the late 1960s, Alfie served as an instructor with 23 SAS (TA) in Birmingham, which brought with it the advantage of allowing him to spend time with Margaret and their three sons. By 1970 he was back with 22 SAS again and in action in Oman.

On completing his 22 years' service, most of which had been with the SAS, Alfie left the army to work as a security consultant in the Middle East, mainly in Saudi Arabia and Yemen. In 1983 he was in Angola, working for De Beers at one of its gold mine sites. It's a big step from coal mining to gold mining, but in this job Alfie stayed firmly on the surface, although the job was not as straightforward as he expected. Angola was at war. The fighting that had begun as a war of independence in 1961 had descended into civil war by the mid-1970s, and would not come to an end until 2002. In 1984, the mine where Alfie worked was engulfed by the conflict when elements of the *União Nacional para a Independência Total de Angola* (UNITA; National Union for the Total Independence of Angola), which included many foreign mercenaries with at least 20 Britons among them, seized the facility. Along with most of the other mine workers, Alfie was taken prisoner and endured a five-week, 300-mile (483km) march to a prison camp. The prisoners had little food and were kept in appalling conditions. After three months in the camp in northern Angola, Alfie was released and repatriated to the UK. Alfie then spent 13 years working for the Brunei Royal Family, maintaining security on their UK properties until he finally retired in 1997.

Alfie died in September 2003 at the age of 73. I will always remember him as being the man you looked to whenever you felt your confidence waver. He was a master at maintaining morale, his vast experience and good humour always there to keep everyone buoyed up. He would have been just as much of a tower of strength on the long march in Angola as he was on the retreat into the Wadi Rabwa 20 years earlier. There aren't many who command the sort of respect that everyone who worked with him had for Alfie Tasker.

Chapter 10

WO1 REGIMENTAL SERGEANT-MAJOR REG TAYLER

The spinning blades of the Sultan of Oman's Air Force (SOAF) Huey kicked up storms of dust that swirled around the helicopter landing pad, the rhythmic chopping of its 48ft (15m) rotor adding to the howl of the Lycoming engine. Waiting ready to board, the soldiers of the SAS patrol turned their heads away from the noise, shielding their faces from the dust and grit that sandblasted their kit. A nod from the pilot signalled that he was happy for them to embark and the patrol moved forward in line, crouched with heads bowed low to keep them well clear of the blades. The SAS is renowned for remaining cool under pressure, but there's more than one way to lose your head!

Moments later, the engine note gathered to a screaming frenzy and the two huge blades adopted their characteristic chattering, the Huey lifting and turning to head out across the parched landscape towards the mountains. The men of A Squadron were used to the noise inside the machine and grateful for the stream of cool air that rushed in through the open doors, a welcome temporary respite from the baking heat of the Omani sun. To any independent observer, they would have looked quite relaxed, taking in the scenery or closing their eyes fully to savour the cold breeze. Another chopper ride to another LZ. They'd had their final briefing;

they knew what they were doing; it was all pretty much routine. There was one, however, who did not appear to have quite the same air of casual confidence displayed by his mates. He wasn't panicking, or showing any signs of losing his nerve, but he was definitely the only one who turned to the man next to him and yelled above the Huey's din.

'Bob!' shouted Reg. 'When we get there – when we land – what do I do?'

Reg Tayler could not have chosen a better man to ask. He was sitting next to Bob Podesta. Bob didn't laugh or even crack a smile. He was calm and serious, giving Reg a look that restored his confidence and banished any nervousness.

'Make sure your weapon is cocked and ready to fire,' said Bob. 'Get down on the ground as fast as you can. Keep your head down until we know it's safe to move.'

Reg's shoulders settled almost imperceptibly. That was all he had to do. Do what the others did. Do what Bob told him and he would be fine. A few minutes later, the nose of the Huey tilted into the air, robbing the aircraft of its forward velocity, and it sank to the ground, its skids barely touching the rocky desert surface before the patrol spilled out, raced clear of the chopper and hit the deck. Reg did as the others did, took up his position and backed up his mates.

While Reg's group secured the LZ, hunkering down behind whatever cover they could find, scanning the surrounding rocks and thorny bushes for any signs of the enemy, their Huey rose out of its dust cloud, clearing the LZ in time to make way for the next chopper. Reg cast a glance at the next sand-coloured machine as it disgorged its troops, the pilot sitting calm and unperturbed as the men sprinted away and the rotors thrashed frantically above him. Reg knew that the pilot fully realized what a tempting target he was for any enemy sniper and marvelled at his cool demeanour. He snapped back to surveying the mountainside in front of him, the chopper dragging itself into the air just as the previous one had done, spending not an instant longer than necessary on the LZ to provide the fastest possible build-up of troops on the ground and the least opportunity for enemy marksmen.

Mobilized by a brief shouted command and a waved signal, Reg and Bob's detachment set off uphill from the LZ. Their job was to take the high ground and provide covering fire for the main part of A Squadron that would sweep forward along the valley to make contact with the enemy that they knew was lying in wait. The object was to force them to withdraw from the area. By now, of course, with the choppers having announced their arrival, the enemy was fully aware of the SAS presence.

Moving quickly between the bone-dry scattering of boulders and scree on the hillside, Reg found himself easily keeping pace with the others, although it was tough going in the growing heat of another sweltering Omani morning. Hardly had the clatter of the chopper's rotors faded into the distance before Reg spotted a spurt of dust erupt on the track followed by the crack of a rifle fired from a great distance, the round arriving before the sound of its discharge. Reg threw himself to the ground and rolled into cover. He raised his head enough to try to spot the sniper's position, narrowing his eyes to squint in the glare of sunshine. He looked over to where Bob had taken cover and heard the others shouting to indicate the enemy location up ahead. Coordinating fire and movement, they moved forward to adopt more effective fire positions. Just as he had been trained to do, just as the others did, Reg hugged his SLR into his shoulder and the weapon bucked as he fired off a volley of shots before he broke cover, sprinting forward to his next position.

As they advanced, the firefight became more intense and the rest of A Squadron, making their way forward on the lower ground, were also trading rounds with the enemy. Having secured a firm base on the hillside, Reg's group continued to engage targets in their own vicinity as well as in support of the squadron down below. Although he was there primarily as a medic, Reg felt no compunction about using his rifle to best effect. Tending to his friends' wounds was one thing, but nailing the men who might cause those wounds was surely the most effective treatment of all.

The firefight continued in sporadic bursts for most of the day, the whine of ricochets and clattering of rock splinters interspersed with waves of fire from Reg's squad. Eventually, with their position swathed in dust and gunsmoke, they decided that, as the rest of the squadron had manoeuvred rather further away than was desirable, they should withdraw to regroup. There was no point in becoming isolated and starting to run low on ammo.

They executed a tactical withdrawal to reunite themselves with A Squadron. Reg knew that his fire party was leaving behind many enemy dead and wounded on the mountainside. On this occasion, his skill at arms had been of greater value than his talent as a medic. The squadron forced the guerrillas to abandon their mountain stronghold and the mission was deemed a success. This had been Reg's first operation, but he handled it like an old pro. He was an integral part of the team.

That, of course, had been Reg's problem. He knew he was part of a team. He knew that all of the guys disembarking from the Huey needed to be able to rely on each other. He wasn't scared or, rather, he wasn't any more scared than any sensible trooper about to be inserted into enemy-held territory should be. He was more worried about cocking things up and letting the team down. Reg cared, but that was no weakness. That was, in fact, one of his many great strengths.

The men who volunteer for SAS Selection come from all sorts of different backgrounds and a wide range of units. There are engineers and signallers, artillerymen, riflemen, guardsmen and quite a number, like me, who join from The Parachute Regiment. There are comparatively few, however, who come from the Royal Army Medical Corps (RAMC). Given the nature of the Regiment's business, though, having a skilled medic at your side can be a great comfort.

Each man in an SAS patrol has a specific skill, whether he be an expert signaller, demolitions man, linguist or medic. At one time a normal patrol would consist of four men, but nowadays they are expected to pack so much firepower and carry so much sophisticated equipment that a patrol is more likely to be six strong. At least one of the six will be a trained medic and that was my job, too. I thought I was pretty good at it, but I could never even have hoped to have the depth of knowledge or the medical understanding of Reg Tayler.

Reg arrived in Hereford in 1965 as a Medical Support and Training Advisor (MSTA) and apart from a short posting to Brecon, he served with 22 SAS until he left the army in 1977. He was a fully qualified State Registered Nurse (SRN), so was, of course, referred to by one and all as 'Sister Reg'. Reg's brief was to ensure that all SAS patrol medics were trained in the latest techniques of administering first aid, had the most modern and effective equipment available and were properly trained to use it. In fact, 'first aid' is something of a misnomer, as the patrol medics were trained to carry out many procedures that went far beyond the conventional understanding of first aid. Treating bullet wounds or dealing with the blast and shrapnel damage inflicted by a grenade or mortar round is more than an average civilian first-aider would be expected to do. We were also schooled in the treatment of tropical diseases and all manner of ailments that could afflict a member of the patrol in a hostile environment – from frostbite to snakebite.

SAS medics are not, however, as well schooled as professional paramedics – their training stretches over three years while ours is only three months. Reg, in fact, had a hand in developing the standard advanced training given to paramedics and the contacts he maintained outside the Regiment ensured that part of our training, and the refresher courses, took place in a civilian hospital. Before he let any of us loose on the medical fraternity, Reg first spent some time at the hospital himself, in order to identify key personnel and ensure that our training stints ran as smoothly as possible. This form of 'work experience' was invaluable in providing us medics with an opportunity to carry out a variety of procedures in a most realistic environment; Saturday nights in a large city hospital often resembled a war zone.

Reg had arranged for Taff Springles, another D Squadron member, and I to be sent on attachment to the John Radcliffe Infirmary in Oxford where one of our patients in the casualty department was a man who had fallen off a ladder while cleaning his windows. He'd landed on his greenhouse and picked up some nasty cuts along with the rest of his injuries. We were dressed in white coats and the poor guy obviously thought we were doctors until he heard Taff asking the Ward Sister what type of thread he should use to stitch one of the cuts. He stormed off to look for a real doctor, warning everyone waiting to watch out for the 'bloody amateurs'. It took a great deal of gentle persuasion to calm him down. We saw him in the pub that night, so he was none the worse for his experience, unlike one poor bloke when I was at St Mary's in Paddington. He had a bad cut on his top lip and, in repairing it, one of my fellow 'professionals' managed to stitch his mouth shut. Needless to say, Reg expected far higher standards from us.

In the classroom, Reg was a great teacher. He had immense enthusiasm for his subject and ensured that his students' learning was informed, interesting and fun. He devised ways of making certain things simple to remember. It's easy to panic when you are faced with a real casualty and forget everything you are supposed to be doing. If that happens, you're about as much use as a chocolate teapot. To help us remember the priorities of life-saving, the initial treatment, he taught us to think of 'ABC' – Airway, Breathing, Circulation. This simple aide-memoire has been universally adopted and is now used all over the world.

Reg also had a great sense of humour. He loved to smile – it let him show off the wonderful set of front teeth he had acquired after he lost his own when he and his old push bike had an argument with the side of a police car. He didn't get too upset, then, when John 'Lofty' Wiseman, the survival training expert, and me 'took him for a ride' one day. We were on one of Reg's medical refresher courses and were being taught how to apply a Thomas' splint. This was a particularly cumbersome piece of apparatus, now much improved, but then tricky to apply and equally difficult to remove. It is used for the treatment of a broken femur and immobilizes the leg.

Lofty and I persuaded Reg that the best way to test whether we'd done it properly was to apply the splint to Reg himself, then he could judge whether it was correctly secured. That done, we sprinkled red ink liberally over the bandages, bundled Reg into a Land Rover and deposited him a few hundred yards from camp, outside the local Post Office. His protests to the passing public fell on deaf ears and, eventually, an ambulance arrived. Fortunately, the ambulance men also had a sense of humour and brought him back to camp. This was in the days when security in the camp was not so stringent and we could come and go at will. At the time it was put down to 'the boys having fun'; nowadays it would probably spark 'an incident'.

As well as training the medics in camp, Reg accompanied the squadrons on operations, remaining on standby at base to give advice in the event of a soldier sustaining a serious injury, the treatment of which required his expertise, even if it was only over the radio. My first encounter with Reg was when he was attached to D Squadron, on operations in the Radfan Mountains of Aden in 1966. He went to great lengths to ensure that the patrol medics were fully prepared to meet all eventualities in that terrain. He took great pride in the knowledge that the medics were the best-trained operatives he could put in the field and loved to hear of their experiences in putting their training into practice.

But Reg wasn't only an HQ advisor. He accompanied patrols in action and had successfully completed the stringent SAS Selection course. To do that you have to be a highly competent, all-round soldier. You can't skip through Selection on the back of your medical qualifications. Reg had to slog his way through the toughest test of a soldier's abilities the army can throw at you.

Much has been written about the SAS over the past two decades, most of it only partially true and some of it complete fiction. SAS soldiers are not superheroes, not indestructible, not infallible. What they do have in spades is dedication and determination. Like everyone else, Reg volunteered to put himself through the test. To understand what he went through to win the right to wear the beige beret and winged dagger badge, you need to have a basic understanding of the Selection process. Whatever the myths and legends, one fact is not in dispute: the SAS is the foremost military unit in the world, an elite force respected and feared in equal measure. Reg wanted to be part of that elite.

Over 60 years ago, the founder of the SAS, Colonel David Stirling, laid down the principles under which the Regiment still operates:

> From the start, the SAS Regiment has had some firmly held tenets, from which we must never depart. They are:
>
> - The unrelenting pursuit of excellence.
> - Maintaining the highest standard of discipline in all aspects of the daily life of the SAS soldier ... a high standard of self-discipline in each soldier is the only effective foundation of Regimental discipline. Commitment to the SAS pursuit of excellence becomes a sham if any single one of the disciplinary standards is allowed to slip.
> - The SAS brooks no sense of class ... we share with the Brigade of Guards a deep respect for quality, but we have an entirely different outlook. We believe,

as did the ancient Greeks who originated the word 'aristocracy', that every man with the right attitude and talents, regardless of birth or riches, has the capacity in his own lifetime for reaching that status in its true sense ... all ranks in the SAS are of 'one company', in which a sense of class is both alien and ludicrous.

- Humility and humour: both these virtues are indispensable in the everyday life of officers and men – particularly in the case of the SAS, which is often regarded as an elite Regiment. Without frequent recourse to humour and humility, our special status could cause resentment in other units of the British Army and an unbecoming conceit and big-headedness in our own soldiers.

Reg lived up to those principles as well as any man I have ever met. He didn't have the best start in life. He almost fell to enemy fire at a time when he had barely learned to walk. A German bomber offloaded its deadly cargo over his home during World War II, and two-year-old Reg was shoved under the kitchen table by his mother just as the bomb struck. His mother's quick thinking saved Reg ... sadly, she died in the explosion. I guess that's something else Reg and I had in common – I was pulled out from under a wardrobe when our house in Brighton was hit.

When Reg grew up, cared for by adoptive parents, he decided to join the army but did not enlist, as so many of us as youngsters imagined doing, in a unit where he could see himself charging around firing a Bren gun from the hip. He did not join to become the next John Wayne or Audie Murphy. He joined to become a nurse in the Medical Corps. Every SAS soldier is a volunteer and anyone in the armed forces can apply, including men from the RAF and the Royal Navy. The Regiment attracts the pick of men from every branch of the services, but few are chosen. You have to have been in the armed forces for at least three years, as mentioned earlier, so you have some maturity and are at least a very good basic soldier. Beyond that, the Regiment isn't too worried about a person's past. They're more concerned with what he is like now and what he will be like in the future.

The ranks coming forward can be anything from private to captain; a lot of NCOs – corporals and sergeants – give it a go, but if they pass, they drop to the rank of trooper. Having worked hard to become NCOs, they find themselves working even harder to become privates again.

Reg went through Selection just a few months after I had done. The trial that we had to face hasn't changed a great deal over the past 40 years, although modern recruits have a far better idea of what to expect than either Reg or I did. Selection consists of a three-week period of progressively severe fitness and endurance tests, designed gradually to wear you down before the final week-long series of tests, which place relentless demands on both your physical and mental capabilities. You must solve a series of daunting problems while force-marching over the Brecon Beacons by day and night, and in all weathers. In the final week you go on one march after another, each one longer than the one before and with progressively heavier kit, culminating in carrying a 55lb (25kg) Bergen and a 10lb (4.5kg) rifle. Forty years ago, Reg was simply issued with the requisite number of bricks from the SAS quartermaster's stores; today the weight in the Bergen is made up with rather more useful items.

When Reg first turned up for Selection he sat in the Blue Room surrounded by hardened professional soldiers in a dozen rows of ten men. The CO's introduction ran as it always did, 'Welcome to the Selection Course. It would be good if you all passed the course – we need the manpower. I will be fortunate if even one out of each row of you passes; it is the standard that we set, not the pass rate.'

Unlike me, Reg did not have the benefit of the advice of ex-Para colleagues who'd passed the Selection course, served in the SAS and then returned to the Paras. They told me that it would be worth spending time on honing my cross-country navigation skills and building up my stamina for hill-walking carrying a heavy weight prior to the actual test. He didn't have the chance, as I did, to spend his spare time in the weeks leading up to Selection on build-up training. Even so, the Selection course itself was far more stressful, both physically and mentally, than I had ever imagined. How did Reg, a medic rather than a Para, manage it? He had the guts to stick it out, is the answer. He had the strength to cope with the gut-wrenching physical exhaustion, when every sinew and muscle feels like it's on fire. He had the determination to keep going on those marches; he put up with the agony of realizing, on reaching the top of a precipice on hands and knees, that over the ridge lay yet another peak to climb. It would have been so easy for him to give up – no disgrace for a medic to bow out of that hell – but then came the thought that he had crossed the Rubicon, that he was closer to the end of the march than to the beginning. Then from deep inside came the stamina to carry on, the conviction that the extra strength had to be found. The reward came the next day, when his name was on the list to carry on with more of the same.

Lofty Wiseman is quoted as saying, 'Death is nature's way of telling you that you have failed Selection.' Even if nature doesn't deliver that message, Selection is only the beginning. You go straight on to a six-month period called Continuation Training, involving training in jungle warfare, weapons and explosives, including demolition and sabotage, ground control of air, mortar and artillery fire, field first aid, combat survival and resistance to interrogation. Throughout the six months you can still be instantly removed and returned to your unit at any time.

Continuation Training culminates in a week of combat survival, living up in the hills on your wits, and precious little else, while being pursued by 'hunter' forces. At the end of the week you face at least 24 hours of continuous harsh interrogation, including every bit of physical and psychological rough treatment that the Geneva Convention allows, and a bit more besides. Only after successfully coming through that – and a surprising number fail to clear that final hurdle – are the surviving recruits regarded as ready for service with the SAS. The handful from the Regiment's Selection intake who finally become 'badged' as fully-fledged members of the SAS are still on probation for the first year of their service, and in the Regimental tradition whatever their rank prior to joining the SAS they all revert to the lowest rank – trooper.

Having made it through Selection, Reg was to serve for the next 12 years with some of the most experienced and professional soldiers in the world, men who had years of special forces experience in Malaya, Borneo, Aden and a host of other places. They had set the standards and developed the techniques that made the SAS pre-eminent, but there was never any hint of complacency; every aspect of our work was under continual scrutiny and our techniques were constantly being refined and developed to keep ahead of the new threats we had to face. Reg took his responsibilities every bit as seriously. He kept abreast of the latest medical developments and applied them to his work with the Regiment. Reg also made himself aware not only of what was happening on operations, but also what was going on within the Regiment and how it affected those associated with it.

Reg's teaching skills were not limited to patrol medics. On his own initiative, he organized courses of first-aid training for some of the men's wives, too. He gave instruction classes himself and arranged for them to be tested and accredited by the local St John's Ambulance Brigade. He was an extremely caring and compassionate person. Although unmarried, he was very much aware of how our lifestyle affected those closest to us. He often went out of his way to visit the sick and wounded and extended his caring to their relatives as well.

This caring and generous aspect of Reg's character is well illustrated by an incident recalled by Dr Phil McCluskie, one-time medical officer to the Regiment. The two were driving along a quiet road in France in an ambulance on an exercise when they turned a corner to find glass and debris scattered all over the road. A set of skid marks led to a delivery van that had smashed into a roadside tree. Reg dashed to the cab and found the driver badly injured and barely conscious. There was no easy way to extricate the man from the mangled wreckage, nor was it advisable until the extent of his injuries could be assessed, so Reg crawled into the tangle of metal to treat the man as best he could. He cleared the van driver's airway and supported his head as the man slipped in and out of consciousness. Reg spoke to him and tried to keep him awake, staying in the wreck of the cab until the emergency services finally arrived. Even then, when he realized that the cab would have to be cut open to free the man, he stuck to his task, giving the driver support and reassurance right up to the moment he was lifted clear of the wreck and loaded into a civilian ambulance.

It goes without saying that any man who would fish a dead, bloated hedgehog out of a garden pond, bury the poor creature then stand to attention and salute over its grave, was something of an animal lover. Reg had many dogs over the years, including a German Shepherd called Clem and a small, grey-and-black dog called Sally of indeterminate breed. It was questionable whether Reg had adopted Sally or vice versa. On one occasion

Reg had delivered a presentation to some visiting 'Top Brass'. Several hours after they departed in the official helicopter, there was a phone call from the Ministry of Defence (MOD) enquiring if a small grey-and-black dog was known to anyone in camp. The description was instantly recognized by the telephonist – it was Sally, who had hitched a lift to London in the MOD's helicopter. Instead of being apologetic, Reg was rather proud that she had shown such initiative.

In 1976, Reg was awarded the MBE (Member of the British Empire) for his services to the Regiment, a thoroughly deserved accolade. This was not the only official praise that he received. After leaving the Regiment in 1977, Reg went to work in Oman and when his contract there was over, he was sent a personal letter of thanks from the sultan, praising him for his work. Reg also spent some time working as a medic on oil-rigs off the coast of Norway, but when he eventually retired he returned to live in Hereford, which by then he regarded as his home. He loved the place and its people and was well-known to many in the town. Local newspapers paid him a fitting tribute when he died following a prolonged illness in January 2004.

Chapter 11

STAFF SERGEANT BOB PODESTA

In the dark alley, the feeble glow from the faltering streetlight failed to dispel the inky shadows that seeped from still corners and cloaked the silent doorways. A man stood alone, waiting, leaning against a wall in the misty light, listening as the echoing click of unhurried footsteps drew ever closer. The figure of a man appeared at the mouth of the alleyway, softly illuminated yet radiating sinister intent. The wide brim of his hat cast a shadow over his face, but even in the half-light, the sharp cut of his pinstripe suit boasted an unmistakeable self-assurance. The extravagance of the wide lapels was matched by the deep cuffs at the bottom of the trouser legs that sat on immaculate spats, starkly white against the gleaming black leather shoes.

As the figure turned to face the waiting man, the streetlight fell on the dull grey form he cradled in his arms. At 3ft (0.9m) long and with its large drum magazine slung beneath the barrel between the two pistol grips, the Thompson SMG was as distinctive as it was deadly. Without a word, the gunman opened up, filling the alleyway with a blaze of muzzle flash and a roar of automatic fire that threatened to shake the walls to pieces. The waiting man, with no time to move and nowhere to run, was flung backwards by the force of the .45-calibre rounds ripping into his body. He landed in a bloody heap, dead before he hit the ground.

The gunman calmly turned and walked away. But this was no Mafia vendetta. This was no underworld 'hit' by the likes of Al 'Scarface' Capone, Lucky Luciano or Bugsy Siegel. The Thompson, nicknamed 'the Chopper', 'the Tommy Gun', or 'the Chicago Typewriter', was being handled by a real expert, but he was no cheap hoodlum. He was Bob Podesta and he's hardly what you would imagine a ruthless gangster to be. He regularly drops by my house, drinks about a gallon of tea and eats all my biscuits! Bob, having retired from the army, had been drafted in by a TV company to work on a documentary about machine-guns. He agreed to dress up for effect when testing some of the weapons and the sight of him decked out like a 1920s racketeer nearly made me die laughing. The TV company couldn't have chosen a better man for the job, though. Bob certainly knows his stuff, having been a soldier all of his adult life and worked with weapons of all shapes and sizes.

When Bob first joined the army, he went into the Royal Artillery. All he had ever wanted to do was to be a soldier and he had been desperate to join up for years. By 1966, having finished his education, he was deemed too old for what was then known as 'boys' service' and too young to join up as an adult. Eventually, he pestered the recruitment office into signing him up in November 1966, just three days after his 17th birthday. His first posting was to Germany where he became part of the British Army of the Rhine (BAOR). During those fretful Cold War years, the BAOR was our frontline against the Soviet threat. It was no secret to anyone in the many bases and camps in West Germany that the communists just across the border in the East had more tanks and manpower than we did. The BAOR was in the unenviable position of knowing that, should the Soviets decide to invade Western Europe, the best we could hope to do with conventional weapons was to hold them up for a few days. The unit to which Bob was posted, however, the 50th Missile Regiment, packed a far stronger punch than any conventional artillery outfit. They were equipped with 8in howitzers and 25ft (7.6m) long Honest John missiles, both of which could go nuclear. In fact, the 50th Missile Regiment provided Britain's only tactical battlefield nuclear capability, and they could deliver some terrifying ordnance. Each Honest John rocket could be armed with a nuclear warhead twice as destructive as the bomb dropped on

Hiroshima in 1945. These were very real and very sinister 'big boys' toys' capable of taking out entire cities – quite a concept for 17-year-old Gunner Podesta to try to get his head round. Of course, the army didn't immediately put raw teenagers in charge of weapons like that, but Bob was there, training with the rest of the unit. Forty years later he was messing about dressed as a gangster with a Tommy Gun, capitalizing on his vast experience of working with the widest range of weapons in the British Army's arsenal, from all manner of small arms and machine-guns, to its biggest, most destructive nuclear missiles.

Missiles and artillery pieces have a fascination all of their own, but Bob is a very active sort of man and needed to be doing something that would present him with more of a challenge than the regular day-to-day duties in the artillery ever could. After a year, he volunteered for the Commando Course. The All Arms Commando Course is run by the Royal Marines at the Commando Training Centre in Lympstone. It is a tough, ten-week course that is open to serving personnel from any part of the armed forces. The course teaches basic skills to a high level as well as providing more advanced military training in things like amphibious assaults and helicopter drills. A bit like SAS Selection, only those with the mental and physical strength to win through will make it. At the most basic level, applicants will be expected to perform a 9-mile (14.5km) speed march carrying at least 30lb (13.6kg) of kit in 90 minutes. There is a 12-mile (19.3km) cross-country yomp (long-distance march) in full kit, carrying a 12lb (5.5kg) rifle. That has to be completed in less than four hours. Every part of the various assault courses come with a time limit attached. Bob not only passed with flying colours, he broke four Commando Course endurance records in the process. He was posted to 95 Commando Light Regiment (RA), where one of his instructors was Ginge Tyler, who had recently left the SAS.

Ginge did, without a doubt, influence Bob's decision to apply for SAS Selection, but for someone like Bob, who wanted to be the best soldier he possibly could be, the lure of the SAS challenge would always have been too great to resist. Bob made it through Selection in 1970, joining G Squadron in August. By the time he celebrated his 21st birthday, he was on active service in Oman during Operation *Storm*.

The SAS has had a long-standing, on-off love affair with southern Arabia both in official and semi-official capacities ever since the end of the Malayan campaign. In October 1958, as the situation in Malaya was being brought under control, D Squadron was pulled out of the humid heat of the jungle to begin a hectic period of retraining to tackle the arid heat of the desert in the Sultanate of Oman. They had just two weeks to get themselves operational with tactics and equipment more suited to their new environment. An attempt was being made to overthrow the sultan and, since he enjoyed the friendship of the British government, steps had to be taken to provide him with protection. A protection treaty had been signed with the Sultan of Muscat (which became part of Oman) in 1789 that gave the British East India Company commercial rights in Oman in exchange for the Royal Navy providing protection from the pirates who roamed the coast plundering the sultan's trading vessels. Britain maintained the relationship with Oman through the reigns of several different sultans up to the 1950s, when Sultan Said bin Taimur, the 13th hereditary ruler of Oman, sat on the throne.

At the time, Britain was following a policy of withdrawing from colonial entanglements in favour of allowing emerging nations the right to self-determination, the right of the people to choose their own governments and their own leaders. Sultan Said bin Taimur was not typical of the new breed of statesmen Britain preferred to see taking their place on the world stage. He did, however, have a couple of very persuasive bargaining tools when it came to retaining the support of Her Majesty's Government. The first was the fact that in 1958 there were a number of oil companies punching holes in the desert crust searching for the black gold. It seemed only a matter of time before they found some. The second was a place called the Musandam peninsula. This is the most north-easterly part of Oman and it sticks out into the Straits of Hormuz. Even if the oil companies never found any oil in Oman (which they did eventually), Musandam commanded a vitally important strategic position, as tankers carrying around half of the western world's oil supplies filed past its rugged shoreline every day.

Although the sultan had British officers and British-trained Omani officers running his armed forces, was supplied with British military hardware, had British troops training in his country and employed the very

British Colonel David Smiley as his chief of staff, the British didn't feel that they could be seen to be providing him with battalions of British soldiers to guard his borders. With the Suez debacle also a recent memory, they certainly didn't want the world's press to start running stories about British soldiers being massacred in the mountains of Oman. And it was in the mountains where the trouble was brewing. On the Jebel Akhdar, or 'Green Mountain', a plateau around 10,000ft (3,000m) high covering an area of some 200 square miles (518 square km), a well-armed force of between 600 and 700 rebels had taken control and had started making forays down onto the coastal plain. They planted mines that destroyed scores of vehicles, including 18 British Ferret armoured scout cars. They were causing the sultan's forces all sorts of problems, not least because their mountain stronghold was notoriously impregnable.

The rebels also had a religious leader, the Imam Ghalib bin Ali of Oman, as their figurehead. Becoming embroiled in a war against Islam was not thought to be a good idea by the British, especially as the imam had backing from Saudi Arabia. The Saudis had been involved in territorial disputes with the sultan, especially over Musandam, for years and the last thing the British wanted was a major confrontation with Saudi Arabia. The solution was to send in the SAS to seize key objectives on the jebel without attracting too much attention from the outside world. D Squadron, led by Major Johnny Watts, started the job in November 1958 and was joined by A Squadron under Major John Cooper in January 1959. A tough time was had by all but the rebels were cleared from the jebel in just ten weeks and the immediate threat to the sultan subsided.

The sultan, it has to be said, was not a terribly popular man. He lived a life of luxury, seldom leaving his palace in Salalah, while the majority of his people lived in abject poverty and fear. Villagers were not allowed to leave their own town without permission from the sultan, even if they were only going looking for work. There was no proper education system, so those who wanted to attend a proper school or university fled the country, many travelling to Eastern European Soviet Bloc states. There was no proper medical care, so people suffered from complaints that simple antibiotics could cure. No one was allowed to wear Western clothes, listen to Western music or to take photographs. The sultan ruled with a rod of iron, yet his people never actually saw him. To be caught defying his laws, however, meant a flogging or being flung into prison. Because of the strategically important land that it occupied and the oil that lay beneath that land, however, Britain had to keep Oman as its friend, even if that meant being nice to the sultan.

Their first Omani adventure in 1958–59 proved that the SAS could operate as an adaptable, low-profile, quick-reaction force to be deployed anywhere in the world under any conditions at a moment's notice. They had successfully transferred from the jungle to the desert and combined with forces already in the area to resolve a situation that had stood every chance of blowing up into a major confrontation.

In Oman, things returned more or less to normal. The poor people stayed poor and the sultan stayed in his palace, but the military planners in the SAS, the 'Head Shed', had no doubts that they would be back in the country eventually. In Aden, bordering the southern Omani province of Dhofar, the build-up to the British withdrawal from the colony had precipitated a power struggle that was causing serious security problems. When the hereditary ruler of Yemen, Imam Ahmad bin Yahya, died in 1962, his son, Crown Prince Muhammad al-Badr, barely had time to warm the cushion on his father's throne before he was deposed in a military coup. The army officers were backed by President Nasser of Egypt, who poured troops and military hardware into Yemen to suppress the crown prince's supporters. The crown prince and his men took to the hills and continued to fight as a guerrilla force. The Egyptian, Soviet and Chinese support for the new regime was worrying for the British, who fully realized that Yemen's intention was to take over Aden when they left. This would then put the Yemenis in an ideal situation to threaten Oman, where the sultan's repressive regime made the country ripe for revolution.

A covert presence was required in Yemen to supply intelligence both to the British commanders in Aden and to keep Britain appraised of the threat level to Oman. It was decided to supply clandestine support to the crown prince's guerrilla fighters in the form of a small mercenary group who would be able to set up a communications and intelligence network. The plan did not have the official support of the British government, but the man asked to organize the mercenary force was none other than the founding father of the SAS, David Stirling. Stirling recruited a number of former SAS officers and men, including John Cooper who had recently led A Squadron in Oman. Cooper had, in fact, been Stirling's driver during the SAS desert campaign in World War II. At one point, the man in command of the mercenary force was Colonel David Smiley, formerly the Sultan of Oman's chief of staff. The crown prince's force also had the backing of the Saudis, the idea of a communist republic sweeping aside an ancient monarchy making them more than a little nervous. Having the Saudis on side, of course, meant that John Cooper and David Smiley were now working with their old enemies from Oman. There was little chance that the royalist guerrillas could defeat the might of the Egyptians, but they did tie down over 55,000 Egyptian troops and a substantial part of Nasser's air force for five years, assets that were sorely needed during Egypt's Six-Day War with Israel in 1967. The Egyptian military would later refer to Yemen as 'our Vietnam'.

What all of this meant was that when Bob and the rest of G Squadron arrived in Oman in 1970, the SAS high command had a very good idea of who the opposition were and the tactics they would adopt. What they needed to know was the enemy strength and how tenaciously it would fight to retain the mountain strongholds. Bob had transferred to A Squadron by the time he was first sent out on a probing mission on the Jebel north of Mirbat early in 1971. The operation involved both A and B Squadrons, split into small groups to reconnoitre the target area.

Bob's group included his good friend the redoubtable Fijian Talaiasi Labalaba (see chapter 12) and after a hard slog through the foothills of the jebel, they finally made contact with the enemy Adoo. Approaching an exposed section of hillside, Bob and Laba slowed to scan the area ahead. The sun-blasted waves of scraggy scrub and crumbling rock looked no different from the miles of parched ground they had already covered, but they both had the feeling that they were being watched, the haunting sensation that raises the hairs on the back of your neck and tightens the stomach muscles. Suddenly, a tattoo of gunfire shattered the mountain air and the patrol threw itself behind whatever cover it could find. Scouring the mountainside for targets, Bob picked out a flicker of movement among the rocks and immediately raked the area with a burst from his General-Purpose Machine-Gun (GPMG; the British Army version of the FN MAG). The others sent two- and three-round volleys in the general direction of the enemy, but the Adoo had chosen their fire positions well and were frustratingly difficult to pinpoint. From the number of rifle and machine-gun rounds that were hammering into the boulders around them, however, it was obvious to Bob that the small SAS patrol was heavily outgunned. It was also clear that they could not afford to hold their ground and risk being outflanked. They had to fall back to a more secure position.

Bob provided covering fire with the GPMG as the patrol began to withdraw. The Adoo, believing they had the upper hand, started moving forward, breaking cover to chase the SAS off the hillside. Bob saw several who appeared to go down under the hail of fire from his GPMG and the deadly accurate rounds squeezed off by Laba and the others. If the Adoo were following, however, he would leave a few surprises for them. As they fell back, Bob planted booby traps to slow up their pursuers. Hand grenades balanced delicately amid piles of stones or strung with trip wires had the desired effect. By the time the group reached a more easily defended position, the Adoo had given up the chase. Bob's patrol had been forced off the mountain, but they had established that the enemy held the area in strength and had left behind a number of dead and wounded Adoo in their wake.

The SAS planners knew that to counter the insurgents they would need more than just firepower: they would need the Omani people on their side. This, in turn, meant that Bob, highly trained in the use of everything from battlefield tactical nuclear weapons to Cherry Blossom boot polish, had to learn a whole new kind of soldiering. During Operation *Storm*, the Regiment was to embark on a major 'hearts and minds' programme, made possible by a drastic change in the country's leadership.

The same sort of violent unrest, encouraged and supported by Yemen, that had flared up in the late 1950s had returned to Oman in the mid-1960s. The sultan's own bodyguards attempted to assassinate him in 1966, and in 1967, when the British left Aden, the warring factions in that territory needed only a little time to settle their differences before devoting their full attention to Oman. In a bold move in July 1970, the Wali (governor) of Dhofar Province arrived at the palace in Salalah, insisting on seeing the sultan. He had come to demand the old man's abdication and had the support of the sultan's son, Qaboos, along with a number of high-ranking British officers in the SAF. The sultan, fearing that the wali's visit signalled another assassination attempt, armed himself with a pistol. He blasted away at the wali, wounding him and unfortunately killing one of his own servants as well. The old man also managed to wound himself in the foot and the stomach before he could be overpowered. The sultan spent the rest of his life in exile in London while his son, Qaboos, became His Majesty Sultan Qaboos bin Said.

Educated at a private school in England, and the Royal Military Academy, Sandhurst, Qaboos made an immediate radio broadcast to his people stating that: 'I promise you to proceed forthwith in the process of creating a modern government. My first act will be the immediate abolition of all the unnecessary restrictions on your lives and activities.'

He was as good as his word and the SAS was there to spearhead his reforms. Before the new schools and hospitals, roads and houses could be built, Bob and the others were there on the ground implementing the SAS's five-pronged plan of attack.

First of all, they had to let the people of Oman know that there was a new sultan and that he was about to bring about great changes in their lives. The SAS carried out leaflet drops with the Omani air force and even handed out small radios so that people could hear Qaboos' broadcasts. They made sure that as many rebel tribesmen as possible came to hear that they were being offered an amnesty and could surrender without fear of reprisals.

Then they had to establish a programme of medical aid, SAS medics working with a newly appointed government medical officer to bring basic health care to thousands of Omanis living in the mountains. More important to some of the people than their own health, however, was the well-being of their livestock. With the help of the RAF, the SAS flew in two Hereford bulls to help improve Omani breeding stock. Agricultural aid also involved bringing in specialist equipment to drill for water or open up defunct wells that the old sultan had concreted over to punish errant villagers.

On the military front, Oman needed an intelligence network not only to keep tabs on the many enemy fighters, but also to monitor propaganda broadcasts by the Yemenis on Radio Aden and find ways to counter it. Finally, the SAS had to raise and train local units to fight for Qaboos against the Adoo. Many of these local soldiers were former Adoo who were promised amnesty if they changed sides to support Qaboos. Since it was his predecessors with whom they had had a problem and Qaboos was now instigating widespread reforms, recruits from among the Adoo came in thick and fast, as much tempted by the £50 reward they were offered for handing over their old Kalashnikovs as they were driven by political ideals.

The SAS 'hearts and minds' campaign worked well in Oman, and special efforts were made in the border territory of Dhofar, the main area of SAS deployment in Operation *Storm*. Like the rest of the SAS in the region, Bob's duties extended beyond simply training the Firquat – they also joined the Firquat, and other regular troops loyal to the sultan, on patrols. One such operation took place in March 1972.

The Wadi Derbat had been identified as harbouring an Adoo stronghold and the plan was that A Squadron would lead one group into the wadi from the south while D Squadron came in from the north, forming a pincer in which the rebel force would be trapped. Having closed on the suspected Adoo positions, however, there were no rebels to be found. The men gathered at a point on the eastern edge of the wadi and patrols were organized to scout the surrounding area and pinpoint the location of the Adoo. Bob set off as part of one of the patrols, heading for a village that lay in the shadow of a hill called Ghaday at the head of the Wadi Nahiz. Picking their way carefully along a rough mountain track in daylight, very much aware that should they be the ones to discover the Adoo headquarters, the mountain tribesmen would easily be able to spot their approach, the tension mounted. The temperature soared as the Arabian sun scorched the landscape.

Then they heard it – the unmistakable zing of incoming rounds and the eruption of rifle and machine-gun fire. The patrol went to ground, taking cover among the rocks, shouting to each other to pinpoint the source of the gunfire. They returned fire, but appeared to be outgunned. They couldn't withdraw without exposing themselves to the Adoo machine-gunners, so they called in an air strike, holding their own until the Strikemasters from Salalah came screaming up the wadi. Flames flared under the aircrafts' wings as they released a barrage of rockets that streaked towards the Adoo positions and exploded in fireballs that were immediately followed by engulfing smoke and dust. The pilots, RAF or ex-RAF flyers on secondment or on contract to the SOAF, then pulled up and swept round to strafe the Adoo with machine-gun fire. The Adoo, having suffered several casualties, withdrew as soon as the planes departed. Bob and the others made their way back to their temporary base in the Wadi to report on the contact. The village beyond Ghaday, it seemed, was where the Adoo had established themselves.

Two nights later, Bob found himself approaching Ghaday once again. SAS patrols, backed by local troops, were to occupy the high ground around the Adoo village under cover of darkness. At first light, they would bring down mortar bombardments, machine-gun fire and air strikes to wipe out the Adoo stronghold. The patrols moved as silently through the darkness as the loose rock and shale beneath their boots would allow. In front of him, Bob could just make out the figure of his patrol commander, 26-year-old David 'Ronnie' Ramsden. The patrols were not marching with full loads of kit, but they were heavily armed. Ronnie had an M79 'Thump-gun' grenade launcher as well as his own rifle and a radio for calling in the air strikes. Bob was armed with a GPMG 'Jimpy' machine-gun weighing around 30lb (13.6km) and strung with a 100-round belt. He carried the gun low on his hip, ready for immediate use, although it was intended to be used in the sustained-fire role once the patrol reached its hilltop vantage point. In the Bergen on his back he had another 600 rounds. Behind him were two of the sultan's soldiers, each armed with rifles and each carrying two 400-round boxes of Jimpy ammo. The last man in the patrol was an SAS trooper carrying his rifle and the Jimpy tripod.

Approaching the Ghaday hill, the patrol had to descend onto level ground for a few hundred yards before they began their climb up the slope. The sky was lightening as dawn began to break over the crest of the hill and the five men advanced through some low bushes. Suddenly a figure appeared in the half-light up ahead. An Adoo had popped up, seemingly out of nowhere, only 5 yards (4.5m) away and fired a salvo of shots at them from his AK-47. Ronnie Ramsden went down. Bob was unsure whether he'd been hit or was taking cover, but he was in no mood for ducking and diving. As the Adoo levelled his Kalashnikov at him, Bob blasted him with a burst from the Jimpy. The Adoo was killed instantly, but Bob was now coming under fire from Adoo further up the hill. He sprayed the muzzle flashes with a welter of fire from the Jimpy and advanced resolutely towards them, blasting away at anything that looked like it might pose a threat. Bob dispatched another two Adoo in a sangar and downed at least another couple before he began to withdraw back down the hill, firing as he went. SAS patrols on adjacent hillsides watched the tracer fire as Bob's patrol retreated down the hill to find cover, and when they had a clear field of fire they opened up to keep the remaining Adoo occupied.

Having reached the bottom of the slope, it immediately became clear to Bob and another SAS trooper that Ronnie had been left behind. He had almost certainly been hit and Bob wasn't about to leave him wounded on the hillside. They both made their way back up the slope, dodging sporadic gunfire, to try to find him. Unfortunately, Ramsden had been killed outright. They carried his body back down the hill. Air strikes were then called in to clear the Adoo from their positions on Ghaday hill.

Bob's swift, valiant action had resulted in the deaths of five of the enemy, including their commander and their quartermaster, with five more later reported wounded. He had also bought time for the rest of his patrol to withdraw. He was nominated for a bravery award, the citation reading:

> Throughout this action Trooper Podesta displayed a complete disregard for his own safety and a devotion to duty of the highest order. His coolness, skill at arms and personal courage were a very fine example and inspiration and there is no doubt that his conduct when surprised and under fire was largely instrumental in inflicting heavy casualties on the enemy and regaining the initiative.

The award that was put forward was the MM, but the one that was finally approved by the Ministry of Defence was an MID, which was 'very strongly recommended' by the commander-in-chief of UK Land Forces.

Bob served a total of seven tours in Oman, participating in a number of vital missions, including Operation *Simba* in 1973. Simba was a defensive line comprised of a number of isolated outposts along the border with Yemen near the town of Sarfait. The purpose of the outposts was to try to restrict the Adoo from crossing over from Yemen, bringing weapons and explosives to supply their fighters already inside Oman. Positions along the Simba Line regularly came under fierce attack from the Adoo.

When information was received that a large stockpile of Adoo weapons had been built up in a series of wadis just inside the Omani border, it was decided to mount a search-and-destroy mission. Once they reached the area of operations near the Simba Line, Bob's job was to provide cover on the flank with his GPMG as A Squadron advanced towards the target. A ferocious firefight developed when the Adoo realized that their precious weapons cache was under attack and Bob was kept very busy raking the enemy positions to give A Squadron the chance to fight its way forward. The Adoo were eventually driven off, leaving behind a treasure trove of AK-47s, mortars, explosives and ammunition.

Bob spent a great deal of time in Oman over the years, including the Regiment's last tour there in 1976, but it was back at base in Hereford in 1971 where I first met him, feeding his legendary appetite in the camp cookhouse. We were both living off the camp, but every morning we would go to the cookhouse for breakfast or a brew before starting work. Bob always tried to get there first so that he could bag his favourite seat facing the main entrance and spot any of his mates coming in. He says that he always knew when I'd arrived by the laughter he heard before he even saw me. I liked to give the lads a bit of morning entertainment before we all got down to the serious business of training. Our paths were to cross many times in the years to come, either on operations or in training, one notable occasion being an escape-and-evasion exercise in France.

Bob is a strong character, both mentally and physically, and a dedicated soldier, although, like many others in the Regiment, he appears very laid-back and calm. When he lets his aggression run free, though, best stand well back. On an annual exercise in France, we had to parachute into an area of the Pyrenees mountains on the border with Spain. The 'enemy' on that occasion was the very experienced, highly professional soldiers of the French Foreign Legion. Our job was to break out of the area without being captured by them and make our way to an RV. The sickener attached to such exercises is that, unlike in real life, you stand almost no chance at all of evading the hunters, and even if you do, you often still have to go through all of the unpleasantness of the interrogation part of the drill. The main difference between the French exercise and the escape-and-evasion element of SAS Selection was that we were in full kit, not the rags and overcoats issued for running around the English countryside. Bob was further hampered by carrying the heavy and bulky 320 radio set (then being trialled for use by the Regiment), putting him at a real disadvantage if he got into a tussle with any Legionnaires. These guys were not out to kill or maim us, but with regimental honour at stake they had every bit as much to prove as we did and we all knew that they weren't going to hang back or pull their punches. They were after SAS scalps and they knew that none of us was going to surrender meekly.

On landing, Bob decided to make his way across a railway line in the hope that he could sneak through the enemy cordon. As he crossed the line, he was jumped by four Legionnaires. Boots and fists were flying as they tried to wrestle him to the ground, but they couldn't hold on to him. He broke away from them, but was soon recaptured. If the Legionnaires thought they were in for an easier ride second time around, however, they were in for a shock. Bob laid into them all over again. This happened three times before he was finally overpowered.

Having been captured, Bob was taken to the interrogation centre where he again showed his determination. Not only did he resist interrogation, giving nothing away, he also managed to escape from his jailors and make it to the RV! The Legionnaires gave him full credit for his performance. They said that capturing him was 'like trying to hold down a wild bull!'

In addition to his time in Oman, Bob took part in four operational tours in Northern Ireland and two in Belize where A Squadron mounted cross-border patrols to help prevent an invasion by Guatemala. He spent the last few years of his service in a variety of different jobs. In HQ Squadron he ran first the Boat Store, then the Armoury and was also sent on numerous foreign training trips as an instructor to countries that included Kenya, Indonesia and Nigeria.

Bob also spent some time as a sniper with the anti-terrorist team and had a period away from the Regiment on a TA posting before his 27-year career in the army finally came to an end when he retired in November 1994.

Chapter 12

SERGEANT TALAIASI LABALABA AND STAFF SERGEANT SEKONAIA TAKAVESI

The lights and sounds from the open area in the Arab township dominated the night, the air filled with the smell of exotic cooking from the various food stalls and music ringing out as the street performers competed for the attention of the crowds. The buzz of a thousand conversations and the calls of the vendors echoed off the walls of the surrounding buildings, where wooden shacks rubbed shoulders with more substantial, mud-walled, whitewashed structures. All of the buildings in the shanty town were bathed in evening shadows, gently disguising their precarious construction and dilapidated condition that was so obvious in the harsh light of the blazing sun during the day.

In fact, the whole character of the Sheik Othman district of the port of Aden was transformed with the setting of the sun. The heavy aroma of the spices in the cooking pots hung in the still air as here, among the maze of buildings, scarcely a breath of the sea breeze penetrated from the coast. The smell of the food at least helped to disguise the daytime stench from the open sewers that ran down the middle of the streets and the piles of garbage that lay festering on the street corners. The hours of darkness also brought some respite from the scorching heat of the Arabian sun, although the night carried with it dangers of its own. The pool of light from the town square weakened as it stretched towards the side streets, leaving long and sinister shadows that crept into the darkness. A few yards away, on the edge of the shadows, two men sat in a parked saloon car, one of a number of ordinary cars scattered around the area. The men watched the crowd milling around, the stark whiteness of the Arab robes appearing almost ghostly in the oasis of light. The two men were dressed in a similar fashion to the people they were so closely observing, although their homeland was a very different place, many thousands of miles away on the other side of the world.

Suddenly, two white-robed men turned away from the crowd. They glanced at the car and took a couple of urgent steps towards it, immediately attracting the attention of the car's occupants. As the Arabs advanced, each reached for something inside his robe and the men in the car caught the unmistakable dull glint of gunmetal. In an instant the men in the car threw open the doors – before their feet touched the ground their Browning 9mm pistols were levelled at the Arab gunmen. The pistols barked and, as though a blanket of silence had been thrown over the square, the voices and the music quickly faded. All eyes turned in the direction from which the brief shots had come and there on the ground, in a spreading pool of blood, lay the two Arabs. The other two men scanned the crowd suspiciously, their weapons still at the ready. In a few moments their back-up would be with them, the area would be teeming with uniformed soldiers and the two men, Troopers Talaiasi Labalaba and Sekonaia Takavesi, would report back to SAS HQ at Ballycastle House in the Khormaksar district for debriefing. Two more terrorist gunmen had been eliminated, but neither the conflict in Aden nor the highly dangerous game played by Laba and Tak were yet over.

I have included Laba and Tak together in this book because that is how I so often think of them, despite the fact that they have not shared each other's company for quarter of a century. I count them both as good friends, going back with Tak as far as my first days with the Regiment. We struck up a friendship when were on the same Selection course together in 1963. Tak, whose parent regiment was the King's Own Borderers Regiment, gave me some useful orienteering tips that helped me through the course. Laba had an equally friendly, generous nature. In the early 1970s we were in Singapore together, spending a few days recharging our batteries during a break from a jungle survival course in Malaya. When I ran out of money, Laba offered to lend me a few dollars, which I promised to pay back as soon as I could get my hands on some cash. Never was a debt so difficult to repay. No matter how often or how hard I tried to insist on paying him, Laba would never accept the money. As far as he was concerned, he had helped me out when I needed it and that was what friendship was all about.

In Aden, Laba and Tak, together with other Fijians such as Jim Vakatali, posed as Arabs to mix with the locals. Although the big men from Fiji towered above the average Arab, their skin colour allowed them to blend in more easily than most Brits. All could speak a little Arabic, but Jim was an expert and would often translate what he heard for the others. When they talked together in Fijian, far from blowing their cover, many locals simply assumed that they were part of a ship's crew from a distant part of Africa. Working undercover, however, is never entirely straightforward and in Aden, telling friend from foe was a frustratingly complicated business.

It was in the townships that Laba and Tak proved their mettle. The two Fijians had all the right attributes for working undercover. They were cool-headed, easy-going professionals from a land that has a long tradition of providing first-class soldiers to the British Army. Fiji was a British colony for a century before becoming independent in 1970 and Fijians are welcomed into the British armed forces in exactly the same way that the army recruits Gurkhas from Nepal. The men from the South Pacific islands do not have their own identity within the British Army in the same way that the Gurkha Regiment does. Instead, they are scattered throughout the service, which is why Tak served with the King's Own Borderers and Laba came to the SAS from the Royal Irish Rangers.

Today there are about 2,000 Fijians serving in the British Army, making them second only to the Gurkhas as the army's largest foreign contingent. Unlike the Gurkhas, however, who are normally small, lean and wiry, the archetypal Fijian tends to be big and powerful. Being large and carrying some bulk can be a disadvantage to some in the SAS, but over the years Fijians like Laba and Tak have proved more than capable of handling anything that the SAS can throw at them. Their first contact with the modern SAS came during the reformed Regiment's initial operations in Malaya. Elements of Fiji's own 1st Fijian Infantry Regiment took part in Operation *Hive*, an attempt to flush terrorists out of the jungle. The Fijians proved, as they had against the Japanese in World War II, that they were experts in jungle warfare. In Aden, Laba and Tak were about to master a completely different martial art in the backstreets of the port.

The Crater and Sheikh Othman districts were the two most volatile areas and the places where assassins who had infiltrated the country from the north were most likely to take refuge. Sheikh Othman was the area closest to the Radfan Mountains and Crater was an enclosed community that was home to several hundred thousand Arabs. At several points during the conflict it would become a 'no-go' area for the security forces. It was in these areas that Laba and Tak's services were most in demand. Grenade attacks such as the one directed at the high commissioner's party at Khormaksar became increasingly common, with army foot patrols, Land Rover patrols, vehicle checkpoints, individual British or Europeans, and even parties of British schoolchildren targeted by the terrorists. British Special Branch officers and their informants were singled out for particular attention.

Laba and Tak would wander the streets and alleyways, sometimes lurking in a car, sometimes blending in as best they could on foot. These operations in Aden became known as 'keeni-meeni' ops, from a Swahili phrase describing the way that a snake slithers, silent and barely visible, through the grass. British servicemen simply took it to mean 'snake-in-the-grass'. But Laba and Tak were not there solely to engage in shoot-outs with the bad guys: their job was to gather intelligence about suspected terrorists, find out which cafés, restaurants or houses they visited, who their associates were and where there were likely to be stockpiles of hidden weapons. They could be assigned to make general observations in an area or to watch for specific targets, men who worked for local politicians or activists from the ever more militant trades unions that ruled the docks. They would then report back and a detachment from the regular army would be sent in to act on the information they supplied. Laba and Tak also had to keep their eyes open for a multitude of potential dangers, or signs of an attack.

There were checkpoints dotted around the different districts in Aden where cars and individuals could be searched for illegal weapons. Patrols on the street could also 'stop and search' if they had good reason. For the committed terrorist, such checks were at worst an inconvenience and at best a potential target. They quickly learned not to attempt to walk around carrying a gun or grenade. They also soon understood that the British soldiers were not permitted to search women unless they had a female police officer with them and the facility for a female suspect to be searched in private. Naturally, such facilities were seldom available, so the terrorists used women to smuggle weapons in their robes to a pre-arranged drop.

Laba and Tak knew to watch for a woman who might loiter near a pile of garbage on a street corner. As the British administration began to crumble in the colony and the militant districts became more dangerous, domestic services such as refuse collection were among the first to suffer. Garbage piles were all too common. A female 'courier' would secrete a handgun or, more often, a grenade in a street-corner garbage pile and walk away, hoping that it looked as though she had just added some trash to the mound. The terrorist would approach the pile of garbage a few moments later, perhaps as an army patrol came into sight, and retrieve what had been left for him. He would then wait for the patrol to pass by. Once the last man had gone, he would throw the grenade before sprinting off up a side alley. Attacks by such 'Cairo Grenadiers', as they were known, caused appalling casualties. In the three years from the start of the emergency to the beginning of 1967, 13 British soldiers were killed and more than 320 were injured, such are the effects of flying shrapnel from a hand grenade.

While keeping their eyes peeled for Cairo Grenadiers, Laba and Tak also had to be wary of groups of children. The terrorists would use a crowd of Arab children as cover during an attack, throwing a grenade or opening fire on their target from the midst of the children, knowing that British soldiers would be reluctant to fire back. The children themselves could also pose a danger. The terrorists were known to supply weapons to young boys and dare them to go out and kill a Brit – and the Brits had prices on their heads. The kids would be offered a few dinah for shooting a soldier, twice as much for shooting an officer.

Laba and Tak also had to deal with the constant danger of discovery. They were certainly compromised the night they were forced to shoot the two Arabs in Sheikh Othman, but there they had enough space to defend themselves. They had to be very cautious when mixing with a crowd on the street. A shoot-out is easier to deal with than a knife in the back.

It was not only the locals of whom they had to be wary, though. There were other undercover groups at work in the townships, also dressed as Arabs. It is no accident that the Swahili 'keeni-meeni' was chosen as a name for the clandestine operations in Aden. The idea of undercover infiltration in this manner was employed by Major Frank Kitson in Kenya during the Mau Mau uprising and further developed in Cyprus and Palestine. The British Army was keen to try it out in Aden, too. Although different units had different areas in which they were supposed to operate, the SAS was not confined to any particular patch and there were systems in place to warn other units if operations were likely to overlap. But mistakes can happen. When an SAS patrol opened fire on a group of armed Arabs in Sheikh Othman, they seriously wounded two members of the Royal Anglian Regiment's newly formed Special Branch Squad. They had no idea there was another undercover unit in the field. Should any of the regular British Army patrols have spotted the SAS Fijians in Arab dress and carrying weapons, they would also have taken immediate action. Laba and Tak were very much aware, therefore, that they were almost as likely to be shot by their own side as they were by the terrorists.

Laba and Tak's keeni-meeni role left them dangerously exposed, but not nearly as much as the non-Fijian SAS soldiers who occasionally worked with them. When Tony McVeigh joined them on operations, his job was not to try to disguise himself as an Arab – quite the reverse. Tony would walk into a market place or shopping street dressed in civvies and wander around under the watchful eyes of Laba and Tak. Posing as a tourist or souvenir hunter, Tony would be the only white person to be seen and would naturally attract the attention of the terrorists or terrorist sympathizers. When they cornered him, Laba and Tak would move in. Poor Tony was just bait, like a little lamb left tethered in a clearing while the hunters lie in wait for the tiger to attack.

The SAS HQ in Aden (although the Regiment had a second base for operations up-country) was in two blocks of flats that had once served as married quarters for RAF personnel at Khormaksar. Here Laba, Tak and the rest of the 20-strong keeni-meeni team ate, slept and planned their missions. Aden provided invaluable experience of operations against urban terrorists that would be put to good use in the years to come, not least in Northern Ireland. It was in Aden, too, that the CQB (Close-Quarters Battle) skills the Regiment had started to acquire were refined and taken to a new level. The idea of the CQB course that John Slim had set up in Kenya was developed at the Cemetery Vale range in Aden. Situated near an Arab burial ground at the foot of Jebel Shamsan, the range was shared with the other services and special ops groups, including the Terrorist Weapons and Tactics Team, known for obvious reasons as the TWATTs. On the range, Laba and Tak practised drawing the heavy Browning pistol from beneath the Arab robes and 'double-tapping' a target from no more than 15 yards (14m). Their techniques for bringing the weapon into play had to be fast and smooth. An instant's delay with the pistol caught in the folds of the robe could mean the difference between life and death.

Laba and Tak had no way of knowing the direct effect that Gamel Nasser's incitements to the Arab peoples and the communist influence from the Soviet Bloc was to have on their lives in the future. Even if they had owned a crystal ball, I doubt if either of them would have given much thought to any predictions it provided. When the Regiment, and the British, left Aden in 1968, the country became a Soviet satellite state, the People's Republic of South Yemen (in 1990, North and South Yemen merged to form today's Republic of Yemen), the military facilities falling into the hands of the Soviets. Laba and Tak, however, had not seen the last of the Yemeni-backed belligerents.

Four years later, on 19 July 1972, the two Fijians were lying on their bunks in their billet in the small Omani harbour town of Mirbat. A low mist hung over the slopes of the Jebel Massif only a mile or so inland, spreading its penetrating drizzle almost as far as the coast where Mirbat nestled on the shore of the Arabian Sea. This was the monsoon season and the thick cloud meant that, at 5.00am, daylight was still some time away.

This suited the Adoo, who crept silently towards their targets in the darkness. Over 250 of them swept down from the mountain, heading towards Mirbat. They divided into specific attack groups, those groups further split into squads of ten men, and made for their start positions, ready to advance on the town from all sides. Mirbat was surrounded.

The Adoo's first objective was an outpost just over half a mile north of the town, standing on a small hill. Halfway between the town and the mountains, the hill towered over the target area and any sentries stationed on the hilltop had to be dealt with swiftly. The eight men manning the outpost were supposed to have died silently, their throats cut as they slept, but things did not go exactly as planned. A shot rang out, cutting through the damp air and, in the instant that it takes to recognize a gunshot, it was joined by a volley that left the sentries in no doubt that they were under attack.

Having lost the element of surprise, the Adoo mortar teams immediately opened up on Mirbat. Inside the town, Laba, Tak and the other seven members of the SAS British Army Training Team (BATT) heard the thud of the mortar explosions and rubbed the sleep from their eyes. Surely the Adoo weren't trying to lob mortars into the town from way out on the Jebel again? The harassing fire rarely caused any real damage and the mortar teams always fled back into the mountains before anybody had a chance to get at them. Then a second wave of shells landed. Laba and Tak exchanged glances. This sounded different, closer. The SAS men scrambled to their stand-to positions to try to see what was going on.

The fishing harbour and garrison town of Mirbat lies on a sandy beach about 40 miles (64km) east of the southern regional capital of Salalah. The narrow strip of coastal plain around the bay is furrowed with wadis cut by water from the summer monsoons rushing down from the nearby mountains to the sea. In the dim light of the approaching dawn, from the roof of the mud-brick BATT house the team could see the wali's fort to the north-east, barely make out the looming mass of the Jebel Ali much farther off to the north and just about identify the Dhofar Gendarmerie (DG) fort to the north-west. This fort housed the 25-strong contingent of the Dhofar Gendarmarie, the local paramilitary police force, who were armed with modern SLRs and boasted one Bren gun in their arsenal. A deep wadi separated the small clutch of buildings that skirted the marketplace, including the BATT house, from the main dwellings of the town further round the bay to the south. Surrounding the whole town, undulating over the uneven ground and cutting through the patchy scrub, was a perimeter fence of barbed wire.

Flashes in the distant gloom identified the location of the Adoo mortars at the base of the Jebel Massif. Their barrage was creeping closer, the rounds now falling at the edge of the town. Smaller flashes from rifles and machine-guns sparked on the Jebel Ali. It was clear from those that the DG sentries in the outpost had been overrun. Most of the fire from the Jebel Ali, including bright green lines of tracer, was directed against the DG fort.

The wali's fort was manned by around 30 Askars, regular troops assigned to the local wali and whose job was security. They searched anyone coming into or going out of the area for weapons or food that might be destined for the Adoo up in the mountains. The Askars were armed with old .303-calibre bolt-action rifles that were accurate in expert hands, but did not provide a very impressive rate of fire.

Heavily armed with mortars, several RPG-7s (Rocket-Propelled Grenades) and at least one Carl Gustav (both originally designed as anti-tank weapons), Kalashnikov assault rifles, heavy machine-guns and grenades, the Adoo were confident that they outgunned and outnumbered Mirbat's defenders. Their intentions were quite simple – take the town and slaughter everyone in it.

The Adoo had suffered some dispiriting defeats at the hands of the sultan's forces and badly needed a resounding victory to rally their disillusioned supporters. They chose Mirbat as a demonstration of their strength because the town was the focal point for the local Firquat, who were being trained by the SAS BATT. The attack on Mirbat was intended to teach the turncoats a lesson and show that the Adoo were not to be crossed. Sacking Mirbat was so important to them that they had assembled their best-trained, most experienced soldiers for the operation. They knew that most of the Firquat were out on patrol in the mountains and wanted them to return to a town that had been razed to the ground, with the butchered bodies of their families lying in the ruins.

It was obvious to the SAS team, under the command of Captain Mike Kealy, that the Adoo's primary target in the village was to be the DG fort, which dominated the town, and the 25pdr field gun dug in outside the fort's main gate. The gun's main purpose was to provide covering fire for the Firquat should there be any Adoo on their tails as they returned from patrols in the mountains. Dug in with its ammunition bunker alongside, the gun was of the type used by the British Army in World War II, reputed to be the finest artillery piece of its size at the time and still a formidable weapon in the right hands 30 years later. Laba decided that those hands should be his. If the gun was captured, the Adoo could lay waste to the forts and the rest of the town. By this point shrapnel from the bursting mortars was screeching over the BATT house and there was sporadic, largely inaccurate, incoming small-arms fire from all sides. Laba left the BATT house and sprinted across the rough ground towards the 25pdr. He took cover where he could, but never for long. The gun urgently needed to be brought into action.

Tak watched his friend disappear towards the fort from his position in the BATT house mortar pit just a few yards from the building. The machine-guns mounted on the roof of the BATT house, one GPMG and one .50-calibre Browning, as well as the other troopers' SLRs, remained silent. There was no point in giving away their exact positions by opening fire when there was barely enough light to identify a target. Tak, however, was busy with the 81mm mortar, pounding the Adoo's mortar positions. As one of the three-man team took fire-control instructions over a walkie-talkie from the mortar controller on the roof of the BATT house, another was frantically unpacking mortar bombs from their containers, removing the safety pins and stacking them ready for Tak to drop them down the tube. In the Fijian's big hands, the deadly 9lb (4kg) shells seemed no more than lightweight children's toys.

Then came the reassuring crash and boom of the 25pdr opening up. Laba had reached the gun pit and was aiming, loading and firing the gun single-handed. Under more normal conditions, the gun would have had a crew of five. As the light started to brighten, the Adoo could be seen advancing towards the wire in the wake of their mortar barrage, which was now creeping forward ahead of them into the town. Using classic assault tactics, one squad advanced to good cover then gave covering fire as the next squad 'leapfrogged' them. Captain Kealy gave the order for the BATT house machine-guns to open fire and the troops in the forts also began to give good account of themselves, although the rate of fire from the ramparts was as nothing compared to the hail of bullets now streaming into the town.

Inside the BATT house, Captain Kealy ordered Pete Winner to contact SAS headquarters at Um al Gwarif, on the outskirts of Salalah, informing them that Mirbat was under attack and that they were taking heavy fire. As Pete worked the Morse key, a mortar round rocked the building. Abandoning normal encoding procedures, he sent the desperate message in plain text. Outside, the Adoo were probing towards the wire, searching for breaches opened by their mortars. No one wanted to present a tempting target by becoming entangled. The exchange of fire continued unabated and the clearing morning mist was reinforced by a pall of smoke and dust. Visibility did, however, slowly improve, although the low cloud made the beleaguered BATT unit's requests for air support almost impossible to fulfil. Reinforcements, however, were being organized. The men of B Squadron in Mirbat had been due to go home on the day of the attack. Their replacements from G Squadron were already at Um al Gwarif and were now emptying the armoury, taking every GPMG and loading as much ammunition as they could carry into the trucks that would take them to the airstrip at Salalah. From there, helicopters would airlift the 22 men and their equipment to Mirbat ... once the mist had cleared enough for the pilots to be able to see where they were going.

Meanwhile, Laba worked hard, crouched behind the armoured shield of the 25pdr, his shirt stained with sweat and blackened with powder. The Adoo were so close that he was reduced to sighting the gun down the barrel, firing into the advancing men at what amounted to point blank range for a gun that was capable of hurling its high-explosive rounds more than 3 miles (5km). There were occasional, and temporary, lulls in the battle when the gunfire subsided from a thunderous frenzy to a more sporadic exchange as the Adoo went to ground. Then, having regrouped, a fresh wave rose to advance on the DG fort and its gun emplacement. They faced a withering hail of defensive fire and the determined barrage from Laba on the 25pdr. When the Adoo had closed to less than 50 yards (46m) from the fort, the rocket-propelled rounds from their RPG-7s and the high explosives from the Carl Gustav blasted enormous chunks of brick and plaster from its walls, leaving gaping holes.

Then a message came through on the walkie-talkie from Laba in the gun pit. 'I've been chinned, but I'm okay.' The message caused grave concern in the BATT house. Laba was not the sort to bother reporting a minor injury and only a lucky few hit by the 7.62mm round from a Kalashnikov ever got off lightly. It was clear that Laba was now in serious need of assistance. Even had he wanted to, there was no way that Captain Kealy could have stopped Tak from going to his friend's aid. Clutching his SLR and a few magazines, Tak left the BATT house, running flat out towards the gun pit. The others gave him covering fire, but still Tak was running into a storm of bullets. A former top-class rugby player, dodging, weaving, diving and sprinting were second nature to Tak and the big Fijian covered the ground at a breathless pace.

Finally flinging himself into the gun pit, Tak gulped in great lungfuls of the smoky air and looked across at Laba. A blood-soaked shell dressing (a gauze-covered cotton pad with lengths of bandage attached) was tied around his face, roughly covering the wound where the bullet had smashed his jaw. Still crouched behind the bullet-ridden armour shield, Laba nodded to Tak, asked for more ammunition, and carried on operating the gun. Once he had made sure that Laba had enough shells to keep him going, Tak decided that what they really needed was another pair of hands. The only place from where he could hope to get more help was the fort. Steeling his body for another Olympian effort, Tak launched himself over the low sandbagged wall of the gun emplacement and dashed towards the door of the fort. Unsurprisingly, when he got there, it was locked. Tak hammered on the door and bellowed to the men inside as machine-gun rounds carved patterns in the masonry around him, showering him with debris. After what seemed like an eternity, the door was opened by Walid Khamis, the Omani gunner with whom both Tak and Laba had trained on the 25pdr. Both men raced for the gun pit.

Tak now knew that they had a chance. With Laba and Walid operating the gun, he could use his SLR to hold off the advancing Adoo. Now they could really start to make a difference. He tumbled back into the gun pit and turned to see Walid collapse on the sandbags. He had taken a round to the stomach and crashed down into the pit, writhing in agony. Laba and Tak were on their own again.

Back at the BATT house a casualty evacuation helicopter had been requested from Salalah and one of the team had slipped out to guide the chopper in to a landing area near the beach. As the helicopter appeared, he threw a green smoke grenade to show that the landing area was safe, but when the aircraft was on its final approach a group of Adoo opened fire, churning up the dust around the landing area. The trooper threw a red grenade to warn off the chopper and its engines roared as it climbed back into the sky with Adoo bullets tearing into its fuselage. The trooper then made his way back to the BATT house. But if one chopper could make the 25-minute flight from Salalah, then so could others. G Squadron was now embarked on three helicopters, heading down the coast to Mirbat.

The situation in the BATT house was now becoming desperate. The mortar crew's targets were so close that it was almost impossible to engage them. The barrel was already raised to its maximum elevation, so the crew set it on the lowest charge, primary charge, and fired; the bomb travelled up almost vertically then dropped down on the enemy. The Askaris in the wali's fort were firing at anything that moved, but the main thrust of the Adoo attack was still towards the DG fort. Having breached the wire in several places, they were moving inexorably closer.

Laba and Tak worked like machines. The gun fired, they opened the breech, ejected the hot shell case, slammed in a new one, rammed it home, closed the breech and fired. Their machine only ground to a halt when Tak reached for another shell and was hurled backwards into the sandbags. He'd been shot in the chest and as he landed another round creased his skull. He was in agony and losing a lot of blood, but he was still conscious. Laba helped Tak prop himself up against the sandbags and handed him his SLR. Then Laba went back to firing the gun and Tak peered down the sights of his rifle, picking off any Adoo who appeared within his limited field of fire.

Automatic fire from the Adoo peppered the gun pit and Laba decided that the time had come to try a different tack. With the ammunition for the 25pdr all but gone, the floor of the gun pit was littered with spent shell cases and steeped in blood. Laba looked around for the small 60mm mortar he knew was in there somewhere. Spotting the weapon propped up against the sandbag wall, he crawled across the floor and reached out from behind the 25pdr's shield to make a grab for the mortar. As he did so, an Adoo bullet ploughed into his neck and Laba slumped to the floor, dead.

In the BATT house, Captain Kealy was worried that all firing from the gun pit appeared to have stopped. Had they been overrun? He had to know exactly what was happening at the fort and what had happened to Laba and Tak. To establish that, he had to get to the gun emplacement and needed someone to go with him. He asked for a volunteer. He got six. The one he chose was Tommy Tobin, a trained medic. By some miracle, they both reached the gun emplacement unscathed. Tommy leapt into the gun pit and Captain Kealy took cover in the ammunition bunker. They were shocked by the scene of carnage before them. Walid Khamis lay on his back, bleeding profusely and obviously seriously wounded. Laba was face down on the floor and Tak was still propped up against the sandbags, drenched in blood, squeezing off carefully aimed rounds from his SLR and grimacing with pain each time the rifle kicked back into his body. Tommy checked Laba, confirmed his worst fears, then turned to pick up his medical pack. At that moment he was shot in the face and fell to the floor, mortally wounded.

Tak called to Captain Kealy for more ammunition and the two men began a desperate battle for their lives. An Adoo popped up at the edge of the gun emplacement, ready to shoot Tak, and Kealy blasted him with his SLR. Another appeared from a ditch close to their position and Kealy cut him down, too. Kealy took out Adoo gunmen as they slunk round the walls of the fort and Tak concentrated on those coming from the direction of the perimeter wire. Although the 25pdr was no longer firing, it was clearly still a primary target for the Adoo as rounds clanged into its metalwork like hammer blows. The Adoo were now close enough to sling grenades, which were bouncing and exploding close to the walls of the gun pit. Kealy froze for an instant as a grenade landed inside the bunker right in front of him. Mercifully, it failed to explode. Then, a new and terrifying sound added its fury to the cacophony of the battle. Two BAC Strikemaster jets of the SOAF came screaming in low over the battlefield, strafing the Adoo with cannon fire.

With the cloud base at no more than 150ft (46m), the jets were hugging the contours of the ground as they made their attack run before peeling off into the cloud and coming round again. Captain Kealy was able to relay fire instructions to the jets via the BATT house over the walkie-talkie and the Strikemasters drove the Adoo back into the cover of a deep wadi outside the Mirbat perimeter fence. A 500lb (227kg) bomb then persuaded them that even the wadi was unsafe for them. Kealy knew, however, that the jets could not hang around forever over Mirbat. One limped back to base trailing smoke from numerous Adoo machine-gun hits and the other soon followed, low on fuel and out of ammo. Kealy used the respite provided by the jets to dress the wounds of Walid, Tommy and Tak, and as he was trying to organize transport to take them to the helicopter LZ for evacuation, he could still hear firing. He knew that the Adoo would be back and that he had to move fast. What he didn't know was that G Squadron had fought its way up through the town and had what remained of the Adoo in full retreat.

The Adoo left behind in Mirbat almost 40 dead and ten wounded who were taken prisoner. It was later learned that there were many other Adoo injured who limped away or were carried off the battlefield only to die from their wounds days later. Altogether, the Adoo probably lost almost half of their elite strike force. It was a bitter blow from which they would never recover and, although the conflict in Oman would continue for almost four more years, history would show that Mirbat was the turning-point that led to the ultimate defeat of the Adoo.

The SAS had lost Laba, and Tommy was to die from his wounds. Tak was seriously wounded, as was Walid. Only one of the DG was killed in the town and another was badly wounded, although almost everyone in both the forts and the BATT house had sustained some kind of minor injury.

Tommy and Walid were loaded onto stretchers for the short trip by Land Rover to the casevac helicopter. Tak refused to lie on a stretcher. He was helped to his feet and walked to the transport under his own steam. The surgeons who operated on him at Salalah declared his injuries the worst chest wounds they had ever seen on anyone who was still alive. Even so, Tak was not to let his injuries end his career with the SAS.

Ironically, Laba had actually left the Regiment long before Mirbat. After leaving Aden, he had returned to the Irish Rangers for a spell of more conventional soldiering, but when the Rangers were stationed in Bahrain in 1969 he ran into some of his old chums. B Squadron stopped off in Bahrain for training prior to deployment in Oman and some of the SAS men were invited to the Irish Rangers' Warrant Officers and Sergeants' Mess, where they met up with Laba and his RSM. They persuaded Laba to rejoin the Regiment and, in return, Laba's heroics with the 25pdr at Mirbat may well have saved the B Squadron BATT unit.

Tak spent some time recovering from his wounds, but his fighting spirit helped him battle his way back to fitness and he eventually returned to duty with B Squadron. He was at Pete Winner's shoulder when they stormed the Iranian Embassy in 1980 and fought in the Falklands campaign. He also saw action more recently in Iraq, although he had long since left the Regiment by then.

In late 2003, Tak was working for a private security company in Iraq and was driving with another ex-SAS colleague in a two-car convoy through the Safwan area near Basra. As always on desert roads, the car in front was throwing up enough dust to rate a mini sandstorm and Tak had only a limited view of the road in front of them. He could see, however, that they were coming up behind another vehicle, a four-wheel-drive truck, and knew that his friend would want to overtake to avoid driving through the same sort of dust cloud that Tak was currently experiencing.

Sure enough, the car in front of Tak pulled out to overtake, but when Tak attempted to do the same, the truck swerved across the road to stop him. There's no such thing as random road rage in a place like Iraq, and Tak could see that the occupants of the truck were four armed Arabs. Three times Tak tried to pull out and pass the truck and each time the truck swerved into his path. Tak's partner had, by this time, realized that something was wrong and was hanging back rather than speeding off down the road. Tak decided to try some off-road tactics and pulled out into the roadside desert scrub to try to outmanoeuvre the truck.

The Arabs leant out of the truck windows and opened fire across Tak's path, forcing him to brake, whereupon his car became bogged down in soft sand. The gunmen's truck slithered to a halt and the Arabs, each armed with the inevitable Kalashnikov AK-47, walked towards the front of Tak's car. Tak sat stock still in his seat as they approached. Then, when they levelled their weapons at his vehicle, he snatched up a machine pistol from the seat beside him and sprayed them through the windscreen. Tak's partner gave him covering fire as Tak dived from the vehicle and tangled with one of the gunmen, clubbing the Arab to the ground with his weapon. He then made for his partner's vehicle, but one of the Arabs managed to get off a shot that caught him in the thigh. His partner bundled Tak into the car and they made off at speed, heading for the British Military Hospital in Basra, leaving the four Iraqis behind – one wounded and one presumed dead. Tak's partner sustained a slight wound to the hand, but Tak's leg wound was more serious and he was swiftly flown back to a private hospital in the UK for treatment.

Both Laba and Tak have become legends within the Regiment and are hailed as heroes in their homeland of Fiji. They are, without doubt, two of the bravest men I have ever known and I am proud to consider myself as having been their friend.

Sekonaia Takavesi, aka 'Tak'.

Pete Winner on patrol in Southern Oman, 1971.

Tommy Palmer with his wife Caroline after receiving his QGM (Queen's Gallantry Medal) from the Queen for his actions at the Iranian Embassy siege in 1980.

Having discarded his hood and respirator after they caught fire, Tommy Palmer enters the Iranian Embassy, 5 May 1980.

Pete Winner changes the clutch on a Land Rover, a week before the Battle of Mirbat (19 July 1972) in which Laba and Tommy Tobin died.

Pete Winner (left) and Joe Farragher carrying out a census of the local villages, southern Oman, 1971.

Tommy Tobin, who died from wounds sustained while trying to help Laba and Tak at Mirbat.

Steve Callan deciphering a message from base in his jungle 'basha' in Borneo, 1963.

Major Glyn Williams, D Squadron commander (centre), coordinating the squadron's operations in the Radfan mountains, Aden 1966.

Steve Callan (5th left, standing) with members of A Squadron in the Borneo jungle.

Pete Loveday takes a breather in the desert mountains of Muscat in 1958, having transferred there directly from the jungles of Malaya.

Pete Scholey (left foreground) with 18 Troop, D Squadron, awaiting heli-lift in Aden, 1966, after a seven-day operation.

Tommy Palmer driving a 'Pink Panther' during desert training in Iran.

Gavin Hamilton.

Vince Phillips, a member of the ill-fated Bravo Two Zero patrol.

Bob Bennett and Roger Cole setting up the 81mm mortar at Mirbat.

B Squadron's 81mm mortar, with the fort at Mirbat in the background.

ABOVE *SAS troopers preparing for a HALO (High-Altitude Low-Opening) jump inside an aircraft using the oxygen masks that are essential to prevent the onset of hypoxia.*

LEFT *A fully-equipped SAS tactical parachutist. The Bergen strapped to the back of his legs would be released to dangle below him on a strap once he deployed his parachute.*

Crash Rescue patrol, Borneo, 1963; l–r: 'Chopper' Essex, Steve Callan, Frank Williams and Ricky Coomber.

A Squadron mobility troop carrying out trials on prototype Pink Panther Land Rovers in Libya, late 1960s.

D Squadron in Aden, 1966. The Regiment operated not only out in the wilds of the mountains but also covertly in the back streets and markets of townships.

(l–r) Pete Scholey, John 'Lofty' Wiseman, Don 'Lofty' Large and Colin Wallace – the 'Old and Bold'!

Chapter 13

STAFF SERGEANT PETE WINNER

The constant electrical hum in the background, which softened all other sounds on the submarine, was perforated by the clicking of rifle actions as the team oiled and checked their weapons. Pete sat in the long, white-painted, corridor-like interior of the sub along with around two dozen other SAS as they prepared their kit prior to a final briefing for their departure from the sub. It was June 1982 and the Oberon-class submarine HMS *Onyx* was playing host to a specially selected SAS team. Somewhere far above them, the Falklands War was raging.

The team's preparations were as thorough as if they were sitting in their own squadron hangar back in Hereford, but there could be no denying that they were actually in a sub, 8,000 miles (12,874km) from home at the bottom of the South Atlantic. The roof and walls were arched, giving the impression that they were crammed inside a giant cigar tube, although wiring ducts, piping, valves, lighting and odd pieces of equipment covered almost all of the interior surface area. Even in the crew areas, where there were flat ceiling and wall panels, every inch of space was decked with lockers for stowing kit. Space was at a premium, despite the fact that, at around 295ft (90m) long and over 26ft (7.9m) wide, this vessel was far from being a small boat. Normally it was home to a crew of just over 60 and the submariners had given as much space as they could and every possible assistance to Pete and their other SAS guests. The team was preparing for Operation *Mikado*, impatiently waiting for the order to go, when the submarine would surface. Then they would move out onto the outer hull of the sub and climb into the small boats sitting on the 'deck'. The sub would drop away beneath them, leaving them to float free and head for shore. At least, that was the plan. Climbing into the boats laden with kit in the dark, the sub rolling in the waves and both the deck and the Gemini inflatables wet and greasy in the freezing, choppy southern sea, was going to be no picnic. And once they were all embarked in the boats, their problems were only beginning.

Two months previously, a 15-man team had left the destroyer HMS *Antrim* in five Geminis. They were to set off across Stromness Bay under cover of darkness, heading for Grass Island from where they were to report on enemy movements in and around the port of Leith on South Georgia. The specially silenced outboard motors of the Geminis had been pre-run in a tank to warm them up aboard the *Antrim*, but despite this, once the boats were in the water three of the motors failed to start. As there was very little wind and only light seas, the run to shore was reckoned to be fairly straightforward and the boats with the dud motors were taken in tow by the two with functioning outboards. Unfortunately, as happens in the Falkland Islands, the weather changed in an instant. A wicked wind whipped up the sea and two of the boats under tow broke free. The three men in each boat were reduced to paddling with their mess tins to try to make it to shore. Only one of the boats did. The three who had been in that boat were so far from where they were meant to be that they had no choice but to sit tight for several days until they deemed it safe to use a SARBE to summon help without fear of compromising the operation. The other boat that had gone adrift was swept out to sea. The three clinging to this boat for dear life spent seven hours drifting helplessly on the open ocean before they were found and rescued by a helicopter. Pete and the others were therefore well aware of the potential problems in transferring from ship to shore in the South Atlantic.

The tension that hung heavy in the air inside the submarine, making the confined conditions seem even more claustrophobic, was not generated solely by thoughts of the trip to shore, however. The mission that lay ahead of them was a truly daunting prospect. Their job was to land on the Argentine mainland at Tierra del Fuego, the Land of Fire, and make for the Argentine air base at Rio Grande. There they were to use explosives and anti-tank rockets to destroy the five Super Etendard jets based at the airfield along with the deadly Exocet missiles with which the aircraft were armed.

It was an audacious plan, bold and daring in the true tradition of the SAS – but it was never to happen. They were in position, ready to go, the sub sitting 2 miles (3.2km) off the Argentine coast with all the dress rehearsals having been completed en route, when the news of the Argentine surrender came through. Having evolved through several different abandoned plans (including one scheme to land two C-130 Hercules aircraft packed with troops on the runway at Rio Grande, just as the Israeli special forces had done at Entebbe in Uganda in 1976), Operation *Mikado* had ended in anti-climax. Pete, however, counted himself lucky to have been there at all. His Falklands War, and his eventful life, had almost ended on his way south before he got anywhere near the action.

It hardly seemed possible that a handful of scrap metal merchants, landing on an island 8,000 miles (12,874km) from Britain to dismantle the rusting remnants of an old whaling station, could precipitate the creation of the largest British naval task force most people in the UK had ever seen. In 1982, however, that's pretty much what happened. The Falkland Islands, including the territories of South Georgia and the South Sandwich Islands, have changed hands many times since the major seafaring nations first became interested in them in the 16th century. Bleak and remote, the islands are comprised mainly of treeless moorland and mountains, with a similar geography to the Orkney or Shetland Isles off northern Scotland. Since 1833, the islands have been under British administration and by 1982 the population of just under 2,000 certainly regarded itself as British, although Argentina has always claimed sovereignty. Most of the islands' inhabitants live in Stanley, the islands' capital and only real town, on the east coast of East Falkland. South Georgia, some 900 miles (1,448km) south and east of Stanley, had a regular population of only about 20 – the scientists of the British Antarctic Survey (BAS) team. The South Sandwich Islands,

350 miles (563km) from South Georgia, are normally uninhabited, Antarctic in climate and actively volcanic by nature.

It was on South Georgia that Constantino Davidoff's scrap metal team arrived on 18 March 1982. Having landed without permission, Davidoff proceeded to raise the Argentine national flag, an act that had almost immediate diplomatic consequences. Davidoff's workers were, without doubt, acting under instructions in order to create a situation that might run to the advantage of the Argentine government. Argentina had threatened the islands on many occasions in the past, the regular naval manoeuvres always having been regarded as 'testing the water' for a military takeover of the territory. The only people on the island when the Argentine scrap men arrived were the scientists of the BAS team and two documentary film makers. A small detachment of Royal Marines from the ice patrol ship HMS *Endurance*, which was on patrol nearby, was landed to protect the survey team. Meanwhile, the Royal Marines permanently based on East Falkland were put on alert. Although they numbered only 60 men, the British government under Margaret Thatcher considered that they constituted a significant enough military presence to deter the Argentines from embarking on any military adventures on the islands. Unfortunately, Mrs Thatcher was wrong.

At the end of March 1982, scheduled manoeuvres by the Argentine Navy with the Uruguayan fleet were shelved in favour of Operation *Rosario* – the Argentine invasion of the Falklands. On Friday 2 April at around 4.30am, Argentine special forces came ashore on East Falkland and less than two hours later they were engaged by the Royal Marines. By 8.00am, the main Argentine force was disembarking at Stanley and, despite the heroic efforts of the Royal Marines, it was clear that they could not hold out against the Argentines. The islands' governor ordered a surrender at 9.15am. The Marines on South Georgia had been called on to surrender when two groups of Argentine special forces came ashore by helicopter near their positions. The Marines' response was to attack. They destroyed one helicopter and badly damaged another before taking on an Argentine Navy frigate with anti-tank missiles, holing the ship below the waterline and knocking out its main gun. Ultimately, however, they knew that they, too, had little choice but to surrender.

The Argentines had taken the Falkland Islands, known to them as Las Malvinas, and were overjoyed. They were confident that the British people, most of whom had never heard of the Falkland Islands and had no idea where they were, would not support British military action in the far South Atlantic. Mrs Thatcher, however, had other ideas. Early in the morning on Monday 5 April, the SAS D Squadron flew out of RAF Brize Norton aboard an RAF VC-10. There were 60 SAS aboard along with 20 support personnel and a hold packed with enough hardware to start a small war – which was entirely their intention. They were bound for Ascension Island. Sticking up in the middle of the Atlantic near the equator, 1,400 miles (2,253km) off the coast of West Africa, Ascension Island is British territory and home to Wideawake, an American air base. It was to serve as the forward mounting base for the planned task force and a refuelling stage for southbound aircraft.

Pete, like me, watched all of the build-up to the Falklands campaign from the training grounds, although I was a bit more of a spectator than he was. Pete was in B Squadron's Boat Troop and B Squadron was being held in reserve. My service with the Regiment was just about coming to an end, but I was drafted in to organize stores and supplies to make sure that B Squadron was ready to go – although if they went, I was also marked down to go along with them. Pete was desperately disappointed to have been left behind. With over 12 years' experience in the Regiment, he was worried that this might be his last chance to take part in a 'real shooting war'. Nevertheless, he went through the training exercises along with the rest of B Squadron. I joined them whenever possible and we made sure that we were all up to speed with all the squadron weapons, hopping in and out of helicopters, getting our feet wet in boats and generally doing everything to ensure that we were ready to move the moment our orders came through.

D Squadron left Ascension Island on 9 April, along with M Company of 42 Commando and a Special Boat Squadron (SBS; a Royal Navy sister unit of the SAS) section, as part of the South Georgia Task Group (SGTG) that consisted of HMS *Antrim*, the frigate HMS *Plymouth* and two support ships, the *Fort Austin* and the *Tidespring*. Their job was simple – retake South Georgia. Two weeks later, before the main task force had actually arrived in the combat zone, South Georgia was back in British hands, the Argentines having surrendered pretty much as soon as the SGTG showed up. This was a real morale booster for the lads in the task force, but a real sickener for B Squadron. It was beginning to look like they might not be needed at all.

Nothing could have been further from the truth. On 4 May the destroyer HMS *Sheffield* was destroyed by an Exocet missile launched from an Argentine Super Etendard strike fighter. The powers-that-be decided that something had to be done about the Exocet threat. If one of the carriers or a troop ship was hit, the retaking of the Falkland Islands would suffer an insurmountable setback. Unless the landings went ahead before the end of May, the southern hemisphere winter would set in, the ferocious weather making amphibious operations impossible. The plan that they came up with was to send in B Squadron, in the original version of Operation *Mikado*. B Squadron was to fly from Ascension Island in two C-130s and attack the Argentine air base that was home to the Exocet-armed jets. Pete and the others immediately set to work carrying out mock attacks on airfields all over the UK. I had to reorganize the stores and equipment they would need for their task. I spent just over a week sorting out the new equipment and making sure it was delivered to RAF Lyneham for shipping on to Ascension. I was ready to join Pete for the last couple of days' training when I got a desperate call from RAF Lyneham. They had loaded our gear on to the two C-130s incorrectly. They needed me there to sort it out. While I was there, Pete and the others returned to Hereford and set off for Ascension without me. Pete was to have what he thought was his last crack at a real enemy, while I was to wait at home.

B Squadron arrived at Ascension to devastating news. A Sea King helicopter had gone down during a routine cross-decking flight, transferring men from the aircraft carrier HMS *Hermes* to the assault ship HMS *Intrepid*. Twenty-two men had been lost, 20 of them from D and G Squadrons. The loss of so many men at once would be a blow to any regiment, but to an outfit as small as the SAS it was devastating. Like me, Pete knew many of those who died. He had been in Dhofar with Sid Davidson, in Northern Ireland with Phil Curass and had played rugby with Paddy O'Connor and Taff Jones. Now he was more determined than ever to strike back at the Argentines. Now it was personal.

Just before dawn on the day after their arrival at Ascension, B Squadron were priming grenades, pushing rounds into the magazines of their Armalites and breaking open liners of linked ammunition for their GPMGs. Carrying all of their personal equipment, they then climbed aboard the Bedford trucks waiting to take them out across the runway to the C-130s. Fitted with probes for air-to-air refuelling, the Hercules transports would be able to take them all the way to the Rio Grande air base – but not back again. They would be abandoned there (provided that they were not shot down by Argentine interceptors or anti-aircraft defences on the way in) with their crews joining the SAS to escape into Chile for covert extraction after the demolition job was complete. It was a simple, direct plan that most regarded as ... a suicide mission. Then, as they sat in the trucks, word came through that the operation was cancelled. Pete couldn't decide whether to be relieved or furious. It seemed as though everything and everyone was conspiring to keep him out of the Falklands. B Squadron was stood down, but the one thing that they couldn't do was relax. They were about to be briefed for a new mission.

Within 24 hours, Pete was heading back out along the runway at Wideawake, carrying not the machine-guns and grenades that he had been preparing for the Rio Grande raid, but a diver's dry suit and flippers instead. The 'suicide' attack on the Argentine air base had been abandoned, but now the two C-130s were to drop sections from B Squadron along with palettes of equipment into the South Atlantic in the vicinity of the frigate HMS *Andromeda*. Rigid raider boats would then pluck them out of the water and deliver them to *Andromeda*, which would take them on to San Carlos Water where they were to reinforce the sadly depleted D Squadron. Dropping from a Hercules into the open sea is not the ideal way to begin a relaxing cruise. The seats in the aircraft are not airline-style recliners. They are simple webbing affairs in the 'passenger area' of the cavernous cargo hold. Pete dropped his kit on the floor, checked his parachutes (main and reserve) then strapped himself into the seat to try to get some shut-eye if he could. The roar from the four turbo-props of the C-130 isn't exactly conducive to restful sleep, but it was to be a long flight. Pete glanced around at the rest of the troop. Some were, to him, little more than kids, almost fresh out of Selection and untried in combat. He knew that they would look to him as the most experienced NCO in the troop if anything unexpected happened. Little did they know that this was his first operational jump into a combat zone too.

When the RAF parachute dispatcher called them to 'Action Stations', Pete struggled into his dry suit. The neck seal has to be so tight to keep out the water that you have to fight to get your head through it. Then it has to be zipped up perfectly. When you are landing in water as cold as that in the South Atlantic, any water penetrating your suit will leave you frozen and dead from exposure in no time at all. Pete strapped on his 'chutes, made sure his fins were easy to get at when he was in the water and fastened a distress light to his wrist. Then, with the tailgate door of the Hercules fully lowered, making the noise inside even more deafening, he watched as the equipment palettes trundled along on their rollers and disappeared out of the yawning doorway. It was his turn next. He was leading the troop out of the aircraft, first in the 'stick'. When the green light blinked on, the dispatcher yelled 'Go!' and slapped him on the back. Pete leapt out into the slipstream of the aircraft and moments later felt the comforting jolt of the parachute opening above him. He checked his canopy and then looked down to see the sinister grey shape of HMS *Andromeda* directly below him. The last thing he wanted was to crash onto the deck of the ship, so he yanked on the steering toggle and veered off to one side. Then he unclipped his reserve 'chute and dropped it into the sea. He could see the water rushing towards him, but judging the distance to the grey surface of the sea when the cloud cover made everything else a dull grey in the fading light was not easy. Pete decided to hit the release and dropped out of the harness just before he hit the water. Clear of the canopy and rigging lines, he inflated his life jacket and struggled into his fins. He could see the other members of his troop drifting down towards the heavy swell and, when he floated up on a wave, he could make out HMS *Andromeda* – far too far away for his liking.

Unfortunately for Pete, having been first out of the aircraft, he had ended up farthest away from the *Andromeda*. When he was down in a trough, all he could see was a wall of water, but when he floated up again he could see the boats picking the others out of the water. After 15 minutes in the water, there was no sign of a boat coming anywhere near him, no matter how hard he waved when he hit the crests of the waves. The closest one came was 270 yards (250m), but it picked up someone else then headed back to the *Andromeda*. The ship seemed to be getting further and further away. Pete's hands and face were going numb with cold and he was starting to tire. He bent the plastic tube on his wrist, cracking the phial inside that allowed two chemicals to mix and glow brightly. He waved the arm with the distress light whenever he hit the top of a wave, but no one seemed to see him. When he realized that he had been in the water for a full 35 minutes, he began to fear the worst. It was growing dark very quickly now and with every minute that passed his chances of being spotted grew slimmer and slimmer. Then, as he crested another wave, a rigid raider suddenly popped into view. Pete waved his arm frantically and the boat veered towards him. A few seconds later, a very relieved and very cold Pete Winner was being hauled out of the ocean.

Pete's problems weren't over when he got to *Andromeda*. One of the C-130s had experienced in-flight refuelling problems and had been forced to turn back, so Pete's troop were the only swimmers to be picked up by the rigid raider boats. One of the equipment palettes, however, couldn't be found. It was floating free somewhere out in the South Atlantic and Pete was told that it would have to be abandoned as *Andromeda* was getting under way. It didn't take Pete long to realize that the kit they had lost contained all of the troop's personal equipment. Without it, they would be about as much use to D Squadron as a patrol of traffic wardens. Pete remonstrated with the petty officer who brought them the bad news, then shoved the man aside and headed for the captain's cabin. Bursting in on the captain of a Royal Navy warship unannounced is simply not the done thing, but Pete certainly got the man's attention and his blunt approach persuaded the captain to resume the search. Tired as he was, Pete made his way out onto the deck, peering out through the freezing sea spray as searchlights played on the water. Eventually, hours later, the ship's radar picked up the palette and it was recovered safely. The *Andromeda* arrived in San Carlos Water the following morning, and Pete's troop joined D Squadron doing what the SAS does so well, operating behind enemy lines, setting up observation posts, laying ambushes and generally making a nuisance of themselves until the day they boarded HMS *Onyx* to prepare for that final version of Operation *Mikado*.

Pete's contretemps with the captain aboard the *Andromeda* was far from being his first brush with authority. The SAS would prefer it if its soldiers maintained a low profile and lived a quiet life when not doing their jobs in training or on operations. It takes a certain strength of character, however, to get through SAS Selection and training and sometimes that character is so strong and extrovert as to be irrepressible. Pete would be the first to admit that he's got himself into a few scrapes in the past. When the Regiment sent him out to Hong Kong in 1977 to work with the Gurkhas and the local police, training them in unarmed combat techniques, Pete became entangled in a bar brawl while out drinking with a couple of off-duty Hong Kong police inspectors. For many years, having seen the sort of trouble that young soldiers can get themselves into when they are out and about in garrison towns, Pete had carried with him a heavy brass knuckle duster. The thing was an antique, a relic from World War I that Pete had picked up somewhere, but it still did its job. When Pete and the policemen were attacked, he slipped the knuckle duster out of his pocket and pushed it onto his hand. He laid out two or three of their assailants as he made his way towards the door, but was wrestled to the ground in the street and was using the 'duster' for its intended purpose when the uniformed police arrived and arrested him.

Although Pete hadn't actually gone looking for a fight, being arrested for brawling is bad enough to warrant serious disciplinary action in the Regiment. Pete, furthermore, had been carrying an offensive weapon, something of which the judge took a very dim view when Pete appeared in court. Rather than impose a custodial sentence on him, the judge gave Pete the option of corporal punishment and Pete chose six strokes of the cane rather than three months in jail. It may have seemed like the easy option at the time, but the punishment inflicted such severe wounds on his backside that he ended up in hospital for a week before being shipped back to the UK on a medical flight. He reckoned he was the only sergeant in the British Army with 12 stripes – three on each arm and six on his arse! When he got home, he was RTU'd – Returned To Unit. Pete went back to the Royal

Engineers, from where he had originally come, but was not out of the SAS for good. The RTU was for 18 months only. When he came back, he lost his stripes – the ones on his arms, at least. The others took ten years to fade.

Had he not been such a valuable asset to the Regiment, the Hong Kong caper would have meant the end of Pete's SAS career, but he had proved many times over that he was one of the best. He had been wounded during Operation *Jaguar* in Oman in 1971 when he caught a ricochet that cut up his hand. A few millimetres' difference would have meant losing his thumb, but Pete took comfort from the fact that a split-second's difference would have meant him taking the bullet in the head.

Pete was also present at the battle of Mirbat in 1972. During the action, Pete had two responsibilities: he had to establish and maintain radio contact with B Squadron HQ at Um Al Gwarif, and also operate a .50-calibre Browning heavy machine-gun (HMG) on the roof of the BATT house, firing at the waves of closing enemy fighters whose objective was to take the 25pdr (see chapter 12 for the details of this battle). Pete sent a quick radio message stating 'situation desperate – send reinforcements', then ran back up to the HMG to engage the enemy, who by this time had closed to within grenade-throwing range of the field gun. Pete kept firing, helping to hold the attackers at bay until an air strike drove them back and reinforcements eventually arrived. The battle of Mirbat raged for almost seven hours and was witness to many acts of individual heroism. The rebels had saturated the defenders' positions with rifle fire from their AK-47s, mortars and rockets. As the source of some of the heaviest defensive fire, Pete had been the focus for a great deal of the enemy's ordnance. When he checked his machine-gun after it was all over, he found that it had scrapes and dents where it had been repeatedly hit by enemy fire, although he had come through it all without a scratch.

Pete was not so lucky when we were in Germany on exercise, thundering across the countryside in our 'Pink Panther' Land Rovers (Land Rovers literally painted pink, one of the best colours for desert camouflage). In fact, he got himself into a bit of a fix. The Land Rover is a wonderful vehicle, but the versions we were using in the early 1970s had their limitations. They have improved a lot, but back then they were heavy, cumbersome, underpowered and had a pretty poor turning circle. The turning circle wasn't such a problem out in the desert, but in northern Europe it could become a liability, making the wagons far less manoeuvrable than we would have liked. In short, they simply didn't always go exactly where we wanted them to go, especially if they were still fitted with the 'balloon' tyres we used in the desert. These were ideal for use on sand, but could be dangerous on the more solid surfaces in Europe. Pete found this out the hard way when he rolled one of the Pink Panthers. Standard procedure when a Rover starts to tip over, as far as I'm concerned, is to get the hell out of it: jump clear and stay clear until the thing stops moving. Pete, however, didn't quite make it out in time and ended up with more than two tons of vehicle lying on his leg. Needless to say, his leg was broken. He wasn't happy. You've never heard a trooper curse to his fullest capacity, running through his entire repertoire of most blasphemous swearwords, until you've heard one who's just had a Land Rover dropped on his leg. Once we managed to get the wagon off him, Pete was whisked away by the medics, heading for a spell in hospital.

I decided that it would be a good idea to pay him a visit as soon as I got the chance. I walked into his hospital ward and spotted him, his leg in traction, lying in a bed adjacent to the only other patient in the room. This was a guy who had been through a rough time. He was an American serviceman who had been badly shot up in Vietnam and was being treated in Germany prior to being shipped home. He had just come out of a coma and had more tubes coming out of him than Piccadilly Circus. When I walked in, smartly turned out in uniform with my beige SAS beret, he glanced at me and I nodded a greeting. He just snorted.

'SAS, huh?' he grunted.

'That's right', I smiled, trying to appear friendly.

'What do you know about soldiering?' he hissed. 'What the hell have you lot done since the end of World War II?'

I then politely began explaining to him exactly what we had been up to, starting with Malaya then moving on through Aden, Borneo and Oman. I was just launching into a few operations in detail when Pete, whom I hadn't even yet acknowledged, roared from the other bed: 'Knock it off, Scholey, before you bore the poor bastard right back into a coma!'

In May 1980, Pete was involved in the most high-profile operation ever undertaken by the SAS, when they stormed the Iranian Embassy in Princes Gate, London, after it had been taken over by terrorists. (See chapter 14 for more detailed background to this incident.) Pete was first in through the French windows on the ground floor at the rear of the building, dashing through the embassy's library as explosions rocked the building and gunfire erupted upstairs. His team's job was to secure the stairwell, clear the basement and prepare to receive the hostages as they were bundled downstairs. For Pete and his team, the greatest dread was encountering booby traps or the explosives with which the terrorists claimed to have rigged the building. Intelligence reports had maintained that the terrorists and their hostages were on the upper floors, but as Pete cleared a barricade from the door to the basement and pulled the pin from a stun grenade, he couldn't help wondering if someone was lying in wait in the gloom of the cellar. Charging down the stairs in the wake of the shock from the 'flash-bang', the troopers shot the locks from the cellar doors and kicked them in. Pete booted one door open and immediately spotted a figure lurking in the shadows. He opened fire and, with deadly accuracy, put 20 rounds into an empty dustbin.

Having cleared the cellar, Pete's group took their positions on the main staircase as the first of the hostages, eyes streaming from the effects of the tear gas, were manhandled down to the exit. Passed from man to man, the hostages were hustled from the building as quickly as possible. The embassy was ablaze and there was still the very real danger that any surviving terrorists (two had not yet been accounted for) could detonate hidden explosives. As the next in line was passed from one black-clad SAS man to the next, a cry went up, 'That one's a terrorist!' The necessarily brusque handling of the hostages was altered to slaps and kicks to keep the terrorist moving towards the exit. Later identified as Faisal, the second-in-command of the terrorist group, the man was almost doubled up as he approached Pete, as though he was hiding something. Then Pete spotted it. Even through the slight misting of condensation inside his respirator eyepieces, the detonator cap of the Russian fragmentation grenade was unmistakable in the terrorist's hand. Pete brought his MP5 SMG to bear, but could not open fire. Hostages and other SAS personnel were in his line of fire. Pete's rounds would pass straight through the terrorist and kill his own mates. Quicker than the blink of an eye, Pete raised his MP5 and clubbed the terrorist to the ground. The man fell down the last few stairs with Pete right behind him and as he hit the floor, Pete emptied a magazine into him, with another SAS trooper opening up too to make sure of the job. The grenade rolled from the dead man's hand. Thankfully for all those in close proximity, Faisal had not had time to remove the pin.

A year later, Pete was called upon to give evidence at the inquest into the siege deaths at Westminster Coroner's Court. Pete was asked to explain why Faisal had incurred 39 bullet wounds. He had to explain about making sure that a terrorist is incapacitated under such circumstances, and about the rate of fire of the MP5, although he was tempted to give the answer that first sprang into his head – 'Because I ran out of ammunition, Your Honour'.

Pete spent the last three years of his service as a member of the CRW Wing of 22 SAS, instructing on all aspects of anti-terrorist training. When he left the Regiment in 1987, he quickly found work as a security specialist and bodyguard, travelling all over the world on jobs for some very high-profile clients.

I am proud to say that Pete remains a close friend to this day.

Chapter 14

SERGEANT TOMMY PALMER

Tommy Palmer braced himself against the bulkhead of the Sea King as it skipped over fences and rocky outcrops, rising and falling, swinging this way and that like some kind of crazy fairground ride, ducking below the enemy radar by following the contours of the hillsides. It was late spring 1982, or it had been when he had left Hereford. Outside, 8,000 miles (12,874km) from Hereford on the edge of the Antarctic, the southern hemisphere autumn was turning to winter in the Falkland Islands.

The Sea Kings that had picked up Tommy and the rest of the B Squadron detachment from their temporary home aboard the Royal Fleet Auxiliary landing ship *Sir Lancelot* had been blacked out for night flying from the moment they took off. It had been late afternoon but already dark when they lugged their kit out onto the wind-swept deck of the *Lancelot* to await the choppers' arrival. The *Lancelot* lay crippled in San Carlos Water, having been hit by bombs dropped from Argentine Sky Hawks on 24 May, one of which had smashed through the starboard side and lodged in the bowels of the ship without actually detonating. Once it had been removed by a naval bomb disposal team, the damaged ship was declared safe and adopted as a base for the SAS QRF (Quick Reaction Force), among others. It wasn't so bad. Tommy had had worse billets in Oman, in Ulster and had spent nights out in the Brecon Beacons where he would have been glad of a bomb-damaged ship to shelter in – not that you were ever likely to find such a thing up a mountain.

Tommy had struggled into his Bergen rucksack and climbed in through the gaping side door of the Sea King along with the others, claiming a space against the bulkhead as the door was slid shut, blocking out any illumination from the lights on deck and plunging them into a gloomy darkness. Their chopper lifted into the air, swinging round to head west before racing low across the water out of San Carlos and across the Falkland Sound into enemy territory on the island of West Falkland. They had now been airborne for what seemed like an age, although Tommy realized it was actually only about 20 minutes. Through a window he caught a glimpse of the countryside, flat and grey in the dim, watery moonlight. Tommy knew that would not be how the helicopter crew was seeing it. They would be viewing the hillsides in psychedelic shades of electronic green through their passive night goggles. The goggles acted as image intensifiers, using all available light, even that from the stars, to allow the aircrews to see in the dark. It wasn't clear as day, and you wouldn't be too happy with the ghostly shapes you saw through the goggles if they were appearing on your TV set, but once you got used to them the goggles were like having cat's eyes. The CRW team used them in the Killing House back at Hereford, a large concrete building with internal rooms which could be used to simulate the various scenarios in which the anti-terrorist teams might have to operate. When the lights went out and the room was full of smoke, a trooper could still spot his targets and pick them off as easily as if they were in broad daylight. Daylight, in fact, came as a bit of a shock after using the goggles. When you took them off as you left the Killing House at the end of the exercise, you had to shut your eyes and blink a few times to stop it feeling like you were staring straight into the sun.

Any sign of sunshine was still several hours away from B Squadron now, however, as the Sea Kings slowed, the noses of the aircraft rearing up slightly before they settled down onto their LZs. The side door was hauled open by the crewman, the chill of the cabin immediately invaded by the far sharper cold of the mountains. Tommy was glad to get out, happy to scurry away from the roar of the two Rolls-Royce engines and the clatter of the Sea King's five huge rotor blades; delighted, above all, to be on terra firma as they adopted their all-round defence position. He'd been in plenty of choppers before. The confidence and skill of the chopper crews always helped to settle any nerves the lads might have about sitting helpless in the spartan interior, crammed shoulder-to-shoulder with their mates. But now every SAS soldier had another anxiety gnawing away at the back of his mind. Now he had to work that little bit harder to stop himself thinking about what would happen if the chopper went down.

Tommy had no fear of flying and had proved many times that he had what it took to cope with the dangers they all had to face when on active service. But, like everyone else around that time, when he climbed into a Sea King from the deck of a ship, he couldn't help but think for a moment about what had happened to the guys from D Squadron when they were transferring from *Hermes* to *Intrepid.* It was only a five-minute cross-decking flight. The last ones to go, they had slung their kit into the Sea King and climbed aboard, pulling on their lifejackets, a few of them in combat gear, most just in the light kit they had been wearing on *Hermes* – boiler suits or fatigues and sweaters. None of them bothered struggling into the cumbersome rubber survival suits. The chopper's side doors had been removed to make it easier and quicker to ferry men and equipment, but that didn't worry any of them, either. They'd done this dozens of times before. It must have come as a relief when the chopper lifted off, as *Hermes* was wallowing around uncomfortably on the kind of rollercoaster waves that washed your last meal around in your guts. At least the Sea King would fly straight and level for a few minutes.

The chopper had lifted off from the rear deck of Hermes and wheeled away to starboard to close in on *Intrepid*, just half a mile away across the heaving waves. *Intrepid* was supposed to have been decommissioned that year, but her retirement had been postponed due to the Falklands War. There was an obvious need for the ship, which had an enormous dock in her stern that could accommodate eight landing craft. Above the dock was the landing deck for which the Sea King was headed. Another helicopter had just touched down, so D Squadron's aircraft made another circuit, waiting while the engines of the chopper on deck slowed to a complete stop and the rotors could be folded away to let the deck crew roll the machine into the ship's hangar.

Suddenly there was a loud bang, the kind of impact that leaves car passengers stunned when another vehicle rams into them. The Sea King lurched sideways. From over 200ft (61m), it dropped like a stone. The men inside were flung across the cabin in a tangle of arms, legs and loose kit. The chopper smashed into the surface of the sea and freezing cold water immediately surged in through the open doorways. Disoriented, shocked, many of them injured, the men struggled in blind panic to fight their way out. Lifejacket straps, pockets and sleeves snagged on unseen obstructions and were desperately wrenched free. For those who made it out of the mayhem, there was little to offer them hope. The Sea King was almost completely submerged, having capsized when it hit the surface. *Hermes* and *Intrepid* appeared as distant lights that vanished as the survivors were sucked down into the troughs between the waves. The South Atlantic froze them so quickly that their arms and legs already felt like lead. They needed every ounce of strength they had to keep on kicking and thrashing to keep their heads above the water. They coughed and retched, spewing up salt water and aviation fuel. The lucky ones made it to an upturned emergency liferaft inflated by the chopper's co-pilot. They clung to the raft, held on to each other. Those who were still wearing lifejackets inflated them and watched as the aircrew struggled to activate their search and rescue beacons, firing flares that rocketed up into the night sky, glowed with faint hope then drifted away on the wind.

They all knew that they couldn't survive for long in the water before the freezing conditions sapped their strength, dragged down their body temperatures and allowed the onset of exposure to drain the life from them. Their training had taught them that much. They knew they had to get out of the water soon, or they would all die. In the end, they were in the sea for 30 minutes before they were picked out by the searchlight of a rescue helicopter. The machine hovered over them as the winchman lowered the harness that would pluck the first of them from the water. By that time a launch from the frigate *Brilliant* was also on the scene. Its crew dragged the exhausted men aboard, most of them too numb with cold even to move their arms. There were just nine survivors. Some of them had been so far gone that they had to be manhandled all the way onto the ship and then laid down under a hot shower to raise their core body temperature and reverse the effects of hypothermia.

D Squadron lost 20 men who perished in the crash. Some had been on temporary attachment with the Regiment for the duration of the conflict. Many more had been Tommy's friends, men he had served with when he was in D Squadron, men with whom he had drunk, trained and fought. The cause of the disaster was attributed to a bird strike that had taken out one of the engines. Tommy thought it strange that a single sea bird could have caused all those deaths. He also knew something of what the survivors had gone through. He'd been in that freezing cold water himself not that long ago. That was how he had arrived in the South Atlantic.

The long journey that had begun in Hereford had paused when Tommy and the others reached Ascension Island. There they had waited for their orders, expecting to join a ship heading south for the Falklands. When they were finally briefed for the task ahead, it came as a shock to find that they weren't destined for a long sea journey at all. They were going to Argentina. The plan was to fly a team by Hercules C-130 directly to the Argentine air base at Rio Grande to destroy the squadron of jets based there and, along with them, the deadly Exocet missiles they carried. In the bar at the American airmen's club on Ascension Island, they had downed flaming Drambuies the night before they were due to fly out. They were letting off steam, fully expecting to be setting off on what some believed to be a suicide mission the next day. Tommy was not one of those doubters. He had great confidence in his own abilities and knew that if any outfit could pull off such a mission, it was the bunch of half-drunk reprobates sitting round the table with him. A raid like that was, after all, what the Regiment was all about. The lure of legendary exploits like that was what had drawn them all to the Regiment in the first place.

Tommy had joined the Regiment from the 33rd Field Squadron, Royal Engineers, when he was just 22, three years after he had first signed up. He had more reason than most to remember his Selection course as something of a nightmare. He thought he was doing pretty well until he picked up an injury and the Selection team had refused to let him continue with the course. Later that year (1973) he was given another chance and went through the whole process again. This time he sailed through and was sent off to do his jump training with the Paras. Nine years on, having been to the Far East and the Middle East, it looked like he was about to head west, if that wasn't an unfortunate turn of phrase, on a lightning tour of a very small part of South America.

Ultimately, of course, they never did pay a visit to the base in Tierra del Fuego. The raid was called off and Tommy, along with Pete Winner and the rest of their group from B Squadron, was dispatched as replacements for the men who had gone down in the Sea King. Ironically, the quickest way to get them there was to dump them in the sea. Tommy had swapped the warm sunshine of Ascension Island for the perishing cold of the South Atlantic Ocean when he parachuted into the sea along with Pete and the others, to be picked up by the Marines from HMS *Andromeda*. The water had been shockingly cold. He had been zipped up inside a survival suit and fully prepared for his ducking, but the cold of the water still came as a real jolt to his system. None of them would have lasted long without the survival gear. Once the *Andromeda* had delivered them to the Falklands, they were eventually transferred to the *Lancelot* and kept busy with operations just like the one he was on now.

After the Sea Kings departed, they surveyed the bleak moorland, making sure that their arrival had not been observed by any hidden Argentines, then formed up for the long trek to their ambush point. Trudging across the damp Falklands mountainside was, for Tommy, very much like being in the hills back home, not in Hereford, but in Scotland.

Tommy had been born in Falkirk in 1950 and had spent a lot of time as a lad roaming the Scottish countryside, becoming an expert poacher. He was well-known in the Regiment as an ace scrounger and I had first-hand experience of his expertise when I was his driving instructor. We had been bouncing over open countryside near Hereford in a Land Rover, as I attempted to teach Tommy the fine art of cross-country, four-wheel driving techniques, when Tommy suddenly slammed on the brakes. Having come close to breaking my nose on the dashboard, I was left uncharacteristically speechless when Tommy simply gave me a grin and leapt out of the wagon. He nipped round the back and reappeared with a shotgun and a large sack. This was rabbit country and there were hordes of the little devils all around. Tommy thought it would be criminal not to bag a few for Lofty Wiseman. As the Regiment's survival guru, he could cook up a fine feast with a handful of rabbits.

The terrain the SAS had to negotiate as they headed for their ambush ground was, of course, not the sort of ground with which even a Land Rover could cope. They stepped over or waded through countless streams that cut into the hillside and criss-crossed the landscape. They cursed as the waterlogged ground on either side of the running water sucked their boots down into the marsh. By the time they reached the hillside above the valley where a previous recce team had observed regular Argentine patrols, Tommy and the others were cold and damp, but fully alert for any sign of the enemy. They spread out to find cover that would give them the best possible fields of fire. Then they watched and waited.

Lying still on the damp, mossy hillside behind the jagged rock, Tommy could feel the chill of moisture penetrating his Gore-tex jacket. He flexed the gloved fingers of his right hand and then returned them to rest on the trigger guard of his M16. The rifle was cold. It made the gunmetal seem impossibly brittle, as though it might shatter when the first round exploded in its chamber. This was a far cry from the blistering heat of the tropical sun on Ascension Island, where he had sat in the shade slotting rounds into the rifle's magazines. Forcing himself to stay alert, he blinked, flexed his toes inside his boots and slowly moved his left hand from the grip around the M203 grenade launcher. He had to keep his mind on the job. There was no point in thinking about how cold he was. Everyone was lying behind his own rock, just as cold as he was. Everyone was in the same boat. Slowly, so slowly that even had anyone been lying right next to him they would not have noticed, he shifted his weight from his right hip to his left, searching for any scrap of comfort he could find on the cold ground. His eyes returned to the target area lying in the valley in front of him. The moonlight made it all seem grey and dead.

From his vantage point he could see down the hillside to the low ferns and bracken that carpeted the valley floor. That was where they would come. That was where they would die. That was his killing ground. He scanned the expanse of boggy ground as far as he could see, searching for any sign of movement, a glint of moonlight on a carelessly unshielded piece of Argentine kit. There was nothing. Tommy glanced across at Pete Winner, lying nearby with a clutch of grenades, pins unsplayed, ready for use, sitting close at hand beside him. Pete caught his eye and slowly shook his head. They'd lain out like this several times before, waiting for targets that never turned up. Even when they did manage to snare an 'Argie' patrol, they never put up much of a fight. They would nail two or three of them and maybe take a couple of prisoners, but the rest legged it from any firefight first chance they got. You couldn't blame them. The Argentines were mostly conscripts who hadn't chosen to be there and weren't willing to risk their necks. Running was the wrong thing to do, though. From the look of most of the prisoners Tommy and the others had seen, they were better treated by our side than they were by their own. The Argentine special forces were different. They were better trained and generally up for a scrap. Maybe some of them would come walking up the valley. Tommy peered out into the moonlight again. There was still no sign of any foot patrol.

Despite the cold, the patrol could not afford to risk compromising their position by attempting to light a fire or brew up some tea. Even when the sun rose and they were lying up during the short daylight hours, they would be on hard routine. No fires, no hot drinks, no hot grub, no cigarettes and no talking. They'd have cold food from their ration packs – pretty unsatisfying stuff and, even when they could heat any of it up in a mess tin over a hexi block, it wasn't exactly a gourmet meal. But hunger wasn't the biggest problem they had to face. The trouble with lying there so long was the sheer boredom. Yet you had to stay alert. You had to keep watching. You had to be ready for anything. If you weren't, then you ran the risk of letting everyone else down. You had to do your job. You had to look out for your mates. At least the cold helped you stay awake. Tommy sucked in a lungful of South Atlantic air and let it out slowly, calming himself, concentrating on the killing zone.

Slowly, the moon and stars grew a little less bright, the sky a little less dark. The first light of dawn began to dilute the night and eventually the sun appeared, bringing with it a harsh, frosty morning. Still they lay there, watching, waiting. Eventually a silent signal was passed from man to man – the ambush was a turkey. This was another no-show. The harsh brightness of the morning, once the sun had dragged itself into the sky, did little to take the edge off the anti-climax. No one feels a sense of relief in a situation like that. When you have invested time and effort into an operation, what you really want is a result. Tommy, never one to be satisfied hanging around with nothing to do, was perhaps the most disappointed. When he was at home in Hereford, even if he was feeling a bit under the weather, he had to get out of the house and take himself off for a run, maybe even have a swim in the river, no matter what time of year it was. Tommy needed to be active. He had taken an instructor's job back in Hereford once, in order to be able to spend more time with his wife and children, but he had hated not being part of a Sabre Squadron and had lasted only 18 months in the new job.

On the Falklands mountainside, their wasted night was followed by another wasted day. They waited out the daylight hours, using their bivvy (sleeping) bags to try to keep themselves warm. When the sun finally set in the late afternoon, they stole away under the comforting cloak of darkness. They had to get out without being spotted by the Argies and without their knowing that they had ever even been there. One night soon they might have to set up this ambush all over again. They made their way back up the mountainside, moving as quickly as they dared, slipping here and there where a frost- or ice-covered rock sent a footstep slithering sideways. Peering out into the darkness, ever wary of walking into the kind of ambush that they themselves had just abandoned, they at last started to warm up, the effort of traversing the steep slopes sending the blood coursing through their veins and re-energizing muscles that had seemed set on hibernation. Once they crested the last ridge before the LZ, taking care not to skyline themselves or present a tempting target for any hidden Argie sniper with a night scope, they fanned out to secure the area. Then it was just a case of waiting for the Sea Kings to come swooping in and ferry them back to *Sir Lancelot*.

Their night on the mountainside had been typical of so many of the patrols undertaken in the Falklands. Not every one culminated with the exhilaration of a contact. There were other compensations, though. When

Port Stanley was finally liberated, Tommy and Pete Winner commandeered a Mercedes wagon for which the Argies no longer had any use and busied themselves organizing a major celebration. Tommy's scrounging skills were put to good use as he called on a Royal Navy contact to supply a few cases of beer. The two cans a day the lads were officially allotted by the Regiment were nowhere near enough for a proper party. There was no way they were going to be able to feast on field rations either, but Tommy had picked up the name of another man who would be able to put some proper food his way – a pile of good steaks was what he had on order. He and Pete also tried to make money at the Post Office in Stanley. Stamps issued by the Falkland Islands postal authorities were highly collectable back home and since the Argies had taken over the Post Office, they had been overprinting them with their own 'Malvinas' post marks, making them even more valuable. Unfortunately, by the time Tommy and Pete got there, the Post Office was back under orderly control. Their party, however, was a great success. There was no doubting Tommy's resourcefulness or determination. He had proved that countless times before, not least during the 1980 siege at the Iranian Embassy in London.

On 30 April 1980, the well-heeled district of Kensington in west London, home to a number of foreign embassies, high-class hotels and some of the most expensive properties in Britain, reluctantly became the focus of the world's media attention. At 11.30 am six men approached the front entrance to the Iranian Embassy in Princes Gate. Overpowering PC Trevor Lock, who was standing guard on the front steps of the embassy, they bundled him inside, producing machine-guns, pistols and hand grenades.

PC Lock had raised the alarm via a 'panic' button on his radio as he was manhandled inside the building and the police were swiftly on the scene, although by the time they arrived the six terrorists had taken complete control of the embassy. Inside they held 26 hostages, including the head of the embassy, Chargé d'Affaires Dr Gholam-Ali Afrouz. Among the hostages were nine visitors to the embassy. These included two BBC staff, the only other British hostage apart from PC Lock being embassy chauffeur Ron Morris.

As the area around Princes Gate was sealed off by the police, the terrorist leader, who identified himself only as 'Oan', announced to the police negotiating team that his group was part of 'The Democratic Revolutionary Movement for the Liberation of Arabistan'. He was quick to issue his demands. He wanted independence for the oil-rich region of Khuzestan in Iran, the release of over 90 political prisoners held in Iranian jails, mediators from Arab embassies to conduct negotiations and the safe passage for the group with an aircraft to fly them to Iraq.

Negotiations with Oan continued for five days, during which the occupants of the embassy were supplied with food and cigarettes and five of the hostages were released. One of these was the BBC newsman Chris Cramer, who had been taken ill. Along with the other hostages, he was able to supply vital information about how well the terrorists were armed, their disposition around the building and the way they had rigged the embassy with booby traps. This confirmed what the thermal-imaging cameras and listening devices, via which the police were already monitoring the situation inside the building along with the SAS CRW team, had already indicated.

The Regiment had been informed of the siege almost as soon as it happened thanks to a former SAS man who was then working as a police dog handler. His call to Hereford had alerted the CRW team, which included Tommy and Pete Winner, who were training in the Killing House that very morning. They had packed their gear and were on their way to London by the time an official request for their presence was passed to Hereford. For five days they laid their plans for an assault on the embassy, codenamed Operation *Nimrod*, waiting for the moment when the police would finally relinquish control of the scene and the Home Secretary would order them to go in.

That order came on Bank Holiday Monday, 5 May, following the sound of gunshots from within the embassy. The body of press attaché Abbas Lavasani was unceremoniously dumped on the front steps of the building and the CRW team was given the go-ahead to implement its assault plan – Operation *Nimrod* was now active. Two squads, Red Team and Blue Team, were to break into the building simultaneously through the front and rear windows. Tommy was to be a member of Red Team, but his part of the assault did not go entirely according to plan.

The windows through which the teams entered were blown in with frame charges or hacked away with crowbar tools known as 'hooligan bars', then CS gas and 'flash-bang' stun grenades were hurled into the rooms. The G60 stun grenade was a formidable weapon specially designed for the SAS. It didn't send out shards of shrapnel like an ordinary grenade, but the magnesium powder and mercury inside went off with an almighty bang and a blinding flash when the device was detonated. The noise and light were enough to disorientate anyone without proper protection for the few seconds an SAS soldier needed to pop up and slot a couple of rounds into him. Barry Davies and Alistair Morrison were the first to use them in anger when they went in with the German GSG9 team to rescue the hostages from a hijacked airliner at Mogadishu in 1977. By the time the assault team on the embassy job used them three years later, everyone was well used to handling them, but that didn't stop the grenades setting the building on fire – this had as much to do with the terrorists having doused the place with kerosene as it did with the flash-bangs. At the embassy, the flash set fire to curtains and then whole rooms went up.

When Tommy went in through his balcony window the curtains were a mass of flames and his respirator and hood caught light. He thought his burning kit was about to turn him into a human candle, but he quickly ducked back out of the window, ripped off the smouldering gear and dived back in again, bareheaded. He now had no protection against the CS gas that was billowing through the building, he had scorch burns to his head and neck and was slapping at his singed hair with one hand to make sure it wasn't still burning. Not that he had much time to worry about that. One of the terrorists was crouched at the opposite side of the elegant room trying to set light to a beautiful floor carpet that had been splashed with kerosene. If he'd waited a couple of minutes, the flames devouring the room from Tommy's end would have done the job for him. Tommy didn't wait. As soon as his feet touched the floor he had his MP5 levelled at the terrorist and squeezed the trigger. Nothing happened. A two-second burst would have been enough to empty most of the 30-round magazine into the man, but nothing happened. All Tommy got was the 'dead man's click' – a stoppage. The terrorist froze for a heartbeat, staring down the barrel of Tommy's gun.

Tommy dropped the MP5 and snatched his 9mm Browning from the quick-draw holster strapped to his thigh. In the split second he took to do that, the terrorist recovered his senses and took to his heels. He dashed through the door into the corridor as Tommy sprinted across the room, the kerosene in the carpet squelching under his boots.

Blinking to clear his eyes of the stinging tear gas and acrid smoke from the blazing room, Tommy pounded out into the corridor. Straight away he spotted the back of the terrorist's shirt, the man racing away from him down the hallway. In his hand, the terrorist now held what Tommy immediately recognized as a Russian fragmentation grenade. The man was heading for a room that Tommy knew was full of hostages. Two more running steps and then he took aim as the man paused for an instant outside the room. That instant was long enough for Tommy to shoot him in the head and the man dropped to the floor. Approaching the man's lifeless body, he was joined by other members of the team and Tommy burst into the room with them, the men in black yelling 'Who are the terrorists?' and dispatching the ones they identified in the room before hustling the hostages down the stairs, out of the building. The whole assault had taken just 11 minutes and, unknown to the SAS team, had been filmed by TV news cameras.

Tommy's wife, Caroline, had been sitting in front of the TV with a cup of coffee watching like millions of others, as the black-clad figures swarmed all over the outside of the embassy. When she had seen him dart out of the window to ditch his burning kit, she had recognized Tommy straight away. She said later that it made a real change knowing where he was for once! A phone call a few minutes later let her know he was okay and then, when he got home that evening, everything was back to normal. Caroline asked him what it was like inside the embassy and Tommy joked about the carpets and how, if they hadn't all been so badly burned, he might have lifted a couple to bring home. Then they let it rest. His work had to stay outside the home as much as possible. That was the way Tommy liked it. His home was with Caroline and their two young daughters. His work was a different world completely.

Two years later, Tommy had been annoyed with Caroline when he had left their house to report to the barracks before setting off for the Falklands.

He had looked back and seen her standing at the window of their front room, watching him walk off down the street. Tommy was a proud man and as tough as they come, but that had been enough to bring tears to his eyes. He had spoken to her about that when he returned home and they agreed to say their goodbyes indoors in future. That was how they had said goodbye shortly after his return from the Falklands, when he set off for a tour of duty in Northern Ireland. Tommy never saw home again. He died in a car crash on the motorway near Lurgan on 8 February 1983, when the vehicle in which he was a passenger left the road and overturned.

Tommy was a great character and a brave soldier, a man I greatly admired. Soldiers like Tommy have made the Regiment what it is today and he will never be forgotten.

Chapter 15

TROOPER TOMMY TOBIN AND SERGEANT PETE LOVEDAY

Little Tommy – we called him 'Little' because he was just that bit smaller than Tommy Palmer – was not what most people might expect a hard-nosed, ruthless, SAS tough guy to be. He was not loud or brash or boastful. He did not have the murderous stare of a battle-hardened combat veteran. Few in the SAS actually do have the look of the archetypal, B-movie action hero. Little Tommy certainly didn't. He was a quiet, good-natured, good-looking young man – and, without a shadow of a doubt, a true hero.

Tommy Tobin joined the SAS from the Army Catering Corps. The Regiment, of course, takes all sorts from all sorts of backgrounds and, should anyone be labouring under the misapprehension that the Catering Corps is nothing but a bunch of overweight cooks and bottle washers, Tommy Tobin was the man to set them straight. A superb all-round soldier, Tommy sailed through Selection and was posted to B Squadron where he became one of Reg Tayler's star pupils, keen to learn and quick to acquire a range of life-saving skills that made him one of the finest medics in the Regiment. In 1972, during the SAS's 'secret' war in Dhofar, southern Oman, Tommy was one of the nine SAS personnel stationed at the BATT house in Mirbat, helping to train the local militia, organizing the town's defences and, especially in Tommy's case, helping to win 'hearts and minds' by providing basic first aid and medical care for the local population.

Medicines, the attention of a trained doctor, hospital treatment or even the most rudimentary health care were things that only the privileged ruling class, the nobility and those closest to them, enjoyed in Oman under the rule of the previous sultan. When the old man's son, Qaboos, had taken over in the summer of 1970, he had promised that all of that would change. Two years on, while the engineers and builders laboured to construct the new roads and hospitals, and medical staff were trained at home and abroad to create the health care system that Qaboos envisaged, SAS medics like Tommy helped to fill the gap, giving the people at least some hope that there was a brighter future ahead. Tommy helped to treat not only the SAF (Sultan's Armed Forces) and local Firquat militiamen, but also their families in the impoverished villages that were scattered across Oman's coastal plain or clung to the precipitous hillsides up in the mountains. Tommy had a soft spot for the kids. He had a new-born baby of his own back home in Hereford.

Mirbat wasn't such a bad place for Tommy to be. There was a beach where the fishermen landed their boats and the sea breeze helped to make the scorching temperatures in that part of the world just a little more bearable. The Adoo would regularly lob a few mortar bombs in from positions somewhere at the base of the jebel, but these generally fell some way short of the town and rarely claimed any casualties that required Tommy's expert attention. The Adoo always scarpered back into the mountains before a Firquat patrol could get close enough to take them on. Like the others, Tommy was anticipating the end of his tour when they would be replaced by G Squadron. He was looking forward to getting home and spending time with his new family.

In the early hours of the morning of 19 July 1972, the very day that B Squadron was due to pull out, Mirbat came under sustained attack from the mortars and heavy machine-guns of an Adoo force determined to overwhelm the town and massacre its inhabitants. Advancing towards Mirbat in strength – estimates have put the Adoo battle group at anything between 250 and 400 – they heavily outnumbered not only the SAS team, but also the local armed units tasked with defending the town. The events that unfolded are described in detail in this book in the chapter on Labalaba and Takavesi, but an element of repetition is necessary here to highlight the heroic part played by 'Little Tommy'.

The SAS team swung into action. As the others manned their positions behind the sandbags that lined the low walls on the flat roof of the BATT house, Tommy worked quickly and methodically at the rear of the mortar pit, flinging open the cases that were packed with 81mm mortar rounds, unscrewing the caps on the individual canisters and sliding the bombs out. Then he checked the charges, removed the safety pins and replaced each bomb in its container nose first, ready for use. He prepared dozens of bombs, carefully slotting the containers into well-ordered stacks, then grabbed his SLR (Self-Loading Rifle) and hunkered down in his own fire position, scanning his field of fire for any opportune targets.

As the battle raged, it became clear to the SAS commander, Captain Mike Kealy, that two of his men, Labalaba and Takavesi, who were manning the 25pdr field gun near the old fort on the edge of town that was the main focus of the Adoo attack, were in serious trouble. The two men were known to have been wounded and now all radio contact with the gun emplacement had been lost. Kealy needed a volunteer to go with him across half a mile of undulating scrubland that was a killing ground for every Adoo who poked his Kalashnikov out from behind a rock. Tommy didn't hesitate. The whole team volunteered, but Tommy knew he was the one that Captain Kealy really needed. He was the medic that his friends up there in the gun pit really needed. He caught the officer's eye and Kealy nodded. Tommy quickly turned and reached for his medical kit. He made sure he had saline and plenty of morphine, and from the medical store he took as many field dressings of different sizes as he could stuff into his pack. Then he slipped the strap over his head and across his body, pulling it tight so that the pack nestled safely on his back.

Grabbing the carrying handle of his SLR, he lifted the rifle into his arms and slid back the mechanism to check that he had a round in the chamber. Then he was ready to go. He and Kealy dashed from the BATT house to the cover of a wadi running roughly towards the fort. This was a less direct route to the gun position than that taken by Laba and Tak, but it afforded them slightly better cover. Then they sprinted from one patch of sparse cover, one shallow ditch, to another with Adoo rounds whistling past their ears, one giving covering fire as the other ran. The constant fire from the Browning .50 calibre and GPMG on the roof of the BATT house swept over their heads to keep the Adoo occupied. With one final, heart-thumping sprint, they both made it to the gun emplacement, Kealy tumbling into the adjacent ammunition bunker as Tommy leapt over the sandbags into the gun pit.

The stench of cordite stung his nostrils and an awful sight met his eyes. The floor of the gun pit was littered with spent shell cases and was awash with blood. Walid Khamis, the Omani gunner, lay in one corner of the dug-out clutching his stomach and bleeding profusely from a bullet wound. Takavesi was propped up against the sandbag wall at the opposite side of the pit, aiming and firing his SLR with one arm, the rifle's barrel resting on a sandbag. Tak was smothered with blood. It had coated his face from a wound somewhere on his scalp and his clothes were heavy with blood from wounds to his abdomen. He still managed a weak smile when he saw Tommy. Incoming rounds continued to slam into the sandbags and hammer at the 25pdr's steel shield. Tak squeezed off another shot, sending some back to the Adoo.

Labalaba lay face down on the carpet of smoke-blackened, blood-smeared shell cases; a dark patch of blood from a gaping wound at the back of his neck sent Tommy's heart into his boots. There was no way the big Fijian could have survived that. Taking in the whole scene in the blink of an eye, Tommy's training kicked in and he prioritized the casualties. Laba was the worst. He had to be checked out first. Dropping his SLR and ripping off his pack, Tommy crouched over Laba's prone form and examined his friend's wounds while checking for a pulse. Laba had a second bullet wound to his chin. There was no pulse, no vital signs, he was dead. Tommy knew he had to move on. He had to deal with the gunner then get to Tak. The gunner would need to be put on a drip and would need a fresh field dressing. He reached for his pack and turned toward the injured Omani.

At that moment, an incoming Kalashnikov round, undoubtedly not even aimed at Tommy but simply loosed off in the general direction of the gun pit, came whistling in over the sandbags. In moving towards the gunner, Tommy turned his head into the path of the bullet. It smashed into the side of his face, ripping away most of his lower jaw. Tommy collapsed forward beside Laba. His part in the battle of Mirbat was over.

The beleaguered garrison fought on, with Captain Kealy and Tak defending their gun pit until air strikes and the arrival of G Squadron drove off the Adoo. Casevac helicopters airlifted Tommy, Tak and the rest of the wounded to be cared for by the Field Surgical Team at Salalah. They were eventually flown back to the UK for treatment and Tommy spent many months in the military hospital at Woolwich. Reg Tayler managed to visit him there, as he did with so many of our wounded, but Tommy's injuries were so severe he ultimately succumbed to his wounds. He died in the hospital and was laid to rest in the churchyard of St Martin's in Hereford, close to the Regiment's base.

Tommy had earned the friendship and respect of his peers during his short time with the Regiment, no mean feat when professional standards and expectations are set so high, yet his achievements reach far beyond even that. Tommy was the purest of all heroes. He put his life on the line not to profit himself or in any foolhardy quest for glory. He made his sacrifice while attempting to help others, he laid down his life for his friends, and there can be no more heroic act than that.

I have brought Tommy and Pete together in this chapter for the simple reason that their careers were so markedly different. Tommy's time with the Regiment was tragically short whereas Pete had what must be the longest SAS career of anyone who has ever served with the Regiment.

Peter Derek Loveday was called up for National Service on 5 January 1950, joining the Suffolk Regiment. The Suffolks had a long and glorious history dating back to the days of King James II, who ordered the Duke of Norfolk to raise a regiment to help deal with the pesky Monmouth rebellion. The duke recruited men from both Norfolk and Suffolk, creating a unit that would endure for the next 274 years, serving King and Queen and Country all over the world, including India, Afghanistan and South Africa. Its 1st Battalion was almost wiped out at Ypres in 1915, suffering more than 400 casualties, but by the end of World War I the Suffolks boasted 23 battalions. During World War II their 1st battalion went to France in 1939 with the British Expeditionary Force (BEF) and returned to the UK, bloodied but unbowed, via Dunkirk the following year. They returned to France as part of the Assault Brigade that fought its way ashore on Sword Beach in Normandy in 1944. Other elements of the regiment served in the deserts of North Africa, and the Suffolks fought a desperate rearguard action against vastly superior Japanese forces all the way down the Malay peninsula before helping to mount the last-ditch defence of Singapore. A large proportion of the prisoners then forced by the Japanese to work under inhuman conditions on the infamous Burma Railway were men of the Suffolk Regiment.

When Pete began his training, the Suffolks were back in Malaya again, heavily involved in suppressing the Communist Terrorists (CTs) who had so much of the rural countryside in their uncompromising grip. The insurgents' cruelty towards the indigenous populations in the isolated jungle regions was legendary, but while they still had the manpower to mount cohesive operations, the security forces were never safe from their attacks either.

Pete found this out for himself when, after only six weeks' basic training, he was dispatched along with the rest of his intake on a troopship bound for the Far East. They travelled via the Suez Canal (still in friendly hands at that time) to Singapore where he found himself organized into A Company, 3rd Platoon, The Suffolk Regiment. It seemed he hardly had time to draw breath before he was trekking through the jungle with a Bren gun, searching for communist camps. The Suffolks had the best tally of enemy kills of any unit operating in the Malayan jungles, even though 70 per cent of them were, like Pete, National Servicemen at only 18 or 19 years of age. Most of their junior officers, too, the men who led them on their jungle excursions, were National Service recruits, not time-served professionals.

Every six weeks or so they would get the chance for a few hours of rest and recuperation (R&R) in Kuala Lumpur, when they would hit the NAAFI bar at the battalion headquarters in Wardiburn barracks for a few beers, before heading into town to banish all thoughts of their tasteless jungle compo rations with a massive plate of steak and chips at their favourite bar, Nanto's. Then they would sink a few more Tiger Beers before rolling back to Wardiburn to sleep it off prior to the journey back up country the next day. If they were lucky, they might get 24 hours extra and a rail warrant to take them as far as Singapore. But the journeys to and from their much anticipated 'rest' breaks could be every bit as dangerous as their forays into the jungle, as Pete was to discover on one rail journey back to base from a wind-down period in Singapore.

It was dark outside as the train trundled up the tracks, heading back north with its cargo of Suffolks, delivering them back to the jungle that had become so much like their second home. The windows were open, but there was little respite from the stifling heat in the carriage. The train lacked any comforts as sophisticated as air conditioning and the Malayan night was warm and humid, so there was no cool breeze rushing in to chill the sweat on their bodies. Where there was a window that would open a few inches, the space served only as a vent to suck the fog of cigarette smoke out of the carriage. When the train rounded a bend and the breeze caught it from the wrong direction, the open windows also let in the sooty exhaust expelled from the steam engine's smoke stack, so they were at times not only an inefficient but also an undesirable form of ventilation.

Pete and the other Suffolks lounged on the hard wooden bench seats, the cotton of their tropical issue uniforms seeming impossibly heavy in the overcrowded carriage. They had stowed what kit they had brought with them in the racks above their heads or under the seats, but finding enough space to stretch or even sit comfortably in a carriage full of 18–20-year-old youngsters all trying to do the same thing was never going to be easy. A few murmured conversations bubbled up here and there, but for the most part they journeyed with only the sound of the engine pumping away up front and the steel wheels clattering over the joins in the track. They had done their partying in Singapore and were now thoroughly exhausted after 25 hours of solid 'rest'. A few of them dozed. Others read and re-read well-thumbed letters from home. Some even tried to scribble their replies.

Pete could feel himself slowly being rocked to sleep by the motion of the train. That was no bad thing. A few hours' extra kip would stand him in good stead when they headed back into the jungle again. Would that be tomorrow, or maybe the next day? Nobody had told them yet. It wouldn't be long, that was for sure. Then, he thought he felt that soporific rocking change just a little. They weren't about to come into a station were they?

Suddenly there was a horrendous screech of metal against metal as the wheels skidded along the rails. The train slowed rapidly, too rapidly. Kit bags tumbled from the racks and drowsy soldiers who had been facing the front were flung onto the floor, the whole train straining to cling to the track and rob itself of its forward momentum. The lights went out. Then the men seemed to float for a moment and the carriage tipped sharply sideways. More kit flew through the air, accompanied this time by the flailing arms, legs and boots of soldiers plucked from their seats and flung across the carriage. Then, with one last lurch, the train came to a complete halt. The carriage was listing, clearly derailed, but still more or less upright and in reasonably good order. The same could not be said for the passengers. In the darkness, Pete could hear the moans, groans and curses of those who had suffered minor cuts, bruises and seriously disturbed naps. But what on earth had happened?

The answer came in the form of the instantly recognizable chatter of a Sten gun, a crackling volley from a handful of .303 rifles and the thump of grenades detonating nearby. The crash of breaking glass filled the air as the windows were shattered and incoming rounds buried themselves in the fixtures of the carriage. The men hugged the floor in the darkness. There was no panic in the carriage. The soldiers just lay dead still, hoping that they were behind substantial cover, praying that they were invisible and impregnable. From somewhere on the train came the comforting bark of a Bren gun returning fire, then another. After a brief exchange, the gunfire petered out and all that could be heard was the sound of orders shouted in the darkness over the mournful creaking of a wounded train. The CTs had struck and melted away back into the jungle, just as they always did. Their attack had achieved more nuisance value than it had serious casualties. Righting the train would cause a greater delay in returning the Suffolks to their jungle patrols than any injuries sustained. Next time the enemy got this close to him, though, Pete would be the one with the Bren and it would be the CTs on the receiving end of the first strike. He'd make damn sure of that.

Pete's platoon, in common with so many others, suffered frequent attacks by the CTs when travelling in truck convoys by road or, as in the overnight journey from Singapore, when on trains. They were constantly frustrated by the fact that the enemy never hung around long enough to put up a proper fight – they followed classic guerrilla hit-and-run tactics, much the same tactics, in fact, so often employed by the SAS.

Soldiering in Malaya with the Suffolks, however, was not all danger and disappointment. Pete found that he enjoyed the excitement of active service and the camaraderie of the men. He felt at a bit of a loose end when his two years' National Service was suddenly over and he was shipped back to the UK. While he went through the bureaucracy of the demob process, he knew that some of his old mates were in Trieste, trying to keep the peace between rival groups of Italians and Yugoslavs, both sides claiming the city and the surrounding countryside as their own, just as they had been doing for countless years before. Those guys were still in the thick of it, still together. He was on his own, contemplating the bleak prospect of trying to find a normal job.

Pete missed the army, so, after a year in 'civvy street' he joined the TA, hoping that part-time soldiering would fill the void. It didn't. Then he heard of the SAS, at that time relatively unknown, which was heavily involved in deep-penetration patrols in the Malayan jungle. In 1953 he applied to join, and passed a very exacting Selection course.

Before he knew it Pete was back on a troop ship en route to Malaya to join A Squadron. He had ten days' training in jungle patrolling, a week on a final exercise, then his para course at the RAF station in Changi. After that, he was back on operations in the jungle. It must have seemed like he'd only just left.

The operational timetable the Regiment adhered to at that time was three months in the jungle, then ten days' R&R leave. This was a tough regime, but for Pete going back to the jungle felt a bit like going home. He revelled in it, completing two three-year tours in Malaya with A Squadron in the 1950s, taking part in all the major operations. This included, of course, participating in the infamous tree jumps. Pete counted himself lucky to survive five of these, three in training and two on operations.

The Malayan operation that Pete regarded as the most satisfying and rewarding was staged in 1954. Pete, of course, was a veteran of jungle warfare by then, but still something of a new boy in A Squadron and the action was to serve as a formative experience for him in learning how the SAS worked. The squadron was deployed to Kajang, an area of treacherous swamp on the west coast of northern Malaya just above Malacca. They had received intelligence that a terrorist group was mounting barbarous attacks against isolated villages, plundering food and livestock and raping and murdering the villagers. The leader of the group, Loon-Kon-Kim, had been dubbed 'The Bearded Terror of Kajang' by the locals.

A local jungle scout was chosen to lead an SAS troop in search of Loon-Kon-Kim's base. Like the rest of his colleagues in A Squadron, Pete was by now more used to operating as part of a four-man patrol, so it felt a little like being back with the Suffolks when the best part of four patrols stalked through the swamp country. Wading through fetid water that could, at times, be almost chest deep, Pete took great care to keep his Bren gun out of the sludge. He was too old a hand to risk any kind of a stoppage when he knew that a close-quarter jungle firefight could erupt at almost any moment.

When they moved across higher ground they were hardly any less wet than in the swamp, the heat and humidity combining to leave their clothes drenched with sweat. Eventually the scout indicated an area up ahead and a series of silent signals were passed down the column. They sank to the jungle floor, Pete resting on one knee, the heavy Bren supported on his left thigh. The scout went forward with the patrol commander, creeping towards a clearing, crawling low in the foliage to find a vantage spot from which they could take a better look at the camp. The troop adopted an all-round defensive formation and waited.

When the recce party returned, the commander described in detail the large camp, which consisted of a collection of bamboo huts. The troop was split into smaller teams that deployed silently around the camp to keep watch, count the number of men in the camp and assess how heavily armed they were. Pete took up his position and got his first view of the camp. The terrorists displayed an arrogant disregard for their own security. They had had an easy ride slaughtering the unarmed villagers in the region and expected no reprisals from that quarter. Camp fires burned lazily, their embers producing wisps of smoke that fought their way skyward through the dense jungle air. A few of the inhabitants appeared from time to time, rifles or Sten guns slung over their shoulders and panga jungle knives dangling from makeshift scabbards at their waists. A couple of well-worn paths where the vegetation was cut back or trodden flat marked the most-used exits from the camp into the jungle. Pete knew that covering those quick-escape routes would be key to mounting a successful attack.

After observing the camp for long enough to establish that their targets were most definitely 'home', a plan of attack was drawn up. They would hit the largest huts first, coming at them from different angles but avoiding catching each other with 'through-and-through' shots – the .303 rounds from their rifles and Bren guns would pass straight through the flimsy huts, even straight through some of the occupants, and they didn't want to end up shooting each other. Part of the troop was detailed as an assault group, some were to provide covering fire and others were to take out anyone attempting to use the escape paths.

From their careful observation it had become obvious to Pete and the others that this was not a regular communist enemy outfit. They were too unprepared for an attack, too careless in their general defence. This group was simply a bunch of jungle gangsters, terrorizing the area for their own ends. They were not the official 'enemy', but the attack would be pressed home nonetheless. Getting rid of them would help to keep the locals 'on-side' and enhance the 'hearts and minds' campaign that the Regiment was waging.

At a given signal, Pete opened up with the Bren, spraying one of the largest huts with a withering wave of fire. The rounds scythed through the bamboo, blasting the frail hut to pieces and laying waste to anyone inside. The terrorist gang was swift to respond, but as quickly as one popped up to bring his weapon to bear, he was cut down by deadly accurate fire either from the men hidden on the edge of the clearing or from those who were now storming from hut to hut, terminating all resistance.

Loon-Kon-Kim's band of cut-throats was wiped out in the attack on their camp. The locals would no longer live in fear of his bloodthirsty thugs emerging from the jungle to prey on their villages. In the months that followed, these villagers showed their gratitude to the SAS by giving the soldiers support and passing on useful information about the activities and positions of the real enemy.

One of the best things about Malaya, as far as Pete was concerned, was the leave time, especially in Penang. He enjoyed many a Tiger Beer at the Sandicroft Rest and Recuperation Centre and Club, and all on '28 bob a week' – just £1.40 in today's money. But there was plenty of serious work to be done, too. At this time, the art of Close Protection (CP) was an emerging skill and Pete was one of the first soldiers to train and then operate as a bodyguard. Part of that training took place with Lofty Large and the rest of A Squadron in Kenya with John Slim. The modern style of pistol shooting they were taught was first developed by former Royal Marine William Fairbairn around 1910 when he worked with the Shanghai Municipal Police. Fairbairn abandoned the traditional 'duelling' stance for aiming a handgun in favour of a combat mode more in keeping with the way he saw men operating during police raids. When they were fired on, they instinctively adopted a protective crouch position and, rather than try pointlessly to drill this out of them, he decided to use their natural inclinations to their best advantage. He taught his men to fire from a crouch position instead of standing erect to take aim, and to fire instinctively rather than waste the split second it took to bring the weapon to bear. He also designed the first killing house to simulate the sort of environment his men would find in the field.

Fairbairn's techniques were further enhanced by another British officer, Grant Taylor, who spent some time on attachment to the FBI in America during the 1920s, gaining experience in the type of urban combat they were forced to undertake when dealing with mobsters. He also took part in Combined Operations commando raids during World War II, on one occasion landing secretly by submarine in occupied France to find the quarters where a group of Luftwaffe pilots were billeted and, along with a colleague, assassinate them. Taylor's CQB skills were put to good use when he joined Field Marshal Slim's Fourteenth Army in Burma. He taught a method of pistol shooting that involved aiming with the body, holding the firearm at stomach height with the forearm parallel to the ground. Like Fairbairn, he advocated the use of live-fire room ranges, sometimes called 'execution sheds', to train men in room and building clearance.

When John Slim, who had trained with Taylor when he served under his father in the Far East, established an SAS CQB training facility in Kenya, he refined the Grant Taylor method, with Pete Loveday and Lofty Large among those who benefited from his experience. For Pete, swapping his Bren gun or SLR for a 9mm Browning automatic came as something of a shock to the system. What they were doing was worlds apart from the infantry weapons training he had had in the past. No longer were they lying on their bellies peering down rifle sights at a target a hundred yards away or more. Here they stood shoulder to shoulder, not as they would on a battlefield, but as they might find themselves in an urban situation. They could hear the report and feel the blast from each other's gunshots as each man stood at the mouth of an open slit trench cut into the hillside, emptying a magazine into a playing card stuck to a man-sized target only 15ft (4.6m) away at the end of the trench. They practised until they could slot every shot into the playing card without taking 'proper' aim.

The double-handed 'instinctive' aim from the shoulder was ultimately adopted as the most accurate method from the crouch and Slim also put Pete, Lofty and the others through a killing house training scenario. These experiments and training methods turned the pistol from being regarded as a largely defensive weapon with limited accuracy into a very effective offensive weapon, as Tommy Palmer proved when he shot a terrorist in the head while on the move during the Iranian Embassy job in 1980.

Demonstrations of the SAS's impressive CQB techniques led to their being in great demand for bodyguarding duties. Pete found himself in far more comfortable surroundings then he had ever known in the Far East when he was part of the protection team for the General Officer Commanding Malaya, and he even acted as bodyguard to Kenyan president Jomo Kenyatta at one time. It was quite ironic for the president to benefit from the protection of Britain's elite special forces when not too many years before he had been accused of being one of the organizers of the Mau Mau rebels that British troops fought so hard against. Such is politics.

Pete's activities were not, however, confined to the 'cushy' job of CP. He travelled with A Squadron from the jungles of Malaya to the barren mountains of northern Oman in 1958, where they fought for five months on the Jebel Akhdar against communist-backed insurgents.

In 1960, Pete was back in the UK, based for a short time at Malvern before the Regiment moved to their home in Hereford. He didn't have long to enjoy a home life, though. He was still an operational soldier and served in the jungles of Borneo during the confrontation with Indonesia, as well as in the battles against Yemeni insurgents in the mountains of the Radfan and the Aden townships from 1963 to 1966.

His experience and good humour were invaluable when he became the sergeant storeman in the quartermaster's department. It's a soldier's worst nightmare when it comes to returning kit you have drawn from the quartermaster's stores and all is not as it was when you were issued with it. James Bond might be able to get away with losing or wrecking valuable bits of kit issued to him by 'Q', but an ordinary soldier is usually expected to stump up for anything he has lost out of his own wages. No-one wanted to see those 'stoppages' deductions on his pay slip. Pete knew exactly how the system worked and he was a master at juggling stores to try to keep him and others out of trouble.

Pete carried on working in the stores until he left the Regiment in 1975, but he found leaving army life behind no easier in 1975 than he had done 22 years before and was back with the Regiment the same year, rejoining his mates as a civilian, still working in the stores. He always had time for a chat or to give advice, and was hugely respected by everyone in the Regiment. Pete was one of the men, after all, who showed that SAS soldiers were more than just the desert raiders so many believed them to be. They were more than merely a bunch of jungle warfare experts and more than a mountain reconnaissance force. Pete helped to prove that the SAS was a flexible, adaptable unit capable of operating under extreme conditions anywhere in the world, including in emergencies on the streets of our own cities.

Eventually, Pete retired in 1996 after an incredible 45 years' loyal and courageous army service – 43 of those years having been spent with the SAS Regiment.

Chapter 16

WO2 SQUADRON SERGEANT-MAJOR STEVE CALLAN

Steve Callan tightened the fingers of his right hand around the pistol grip of his SLR and tugged at the straps of his Bergen with his free hand, shifting the weight of the radio packed on his back as he followed Staff Sergeant Frank Williams through the gathering gloom of the late afternoon. The mountainous jungle of north-eastern Sarawak was a challenging place to be. The inherent dangers of patrolling in the jungle, the arduous heat and humidity, the poisonous insects, the vegetation that clawed at your skin through the thin layers of sweat-drenched clothing, and the strength-sapping terrain with its precipitous slopes and raging mountain torrents, all combined to make the trek they had undertaken one of the most physically demanding he had ever experienced. The fact that they were only a stone's throw from the border with the Indonesian state of Kalimantan and could expect to run into an enemy patrol at any moment only served to heighten the tension. Under normal circumstances, such an encounter might have been exactly what they were looking for, but this was no normal patrol.

A normal patrol would have seen them traversing the dense jungle slopes slowly and with great caution, wary of making the sort of noise that would alert any Indo ambush team to their presence. While Steve and the others remained very much conscious of the enemy threat, on this occasion they pursued their course with a far greater urgency. This was a rescue mission.

On 4 May 1963, a Belvedere helicopter had taken off from Bakelalan, a mountain base in Sarawak right on the Kalimantan border, on a flight to visit tactical patrols (concerned with gathering intelligence and engaging with the enemy) in the jungle. On board were Major Ronald Norman, second-in-command of the SAS Regiment; Major Harry Thomson, the operations officer; Corporal 'Spud' Murphy and six others, including the RAF crew, Mr M.H.Day of the Foreign Office and Borneo Company official Mr D.Reddish. The Bristol Belvedere was a twin-rotor, heavy-lift helicopter with two powerful Napier turbines and was capable of flying on just one of its engines. The type had been in service with the RAF for two years and was of proven reliability in the jungle, the natives having christened it 'Long House', as its cigar-shaped fuselage reminded them of their own long huts. On this flight, however, something had gone drastically wrong with the stalwart Belvedere and the chopper had gone down.

As soon as news of the crash was received, Frank Williams, who had been due to join the flight but was recalled to the operations room just before take-off, put together a four-man crash rescue team, including himself. Top of his list for the patrol had been Steve Callan. Frank knew he would need an expert signaller, and Steve was the best in the business. The other members of the team were Rickie Coomber (medic) and 'Chopper' Essex (lead scout). A local jungle tracker led them through the mountains and down into the Trusan Valley towards the isolated village of Long Merarap, the area where they expected to find the crashed Belvedere.

Steve paused and sank to one knee as a silent hand signal was passed from man to man. Something was wrong. The normal jungle background noise was strangely hushed. He peered through the maze of giant tree trunks and tangles of hanging vines to his left and right. He saw no sign of movement, no hint that they might have stumbled upon a lurking Indo ambush squad. Frank signalled to Steve to move forward and Steve passed the signal on to Rickie Coomber, crouching among some tree roots a few paces behind him. After a few steps, Steve noticed a new, alien scent in the heavy jungle air. It was like the smell of a dampened bonfire, the dank aroma of an extinguished blaze. Then, glancing up towards the jungle canopy, he could see broken branches and, before long, he spotted the dull glint of metal. There was wreckage in the trees and, as the patrol came closer to the site of the crash, more charred and twisted metal mixed with burnt and broken tree limbs on the ground. It became clear that the helicopter had exploded. They spread out to comb the area in search of survivors, but it didn't take long for their efforts to confirm that there were none. All nine aboard the Belvedere had perished. The patrol shared the gruesome task of recovering all of the bodies, gathering them in one place so that they could all be buried at the scene of the crash.

Steve also had the onerous task of reporting back to base that they had found the crashed chopper. It was not possible for the small team to work out why the aircraft had gone down, nor were they in a position to gather any evidence. Having put in a massive effort to reach the crash site, their job was now to get themselves safely out of the jungle again. This was not the first jungle sortie in which Steve participated, nor was it to be his last operational patrol but, for the worst possible reasons, it was one of the most notable.

Highly intelligent and a thoroughly professional soldier, Steve was the nicest, most straightforward bloke you could ever hope to meet. I came to know him really well when I worked with him in the mid-1970s in 'Ops Research'. Those who know no better seem to think of the SAS's Operations and Research Wing as some kind of dumping ground for soldiers who are past their prime. That is really not the case. It is true, however, that to be of any use in Ops Research, you need to have a good deal of experience in all aspects of SAS soldiering.

The job of the Ops Research team, which usually consists of only a couple of senior staff, is to source or develop specialist equipment that could be of use to the Regiment on operations. Obviously, you need recent operational experience to know which bits of kit are going to work in the field and which bits your mates are going to curse you for lumbering them with. On the equipment front, Ops Research looks at everything from new weapons and vehicles to new boots, clothing or field rations. Some of these things are developed 'in-house' by the Ops Research team, but they also spend a great deal of time evaluating equipment from a variety of different manufacturers and suppliers.

Another aspect of the Ops Research job is to visit airfields and military installations at home and abroad to assess their suitability for use by the Regiment. We looked at airfields and heliports, working out flying times to and from different potential locations where the Regiment might feasibly have to be deployed. We looked at airport security and the length of runways at different places around the country, working out not only which ones could take troop transports or supply planes, but which ones could accommodate passenger jets in the event that they had to be diverted in an emergency. It was vital to be able to know where a hijacked aircraft could be sent and what facilities were there so that the SAS could control the situation once the plane was on the ground. I accompanied Steve on countless car trips all over the UK looking at different bases and buildings. He had all sorts of contacts not only at regular military facilities, but also in research establishments, some top secret, with whom he worked either in an advisory capacity or as a 'client', with them helping him in his own research on projects for the Regiment. If he hadn't joined the SAS, Steve would almost certainly have been working as a boffin himself, as he was a talented designer and engineer. His range of contacts was also quite amazing. On one trip with Steve, we met a man called Jack Roberts who had designed PLUTO, the pipeline under the ocean that supplied fuel from England to France for the Allied forces that landed in Normandy on D-Day during World War II. Jack also designed the bomb disposal robot that has famously been seen many times on TV tackling suspect devices in Northern Ireland.

Steve and I had a very strange experience on one of our trips during the mid-1970s when we were invited to take a look at a facility in the Home Counties. Prime Minister Harold Wilson was resident in 10 Downing Street at the time and outlandish rumours were being circulated by conspiracy theorists accusing both Wilson and his private secretary, Marcia Williams (now Baroness Falkender), of being secret Soviet agents. At the time there was a great deal of social and industrial unrest, with Conservative Prime Minister Edward Heath's government involved in a protracted confrontation with the miners just before Wilson came to power in 1974.

This was the time of the 'Three-Day Week' when businesses closed down to save power, and there were regular blackouts in homes all over the country when power stations went offline due to a lack of coal. During that time troops were actually deployed at Heathrow on an anti-terror security exercise. Conspiracy theorists continue to propose, even today, that that exercise, and others during this period, were 'rehearsals' rather than mere exercises and that some shady background organization within the establishment was demonstrating that a military coup could easily be organized in Great Britain if what they saw as communist-backed industrial action was not brought under control.

The installation that Steve took me to see was incredibly well disguised. Even people living nearby would never have known it was there. The entrances blended in quite unobtrusively with their surroundings, but what they concealed was breathtaking. Deep underground, there was a highly sophisticated bunker system housing an operations centre that was, to Steve and me, like something from a science fiction movie. There were living and sleeping quarters for a sizeable number of men; a gymnasium; a dining hall; a medical ward with an operating theatre attached; a briefing room that doubled as a library and cinema; a small-arms range and combat training hall; an armoury; a high-tech operations and communications room and storage facilities for food, ammunition and explosives. The whole bunker system was blast-proof and fitted with gas and chemical detection systems as well as closed-circuit television (CCTV) surveillance of the surrounding area. You could have run a war from that place, yet it was empty, mothballed, unused.

Steve and I were a bit mystified about why we had been shown the place. It didn't appear to be part of any normal 'Cold War' nuclear defence facility that we knew about. It wasn't until much later that we began to hear all the weird conspiracy theories about a 'military coup' and started to wonder if someone might have wanted to get the place 'checked out' by the SAS prior to its use as a secret command centre. Or were we just buying into the coup fantasy? It's more likely that one of Steve's contacts just wanted to let him see it. After all, what's the point in playing caretaker to a complex that any James Bond villain would be proud to call his own if you can't show it off once in a while?

The bunker was just one of the things that made for so many strange days with Steve in Ops Research, but most of the work that this remarkable man undertook really was of genuine benefit to the Regiment. Steve had wanted to be a scientist from the time he was a schoolboy and on leaving school he started a degree course at the University of Wales, Cardiff, his home town. He suffered from the inevitable student malaise of never having enough money to get by and became hugely frustrated when he saw his brothers and friends, all of whom had jobs, splashing money around, never short of a few pounds for a good night out. In the end, being broke all the time became too much for him to bear and he dropped out of university.

Steve's technical aptitude was, however, put to good use when he joined the Royal Corps of Signals and he was able to resume his higher education when the Signals sponsored him through a degree course in electronics at Bristol University. The Regiment can always find a place for a talented signaller, provided he can hack it on the Selection course, and by 1959 Steve was a highly proficient all-round soldier. On passing Selection, he was badged as a member of A Squadron.

Steve served on operational tours with A Squadron in Oman, Aden, Borneo and Northern Ireland. He was even awarded a Malaysia bar to his General Service Medal (GSM) when the Indonesians made a landing on the Malaysian peninsula during the Borneo campaign. You have to be on active service in the conflict zone to receive such an award and Steve qualified even though he was actually on a Malay language course in the operational area at the time. Steve's greatest contribution to the Regiment came later when he joined Ops Research. He was posted there when the powers-that-be recognized his ingenuity and enthusiasm for all things scientific and technical. He was very keen to evaluate and improve equipment by observing it in use by the squadrons when they went on operations. And that's precisely what he was doing when he was attached to D Squadron on their tour in Aden in 1966.

It would seem a bit odd, spotting a soap dish lying by the side of a mountain track in the middle of the Radfan. The barren terrain wasn't the sort of place where anyone would have much use for a bathroom accessory. The terrorist who had trekked for days with his comrades through the mountains to infiltrate secretly from Yemen into the Aden Protectorate was tired and thirsty, but he remained alert enough to spot this alien object, so curiously nestled behind the small stones at the side of the track. Was it really a soap dish – the kind of thing he had seen during his many visits to the market in Crater? Those may well have been the last thoughts that passed through his mind before the soap dish erupted in a blinding flash, sending a hail of deadly shrapnel screeching towards him. The ambush was sprung. Had the shrapnel not ended the terrorist's journey, he and his friends would then fall before the withering fire of the SLRs and Bren gun of the SAS patrol. Steve Callan's home-made Claymore had worked a treat.

At the time Steve was in Aden, the US troops in Vietnam had recently been issued with their new Claymore mine. Steve managed to acquire one to have a look at. The Claymore is a devastatingly effective weapon. Its primary use is in an ambush situation. The mine has to be sited very carefully and can be camouflaged with loose leaves or undergrowth, its trailing wires covered with a scattering of earth or vegetation to hide them from view. The weapon consists of a box about 8in (20cm) long with a heavy steel backplate and a plastic front cover. Inside, the backplate is lined with explosives and the space between the explosives and the plastic cover packed with steel balls. The plastic cover is marked 'Front Toward Enemy' to make sure you place it facing the right direction. When the explosive is detonated, the shrapnel – around 700 steel balls – is sent hurtling out in a spread pattern that forms a 60-degree arc. If you are caught inside that arc at anything less than 55 yards (50m), you don't stand much chance. At up to 110 yards (100m), you would still have problems passing through an airport metal detector. The Claymore was designed by a man named Norman MacLeod and named after a type of heavy Scottish sword, but it was based on research by the Germans in World War II who discovered that the force of an explosive detonation could be directed away from a heavy backing surface. They tried to develop this into an anti-tank weapon, but it was the Americans who picked up on the idea to use as an anti-personnel device.

When Steve got hold of one, he dissected it, examined it and decided to try to make his own. This was in the days when Ops Research's equipment consisted largely of parachute cord, masking tape and any other bits and bobs that could be found lying around. To make his Claymore mine, Steve started with a plastic soap dish. He removed the lid and put a strip of plastic explosive around the inside of the base, then filled the base up with plaster of Paris, liberally laced with ball-bearings. He then replaced the lid and secured it with masking tape. A meat skewer was used to make a small hole in the base through which an electric detonator was fed and embedded in the plastic explosive. Then it was a case of retreat as far as possible and 'heads down' when the detonator wires were touched to a hand-held battery. Amazingly, it worked. Steve then set about making up several of these, which the squadron used unofficially. That was not the end of Steve's ingenuity, however. Using another soap dish he devised an electrical switch that could be used to detonate the mine.

Flushed with success, Steve returned to the Ops Research building in Hereford to continue work on the detonation device and came up with a formidable piece of equipment that was named the Callan Switch. He once showed me his original plans of how it worked. It looked very complicated to me, but he understood it perfectly. It was a box of electrical tricks with switches and buttons that provided for a variety of settings. This device, when modified and refined, later became known as the Shrike Exploder and is used extensively by armies all over the world. Its effect can be seen in many military and action films, but it was a real and deadly piece of equipment. It could be used with all sorts of explosives as well as the Claymore mine and could be set to detonate up to 30 or 40 mines, either individually, in groups, in sequence or all together. For his original invention, Steve was given £30 by the government, which he donated to an army charity. His device was later sold on by the government to a commercial organization in Devon, who developed and marketed it. The Shrike is currently in service with the armed forces of over 40 countries worldwide. He may not have made a fortune from it, but Steve was later awarded the MBE for his 'outstanding contribution to the SAS and the Government for work in operational research'.

Another of Steve's inventions came as a direct result of requests from squadron members on operations. In the jungles of Borneo, they found that when resupplies were dropped to them from aircraft, the parachutes and their rigging lines would often become entangled in the tops of the trees. As the jungle canopy was so high and dense, the supplies were inaccessible. Flares were sometimes fired at the parachute to try to set it alight so that the supply box would then drop to the ground. Apart from the dangers of setting the jungle canopy ablaze and the problems of smoke and flames advertising your position to the enemy, by firing a flare you also ran the risk of setting light to the supplies themselves. You wouldn't want to be standing under a consignment of ammo or explosives when it went off.

Steve took a look at the parachute delivery system to try to work out some improvements. When the supply boxes left the aircraft, they were attached to the parachute by means of a long strap, which unfurled as the parachute deployed, allowing the box to swing free below it. While in the Malaysian jungle with one of the squadrons on jungle training exercises, Steve experimented with an ingenious solution to the tangling problem. Having played around with different kinds of detonator fuse cord to establish their rates of burning, he reasoned that a length of fuse could be fixed to the strap where it was joined to the parachute. When the fuse burned down to the strap, it would cause the strap to burn through and the box would be released to fall down through the trees, leaving the parachute on the tree-tops. Even if the patrol wasn't waiting directly underneath (unadvisable with falling supply boxes coming at you) the parachute would act as a marker for the retrieval of the box, which would be somewhere directly below. The height at which the aircraft was flying was taken into account when calculating the length of the fuse required, so that the box was timed to be released just as it reached the top of the trees, making it less likely to get caught up in the branches along with the parachute. The system was perfected and developed into an integral part of our supply equipment that became known as the Jungle Line Supply System (JLSS). It was basically a very simple idea, but was invaluable to the troops on the ground.

I joined Steve in Ops Research after I finished my time in a Sabre Squadron, and worked with him on all sorts of routine evaluations of many items of clothing and equipment that the Regiment was considering using. Soldiers would, for example, be asked to wear a new type of boot and report on its durability, water resistance and comfort. The reports would then be collated and comparisons made with other boots before a decision was made about the best type to buy. Having trekked around in everything from the old standard-issue hob-nailed boots to parachute jump boots, Steve and I had the experience to be able to evaluate the soldiers' reports sensibly.

As well as routine work on things like boots, some of the projects we were involved with can only be termed weird and wonderful and, as in any research, did not get past the experimental stage. One of the projects was a device to help the men on vehicle patrols in Northern Ireland. When on patrol in the winding lanes of the border country you had to be constantly alert, even if you were in an ordinary unmarked car, for a carefully concealed ambush. The stone walls, ditches and hedgerows in the undulating countryside meant that you could seldom see too far ahead, so it was easy to round a bend and find a vehicle checkpoint staring you in the face. From a distance, especially at night or in poor weather conditions, it could be difficult immediately to tell if the checkpoint was one of ours, or one of theirs. The IRA mounted vehicle checks just as the Royal Ulster Constabulary (RUC) and army did. The big difference was that at an IRA checkpoint, as soon as they realized who was in the car, an ambush would be sprung and you could end up sharing an already packed car with more 5.56mm Armalite rounds than is ever going to be comfortable.

Steve knew that magnesium flares had been used to great effect in mapping previously uncharted territory, such as the jungles of Borneo. They were fitted to the undersides of Canberra bombers and, when lit, acted as a camera flash, equivalent to a quarter million candlepower, for aerial photography. The photographs were then studied to put together maps of the area. What we tried to do in Ops Research was to fit much smaller magnesium flares just below the headlights of a car. The idea was that if a vehicle patrol came upon an illegal vehicle checkpoint, it could electrically ignite the flares via a foot pedal inside the car. The resulting blinding glare would dazzle the men manning the checkpoint. This would give the soldiers in the car a chance either to drive through the checkpoint, reverse at speed to get away, or pile out of the car and take out the terrorists while they were still wondering whether it was evening, morning or next Wednesday.

Another idea Steve investigated was to fit steel bars 2 or 3ft (0.6 or 0.9m) long to the underside of cars on either side. If anyone attempted to hijack the car, the bars could be hydraulically operated from inside the car to shoot out and take the legs from under the hijackers. Neither of these James Bond-type projects got much further than the drawing board.

One of the more adventurous projects we worked on was to produce an incendiary device that instead of going up in one great ball of flame (in the hope that it would set fire to everything around it) would burn for a much longer time. This would allow it to carry on feeding any fire that it started and could, under certain circumstances, prove more effective. Our effort involved boiling a gallon of petrol over a single Bunsen burner then mixing in soap-flakes (using a very long stick). As the soap mixed with the petrol, a thick, jelly-like consistency was achieved. The mixture was then ladled into (yet another) soap dish and allowed to cool. A time pencil detonator was inserted into the incendiary gel, and strong magnets attached to the underside of the dish, the theory being that it could then be attached to anything from a car or truck to a gas tank or elevator. We made a lot of pretty fires testing these out in safe areas on the base and we both lost our eyebrows a few times, too.

When we were travelling around, the long journeys could be quite exhausting, but Steve never seemed to flag. He was a thorough workaholic who was incredibly enthusiastic about every aspect of his job. On away trips, he was always reluctant to take long breaks, always eager to get on to the next part of the trip and sort out whatever lay in store for us. Part of that motivation was a thirst for knowledge. Steve never stopped learning and never stopped wanting to learn more. Looking back, I think one of the reasons I found those long trips so exhausting was because I was having to keep up with Steve all the time, but it was always fun, nonetheless.

Steve left the army in 1983 and set up his own research and development company. Sadly, he died shortly afterwards of a heart attack at the very young age of 42. I have absolutely no doubt that, if he had been given just a little more time, he had the drive, enthusiasm and talent to have become enormously successful. But you'd always want to steer well clear of one of his soap dishes.

Chapter 17

CAPTAIN GAVIN HAMILTON

I never had the honour of serving on operations with Captain Gavin Hamilton, but knew him to be a very likeable man who very quickly gained the respect of the men who served under him. Gavin John Hamilton joined the Regiment from the Green Howards in January 1981 as the new commander of D Squadron's Mountain Troop. At the age of 28 he was an experienced soldier and mountaineer, leading his troop on two successful assaults on the summit of Mount Kenya (the Kirinyaga that Mountain Troop had first climbed 20 years before) on training exercises in the few short months he was with the squadron prior to the eruption of the Falklands War in the spring of 1982.

While I was messing around with B Squadron's equipment, loading and unloading C-130s at RAF Brize Norton, Gavin Hamilton and D Squadron were already on their way to the South Atlantic. He and his men were to be among the first SAS detachments to be deployed in the campaign to wrest the Falkland Islands back from the Argentine invaders. I ended up having to watch it all on TV back home, left behind to mind the shop while so many of my friends went off to war. You could sometimes worry about your mates when you knew they were under the command of certain young officers. Mainly you worried that they might murder them. There were no such worries with Gavin Hamilton. He was one of the best.

The initial stage of the Falklands campaign focused on the retaking of South Georgia, a wind-blasted island over 600 miles (966km) south-east of the main Falkland Islands group. Around 100 miles (161km) long but only 18 miles (29km) wide, South Georgia is a land of barren mountains that rise to over 9,500ft (2,896m) and are cloaked in glaciers. Although remote and inhospitable, the wide bays along the island's north shore formerly provided safe anchorage for the whaling fleets and are scattered with small settlements. It was at the old whaling station of Leith in Stromness Bay that the Argentine 'scrap metal merchants' had first landed and laid claim to the island in March. Following the full military invasion of the Falklands and South Georgia on 2 April, the Argentines were now in possession of strategic buildings strung out along the coast, including the BAS (British Antarctic Survey) team's base at Discovery House in Grytviken. They were also in possession of the island's thousands of penguins and colonies of seals, whether they wanted them or not. My guess is that the seals and penguins probably didn't give a stuff who was in charge, but they were about to be liberated, whether they wanted it or not.

D Squadron had flown out to Ascension Island from Brize Norton on 4 April. There they embarked on the Royal Fleet Auxiliary ship *Fort Austin* to head south with the lead elements of the naval task force. On 12 April Hamilton and his men transferred by helicopter to the 'Red Plum', the scarlet-hulled ice patrol vessel HMS *Endurance*. They had been tasked with landing on the Fortuna Glacier in the mountains to the west of Leith, then making their way down towards the coastal settlements, where they would set up observation posts watching Leith and the nearby whaling stations of Stromness and Husvik to determine Argentine troop strengths and dispositions. They were also to identify suitable beach landing stages or helicopter LZs on the shore of Fortuna Bay, an uninhabited inlet on the other side of the mountains from the target settlements. As the Argentines would be expecting and guarding against approaches from the sea, the route down from the glacier was regarded as the best way to establish the OPs covertly.

Hamilton and his men pored over maps and charts, examining every known aspect of the glacier and their probable routes down the mountain. They spent hours studying street plans of all of the settlements and consulting with personnel who had visited the areas to create detailed room plans of key buildings. Hamilton made sure that they all prepared thoroughly for their forthcoming mission. Everyone was given photocopies of the maps and plans to study. Then they carefully prepared the kit they would need. They knew that they were to face Antarctic conditions on the glacier and in any form of polar warfare, survival skills are ten times more vital than combat expertise. They were to take skis, snowshoes, crampons, ice axes, tents, winter warfare clothing, sleeping bags and waterproof bivvy bags. They would have four pulks – a kind of supply sled with a harness that allows it to be dragged across snow and ice. They would take turns in pulling the pulks, each of which would be loaded with around 200lb (91kg) of equipment. In addition to that, each man would carry around 80lb (36kg) of kit himself. Their preparations were meticulous and they were in confident mood when the helicopters ferried them to their base of operations aboard the County-class destroyer HMS *Antrim*.

As dawn broke on the morning of 21 April, a Wessex 3 equipped with radar that allowed for all-weather flying took off to reconnoitre the Fortuna Glacier landing zone. The weather was unpleasant, with wind-driven rain sweeping across the glacier, but the chopper, affectionately known as 'Humphrey', made it to the LZ where the Royal Navy pilot, Lieutenant Commander Ian Stanley, judged that conditions were still good enough for the mission to go ahead. He returned to the *Antrim*. At noon he took off again, with Hamilton and three of his men aboard. Two Wessex 5s each embarked six more of D Squadron and followed Stanley's lead all the way to the glacier. As they made their approach, the weather conditions quickly deteriorated. To avoid being spotted by any Argentine patrols, their route to the glacier took them across Possession Bay and Antarctic Bay to the north-west of their target. Heavy cloud and torrential rain, which soon turned to icy snow as they crossed open water near Possession Bay, forced them to return to *Antrim* where Hamilton and his men waited impatiently for the weather to improve so that they could try again. Twice they attempted to reach the glacier and twice they were forced back by appalling weather and zero visibility. On their third approach, the choppers forced their way in and disgorged their passengers, all grateful to escape from the bucking, weaving machines and get their feet on solid ground. But their problems were only just beginning.

Mountain Troop dragged their kit out of the choppers, battered by winds in excess of 50mph (80km/h). The helicopters wobbled into the air and headed off back in the direction of Antarctic Bay, leaving the troop to fend for itself. They began to make their way across the glacier in a slow, painful trek, during which they frequently halted in maelstroms of fresh snow that swirled all around them. The disorientating effect of a 'white-out' leaves you unsteady on your feet. You can't tell which way the ground beneath your feet is sloping. You can't even tell which way is up or down. That brings on a dizzy feeling that, combined with the wind roaring in your ears and the mind-numbing cold, leaves you unable to move. Neither was there any escaping the wind by turning your face away from its icy blast. The wind direction was changing almost with every laboured footstep the men took, one moment blowing up the mountain, the next racing down its slopes. Every gust whipped up spindrift from the surface of the glacier, fresh snow and old snow charged with needle-sharp ice particles that raged against the outer fabric of their snow suits. The ice and snow clung to their equipment, penetrating the actions of their weapons and freezing them solid. Even if they could have seen an Argie to shoot at, their M16s and GPMGs were, for the moment, completely useless.

Their progress across the glacier was further slowed by the need to probe constantly for crevasses hidden beneath thin crusts of snow and ice. One large crevasse, rising through a high vertical slab of glacial ice, provided them with partial shelter from the storm. In five hours they had managed to cover only a few hundred yards and Hamilton decided that they would have to make camp for the night in the hope that the storm would lift. In attempting to pitch one of their two-man tents, the wind snapped the flexible tent poles and whisked the entire structure off into the night. Another tent was successfully erected and five men crowded into it, leaning against the walls to keep it upright. The others crawled into sleeping bags inside bivvy bags, and attempted to find shelter under the pulks. The next morning Hamilton knew that if he was not to start losing men to frostbite or exposure, he had to get them out of there. He reported by radio that they had been unable to move off the glacier and requested that the whole troop be evacuated by helicopter.

The same formation of three helicopters that had landed them on the glacier set out to pick them up, but was again driven back by the atrocious weather conditions. Eventually, when it seemed like the wind had died enough to let the rescue choppers in, 'Humphrey' led the two Wessex 5s up onto the glacier at around 1.30pm. The brief clear spell was not to last for long and they were still experiencing winds gusting at up to 70mph (113km/h), making controlling the aircraft near the ground especially hazardous. The three choppers were guided in by a SARBE radio and flares were lit to try to give the pilots some idea of wind direction, although the green smoke swirling around the LZ seemed to confirm only that the winds were as unpredictable as ever. Mountain Troop clambered aboard as soon as the choppers made their tentative landings, hauling most of their equipment with them. The flight then lifted off unsteadily, with 'Humphrey' taking the lead. After only a few seconds, one of the Wessex 5s was engulfed in a white-out squall and the pilot struggled to keep the chopper's nose from ploughing into the ice. The aircraft drifted across the glacier, tipped the ice and crashed down on its side. Amazingly, no one was seriously injured. The men clambered from the wreckage and were picked up by the other two choppers. The pilots dumped fuel and Hamilton ordered his men to abandon their equipment to give the overloaded choppers the chance to get off the ice.

'Humphrey' led the way once more but, like some sickening replay of the previous take-off, the second Wessex 5 vanished in a squall of snow and ice, hit a ridge on the glacier and tipped over. Just as before, its passengers and crew escaped with no serious casualties, but they were forced to watch as Ian Stanley wheeled 'Humphrey' away from the crash site and headed back to the *Antrim*. The Wessex refuelled in record time and immediately set off back to the glacier, covering the 30-mile (48km) trip flat out. With zero visibility and howling gales on the mountain, however, Stanley was forced to turn back. Radio contact confirmed that the men remaining on the ice were in reasonable shape. They scavenged what they could from the crashed Wessex to protect themselves from the elements and settled in to wait. As soon as a break in the weather appeared, 'Humphrey' was back and this time Stanley was able to coax the Wessex down onto the glacier. The crash survivors crammed themselves in and, desperately overloaded with 17 on board (including Stanley and his navigator), 'Humphrey' struggled into the air. When they reached the *Antrim* the extra weight meant that the Wessex came in like a brick and crash-landed on the deck, but Ian Stanley and 'Humphrey' had brought all of Gavin Hamilton's troop back alive.

It was an inauspicious start to D Squadron's Falklands War. They were bitterly disappointed at not having been able to follow through with the plan, but hugely relieved to be back on *Antrim* alive and, apart from a few cuts and bruises, in reasonably good shape. I've had quite a few hair-raising moments in helicopters and can well imagine the feelings of panic and sheer terror that gripped the men in the Wessex 5s when they realized that they were going to crash. Those who went through the nightmare twice deserved to have picked up more than a few grey hairs. On board *Antrim*, however, their feelings turned to relief and profound gratitude to the helicopter crews who had risked their lives to pluck them from the glacier. They all piled into the *Antrim*'s wardroom to buy drinks for their rescuers. Normally the wardroom is strictly for officers only, but these were far from normal circumstances. D Squadron truly appreciated the courage shown by the helicopter crews. Ian Stanley was to be awarded the DSO for his actions that day.

For any normal person to have gone through such an ordeal, the sheer stress and utter exhaustion would have wiped them out for weeks. All Gavin Hamilton and his men wanted to do was to get back into the fray and prove themselves in action. They got their chance just three days later when Mountain Troop found itself back on the Wessex heading to South Georgia. They were landed just a short march from the BAS station at Grytviken where, along with a mixed force of Royal Marines, they witnessed the surrender of the Argentine garrison.

After a lengthy period of planning and preparation, they were back in action again on the night of 14 May, when Hamilton led his troop on a daring raid that bore all the hallmarks of a classic SAS operation in the North African desert in World War II. The Argentines had established an air base at Pebble Island, an irregular strip of land in the north of West Falkland. A Harrier pilot had picked up radar signals from the base, which was previously believed only to be a facility that was home to a few engineers preparing an airfield to act as a back-up for the main air base at Port Stanley. D Squadron proposed a plan to raid the base, but it was considered too risky and the plan was turned down until firm intelligence from a reconnaissance team confirmed that it was home to 11 aircraft. The planes included a number of Pucaras, heavily armed ground-attack aircraft that posed an obvious threat to future operations.

In fact, Pebble Island had become a place of strategic significance to the Argentines. Before the war the whole island was entirely given over to farmland and was home to around two dozen people and several thousand sheep. Now the low-lying area of the island was in the process of becoming a vitally important air base. It was over 100 miles (161km) closer to the Argentine mainland than the runway at Port Stanley, making it an ideal staging post for the resupply of troops on West Falkland, especially when Port Stanley started to come under regular air attack. The raid was approved.

Three Sea Kings delivered 45 men of D Squadron from the task force's flagship aircraft carrier HMS *Hermes* to an LZ that was less than 4 miles (6.4km) from the airstrip. There they were met by the Boat Troop reconnaissance team who led them in to the target. The group was heavily armed with 81mm mortars and Light Anti-Armour Weapon (LAW) rocket launchers. The LAW fires a 66mm High-Explosive Anti-Tank (HEAT) round that can penetrate over 10in (25cm) of armour. A direct hit from one of those would be more than enough to destroy any aircraft on the ground. The men also carried their usual M16s and M203 grenade launchers and their GPMGs. They shared the loads of mortar bombs and demolition explosives. Once they were in position ready to launch their attack, one troop was to cover the two entrances to the airfield, one was to stay in reserve in case any surprise opposition materialized and a third, Gavin Hamilton's Mountain Troop, was to hit the airfield itself to destroy the aircraft.

As a prelude to the attack, the twin 4.5in guns of the destroyer HMS *Glamorgan* laid down a barrage on the Argentine defences, directed by a naval fire support officer. The mortar team began dropping rounds on the enemy as well and, with the suppressing fire from the attack team also persuading them to keep their heads down, there was little in the way of opposition from the Argentines. Hamilton had limited time to carry out his task of destroying the aircraft – *Hermes* and *Glamorgan* had to be far out to sea in safe water before daybreak. The SAS soldiers blasted the aircraft from a distance with the LAW rockets, grenades and their M16s before Hamilton led a team out among the parked planes to place demolition charges. Blazing fuel and ammunition dumps that had been hit during the naval barrage cast flickering pools of light out across the darkened airstrip, with smaller fires from already burning aircraft providing enough light briefly to illuminate the ghostly figures as they flitted from one plane to the next. One man was hit by shrapnel in the leg, another suffered concussion when a mine exploded among them, but with their job done Hamilton led all of his men off the airfield towards their RV. There was a brief skirmish with an Argentine squad as they exited the airfield, but they quickly drove them off with automatic fire and grenades, making their way back to the LZ without further incident. Later, they learned that the Argentine garrison defending the installation was three times as strong as the raiding force. This fact only served to heighten the elation. The raid had gone like a dream and, with only two relatively minor casualties, it had been an enormous success. They had wrecked six Pucaras, four training aircraft and a Skyvan transport. In his subsequent Military Cross (MC) citation, Hamilton was described as having:

> led his troop on the successful and brilliantly executed raid on Pebble Island in the Falklands Islands when eleven enemy aircraft were destroyed on the ground. Acting quickly and decisively and with great courage and coolness, he personally supervised the destruction of seven of the aircraft.

After a shaky start on the glacier, Mountain Troop was now brimful of confidence, but their high spirits were not to last. Four days later, while preparing for a raid on the Argentine stronghold at Darwin, the Sea King was lost in the cross-decking incident. Many of those lost were Hamilton's men. They had survived the helicopter crashes on the glacier and the Pebble Island raid only to perish in a freak accident. Gavin Hamilton's reaction was to take it out on the Argentines. He took the remainder of Mountain Troop ashore a day after the accident as part of a contingent of 50 or so whose job it was to approach the Darwin/Goose Green area from the east. There they were to attack the Argentine garrison to make the enemy think that a major landing was taking place from the Choiseul Sound. This was to cover the fact that the real landings on East Falkland were actually taking place 20 miles (32km) further north across the mountains at San Carlos Water.

Once again, the squadron was heavily armed, each man's load of around 80lb (36kg) consisting mainly of ammunition, not only for their GPMGs and M16s, but also for their faithful mortars and M203s as well as rockets for their Milans. The Milan is a wired-guided anti-tank weapon that packs an awesome punch. During the 1991 Gulf War, SAS patrols used Milans mounted on their Pinkies (Land Rovers painted pink as desert camouflage), but for the attack on Darwin they were fired from portable tripod 'firing posts'. Highly accurate even in the dark, when an infra-red night sight is used, the Milan's missile can be guided onto its target. When the weapon is fired the missile is blasted from the launcher by an explosive charge whereupon the rocket motor ignites and it scorches towards the target. Small in-flight adjustments to its trajectory can be made simply by keeping the target in the launcher's sights, as the missile is controlled electronically via a trailing command wire. It's a fantastic piece of kit to have in your armoury, but it's no lightweight. The Milan is usually manned by two men, the gunner who carries the firing post and the loader who lugs two missiles. Neither of them gets off lightly. The firing post weighs in at over 36lb (16kg) and the missiles are almost 15lb (7kg) each. It doesn't take long to make up an 80lb (36kg) load when you are packing that sort of ordnance.

The weight they were carrying mattered a lot this time round. On the Pebble Island raid they had only a few miles to cover. To maintain the element of surprise on the Darwin job, their approach to their attack positions involved a gruelling 20-hour route march over rough terrain, in freezing conditions, in the dark. Nevertheless, with Gavin Hamilton urging them on every step of the way they made it on schedule. The single 4.5in gun of the frigate HMS *Ardent* provided the backdrop to the attack this time round, and from the hillsides surrounding the buildings that housed the Argentine soldiers, D Squadron let rip. Their brief was to make as much noise and do as much damage as possible to make it seem like they were a much larger invasion force. Had the Argentines known that there were so few attackers, the 1,200 men in the garrison buildings might have been tempted to make more of a showing. Hamilton ordered his men to change position constantly and present a widely dispersed formation to make it look like they were covering far more ground than they really were. They kept the Argies pinned down until dawn, then broke off the engagement to make their way north and link up with 2 Para, who had landed on the other side of the mountains without a hitch. Hamilton's fortitude and unstinting resolve during the raid earned him a further mention on the MC citation:

> Later, even though his troop had lost half of its strength in a helicopter crash the previous day, Captain Hamilton led the remainder of his men on a highly successful diversionary raid on Darwin in order to cover the main amphibious landings on East Falkland. That he was able to do this after such losses is an immense testimony to his resilience and leadership qualities.

Within a few days, Gavin Hamilton's mob were back in the thick of it again. As the main battle groups closed on Port Stanley by working their way round the coast in a kind of pincer movement, any Argentines on Mount Kent, between the two prongs of the pincer, could clearly have caused a major problem. An SAS reconnaissance patrol had been on Mount Kent since 1 May, living in freezing conditions to man their OP and running the constant risk of being spotted by the enemy as they reported on Argentine activity. It was decided that a larger force would be inserted to occupy the mountain, until reinforcements became available to take over the mountain in strength and use it as a base for the final push on Port Stanley. D Squadron was sent in and quickly established itself, mounting ambushes and becoming involved in regular firefights with Argentine special forces. Gavin Hamilton made the hillsides Mountain Troop's killing ground, lying in wait on the slopes to devastate any Argie patrol that dared venture up onto the high ground. Again, Hamilton's citation says it all:

> Next, Captain Hamilton deployed with his Squadron to a position 40 miles behind the enemy lines overlooking the main enemy defensive positions in Port Stanley. Again, his leadership and courage proved to be instrumental over the next seven days of continuous operations in seizing this vital ground from which the attack on Port Stanley was ultimately launched.
>
> On 27th May he identified an enemy probe into the squadron position and in the ensuing battle captured a prisoner of war.
>
> The next night, he and his Troop successfully held off another enemy attack and by doing so enabled 42 Commando to fly in as planned to re-inforce the position – an important step in the repossession of the Falklands. On the following day he ambushed another enemy patrol wounding three and capturing all five members of the patrol.

Four days after he was relieved on Mount Kent, Hamilton was inserted by helicopter with three of his men onto West Falkland. Their job was to set up an OP to establish the strength of the Argentine garrison at Port Howard. They made their way through the darkness to another bleak and miserable mountainside, heading to where they believed they would be able to establish an LUP that would be safe from the prying eyes of daytime patrols. This they did and, during the daylight hours, they were able to keep watch on Port Howard, sending back reports about enemy movements. It was a monotonous business that avoided being utterly tedious only because they knew that they had to be constantly on their guard against discovery by the enemy. They were on hard routine and could have no fires to warm them or to heat up their drinks or rations. All they could do was lie in their hide and keep watch on the town below.

After a while, Hamilton identified a better position for clearer observation. He decided to move forward to the new position with his signaller under cover of darkness. From there they could watch the port during the day and then move back to the main hide when darkness fell, returning to the forward position again before dawn. The spot he chose was just a little over 1.5 miles (2.4km) from the target and he could send reports that were more precise, more detailed.

Five days after they first arrived on the mountainside, Hamilton made his way through the darkness to the OP with his signaller as usual. It was bitterly cold and he doubted if the temperature would improve much, even when the sun came up. It was now early June and well into the southern hemisphere winter, so the cold was to be expected. It still wasn't as cold as it had been on the Fortuna Glacier six weeks ago. That had been spectacularly cold, even for the men of his troop, who were all well-used to sub-zero mountain temperatures. He slid down into the mossy slit behind the rock where they had set up their OP. His signaller slithered in behind him. There was only half an hour until sunrise, then they could take a look at what Galtieri's boys were up to today.

Hamilton rubbed his eyes as the feeble rays of the sun crept over the mountains far away across the Falkland Sound on East Falkland. Over there most of the island was already back in British hands. Surely it wouldn't be long now before the Paras or the Marines kicked the Argies out of Port Stanley? He stared down towards his own port – Port Howard – to see if anyone was awake down there yet. Then, out of the corner of his eye, he picked up a slight movement on the hillside far off to his left. What was it? A rabbit, perhaps, or a deer? He lifted his binoculars to his eyes to take a closer look. At first he saw nothing out of the ordinary, but then there was another flicker of movement, and another. And they were no deer or rabbits – not unless deer and rabbits had started carrying rifles to shoot back; those were men. He glanced urgently at his signaller and nodded in the direction of the enemy soldiers. The other man confirmed the sighting, but Hamilton was already scouring the hillside to their right. It could be a patrol creeping around over to the left. They might be able to let them pass by if they stayed put and stayed hidden. If there was movement on their other flank, however, it could only mean one thing – they'd been rumbled.

Hamilton caught his breath. Sure enough, over to the right, he could see soldiers closing on them. They knew the hide was there. How had they spotted them? A glint of sun on the field glasses, just as always happened in old movies maybe? He thought he had been more careful than that. Perhaps an Argie night patrol, listening in the darkness somewhere on the mountainside, had heard them moving about one night and been able to take a covert look during the daytime? Whatever had happened, they'd been spotted. The signaller was now staring apprehensively off to the right as well. He'd seen them, too.

'Bug out,' said Hamilton, 'before they've got us surrounded. You go first, I'll cover you.'

He snatched up his M16 and took aim at the closer group to their left. He'd drop a target if he could, but if none presented itself then he would send a couple of shots over to keep their heads down.

'Go!' Hamilton yelled. The signaller launched himself out of the depression and started sprinting up the hillside, hearing Hamilton snap off a couple of shots as he did so. The return fire did not come immediately. The signaller had enough time to reach a rocky buttress and dive behind it. Then he brought his rifle to bear on the platoon of soldiers approaching from the right and gave them a short burst. Hamilton came thundering up the slope towards him and flung himself down on the damp heather. He twisted himself round to bring his rifle to bear on the left-hand group and the signaller made another run as he squeezed off a few more rounds. And so they continued up the hill, sometimes leapfrogging each other, sometimes finding different scrapes of cover, but ducking and wincing as the incoming rounds whistled in ever closer and the figures in their rifle sights grew ever larger.

Hamilton reasoned that by now the other two men in his patrol would, if they had any sense, have legged it for the emergency RV, having heard the gunfire and assessed the situation. There were no reinforcements that would come charging over the ridge. They were too isolated out here for anyone to be able to reach them quickly enough. They were on their own. They had to fight their way out. There was no other option. He sprayed another burst, ejected his magazine and slotted another one into its place. From his cover position the signaller opened fire and Hamilton scrambled to his feet. That was when it caught him – a hammer blow in his back. Damn! He hadn't presented a target for them, he'd just got up at the wrong time. He'd caught a round that would have gone whistling over his head if he'd waited another split second. He staggered up the slope and collapsed into cover.

His friend looked across at him from his position a few yards away. He could see that the boss was wounded. He reached for a field dressing, but Hamilton waved him away. He knew now he wasn't going to make it off the mountainside.

'You go,' he said. 'I'll keep them busy.'

Raising his rifle, Hamilton fired off a burst and the signaller dashed for another scraping of cover. He could see the boss continuing to fire, saw him rise up for a better vantage and take another round. Still he went on firing.

Gavin Hamilton fought to the bitter end, as the citation for his posthumous Military Cross describes:

> On 5th June, he was deployed in command of a four man observation patrol into a hazardous position again behind enemy lines on West Falkland to carry out observation of enemy activities in Port Howard.
>
> He managed to establish himself in a position only 2500m from the enemy, from where he sent detailed and accurate reports on the enemy. Shortly after dawn on 10th June he realised that he and his radio operator had been surrounded in a forward position.
>
> Although heavily outnumbered, and with no reinforcements available, he gave the order to engage the enemy, telling his signaller that they should both attempt to fight their way out of the encirclement. Since the withdrawal route was completely exposed to enemy observation and fire, he initiated the fire fight in order to allow his signaller to move first.
>
> After the resulting exchange of fire he was wounded in the back, and it became clear to his signaller that Captain Hamilton was only able to move with difficulty.
>
> Nevertheless, he told his signaller that he would continue to hold off the enemy whilst the signaller made good his escape, and then he proceeded to give further covering fire. Shortly after that he was killed.
>
> Captain Hamilton displayed outstanding determination and an extraordinary will to continue the fight in spite of being confronted by hopeless odds and being wounded. He furthermore showed supreme courage and sense of duty by his conscious decision to sacrifice himself on behalf of his signaller.
>
> His final, brave and unselfish act will be an inspiration to all who follow in the SAS.

Gavin Hamilton was an inspiration and a desperately sad loss to the Regiment. All of those who knew him appreciated his courage and dedication. Some who never knew him at all also understood something about the man. When the Argentine commander of Port Howard was interrogated after the surrender, he said that he wanted to recommend 'the SAS captain' for the highest military honour we could award him because he was 'the most courageous man I have ever seen'.

Gavin John Hamilton was indeed an extraordinary man and a superb soldier.

Chapter 18

SERGEANT VINCE PHILLIPS

Most people in the Western world had little knowledge of, and even less interest in, the political tension that had built up between the oil-rich Arab states of Iraq and neighbouring Kuwait over the summer of 1990. Those distant from the region were weary of hearing about its armed conflicts, of seeing images on TV news bulletins of bombed-out buildings and smoke-blackened, battle-damaged military hardware smouldering somewhere on a featureless desert plain. Iraq had fought an eight-year war against another of its neighbours, Iran, with battlefield images appearing almost nightly on our TV screens, yet most people living in the comfort and safety of the West would still have struggled accurately to pinpoint the exact locations of those countries on a map of the Middle East.

The same could not be said of the men of the SAS. Their regular briefings and bulletins about conflicts all over the world were staged for more than just satisfying an interest in current affairs. Any major confrontation, as well as plenty of minor ones, could represent a situation into which they might be drawn and thus became background 'homework', knowledge to be absorbed and stored away for future reference.

The problems between Iraq and Kuwait had arisen due to Iraq's precarious financial situation. The war against Iran had cost billions of dollars and Saddam Hussein's dictatorship was utterly bankrupt. A huge part of Iraq's war debt was owed to its neighbour Kuwait, which had helped to finance the conflict with Iran, and Kuwait was determined that Saddam should repay his debt. With his overdraft far outreaching the income generated by his oil sales, the simple answer for Saddam to balance his housekeeping budget was to raise the price of his oil. As a major supplier to the rest of the world, even a small increase in price would be enormously lucrative for him and, since Iraq was practically floating on a sea of the stuff, there were obvious long-term benefits.

The production and price of oil is, however, carefully controlled by the oil-producing nations through the Organization of Petroleum Exporting Countries (OPEC). Fluctuations in oil prices can seriously affect the economies of countries all over the world and Kuwait opposed Saddam's proposed price rises. Kuwait also increased its production of oil, threatening a price drop – just like every other commodity, when there is more oil in the marketplace, the price goes down. For Saddam, this meant draining more of his oil reserves simply to maintain the same level of income. He viewed the Kuwaiti move as an act of aggression against Iraq and the two countries went nose-to-nose.

Knowing that he couldn't repay the cash he had borrowed from Kuwait during the war, a small matter of $14 billion or so, Saddam decided to try to deal Kuwait out of the diplomatic game by raising the stakes. He accused the Kuwaitis of stealing his oil. He wasn't just saying that they were sneaking across the border in the dead of night to siphon fuel out of one of his many limos; he had them down for wholesale theft of millions of gallons. A major oil field straddles the border between Iraq and Kuwait. The Iraqis had always taken their oil from the northern deposits, while the Kuwaitis extracted the black stuff from their own side of the border. Saddam, however, accused them of 'slant drilling'. He maintained that instead of drilling straight down to their own part of the oil field, the Kuwaitis had been boring at an angle that took them over the border, deep underground, to poach his supplies. It has been known to happen. Saddam claimed that Kuwait had filched $10 billion of oil over the preceding ten years and further demanded over $2 billion in compensation for the crime, taking the reparations remarkably close to the debt that he actually owed to Kuwait.

For Vince Phillips and the men of A Squadron, the bickering between Iraq and Kuwait was of passing interest, but little more than that. It was another potential hot spot that someone would be monitoring. They would hear quickly enough if they were to be dragged into it in any way. In the meantime the Regiment, although not committed to a major conflict, was as busy as ever with anti-terrorist duties and training exercises all over the world. Small teams had been at work in a training or advisory capacity in Liberia, Thailand, Ethiopia and Columbia and they continued to fulfil a demanding role in Northern Ireland.

It wasn't until Saddam pulled his next move that the situation in that part of the Middle East became of serious interest to them. The Iraqi dictator amassed an army of 100,000 men on his southern border with Kuwait. This was seen as further sabre-rattling from Saddam, but there was a clear threat that he would launch an invasion of the far smaller Gulf state. Having convinced American and British diplomats that this was, indeed, just a show of force, he then took everyone by surprise, including the Kuwaitis, when his tanks rolled across the border in the early hours of 2 August 1990.

As they waited for the inevitable call to 'stand by' and so begin preparations for deployment somewhere in the Middle East, Vince Phillips and A Squadron could do little more than watch, like the rest of the Regiment and the rest of the world, as the drama unfolded in Kuwait. Vince was a highly experienced, highly proficient soldier with eight years' exemplary service in the SAS, having attained the rank of sergeant. He had been in the army since 1972, having joined the Royal Army Ordnance Corps (RAOC) at the age of 17. On completion of his basic training he was posted to Bicester, but within a year he had moved on to 16 Para Heavy Drop Company, completing his parachute course successfully towards the end of 1973. When that unit was disbanded in 1976, Vince volunteered for the All Arms Commando Course at Plymouth and passed with flying colours. He served with 3 Commando Brigade for seven years before applying for SAS Selection and passing the course in 1983. This achievement gave him the unusual distinction in the British Army of having earned the right to wear either the maroon beret of an airborne soldier, the green beret of a commando or the beige beret of the SAS. To attain any one of these requires phenomenal commitment and sacrifice, well above average intelligence and huge amounts of guts and determination. To attain all three demonstrated that Vince possessed all of these qualities in abundance.

Vince was posted to Boat Troop of B Squadron at first, then was seconded to the SBS for a year before returning to the Regiment as part of A Squadron's Mountain Troop, where his fitness and endurance became legendary. Like the rest of the Regiment, he saw the events unfolding in the Gulf as a potential opportunity to put his training and experience into practice, but was forced simply to wait and watch as Kuwait fell before the weight of the Iraqi onslaught.

At the time, Saddam commanded one of the largest standing armies in the world and the forces that he unleashed on Kuwait included four divisions of his elite Republican Guard, as well as special forces units that amounted to another entire division. In the air he fielded a squadron of Soviet-supplied Mil Mi-25 helicopter gunships – the 'Hind' – armed with anti-tank missiles, rocket pods and a four-barrel 12.7mm cannon mounted in the nose. Helicopter troop transports raced commandos ahead of the advancing army to capture Kuwait City, and his MiG jet fighters and bombers were deployed to supply ground support and disable the two main Kuwaiti air bases.

Although they had been caught on the hop, Kuwaiti Mirage and Skyhawk fighter jets were scrambled to engage the invaders. They suffered heavy losses, with 20 per cent of the Kuwait Air Force (KAF) destroyed or captured before they were ordered to evacuate to Saudi Arabia and Bahrain. Some of the jets took off from motorways adjacent to the air bases while Iraqi tanks trundled down the runways. In central Kuwait, the 35th Armoured Brigade deployed its Chieftain tanks in a delaying action against the advancing Iraqis at Jahra to the west of Kuwait City, but they could do little against Saddam's vastly superior forces. Other elements of Kuwait's heavy armour that were in a position to do so were ordered, like the air force, to evacuate to Saudi Arabia. Of the small Kuwait Naval Force (KNF), only two missile ships managed to escape capture or destruction, one engaging at least three Iraqi vessels before fleeing.

By the end of the morning of 2 August, Iraqi tanks were in Kuwait City and it was clear that Saddam's *Blitzkrieg* had succeeded. Tanks were advancing on the royal residence at the Dasman Palace, although the emir had already been evacuated to Saudi Arabia. His younger half-brother, however, remained in the palace with a cadre of guards to mount a last-ditch defence. He was shot dead, his body then laid in front of a tank and crushed. Kuwait was now in Saddam's hands.

Over the next few days, Iraqi soldiers stripped Kuwait of anything of value that could be shipped home to Iraq. Shops and houses were looted and the population of Kuwait City lived in terror of the brutal soldiers who rampaged through their streets and homes. The UN was quick to condemn the invasion and instigate sanctions against Saddam. The US was equally quick to begin a build-up of forces in the area, shipping men and equipment into Saudi Arabia, ostensibly to prevent Saddam now turning his army against the Saudis, too. US men and equipment began arriving in Saudi Arabia just four days after the invasion, as the international coalition that would make up Operation *Desert Shield* and ultimately *Desert Storm* began to assemble.

There followed five months of frustrating diplomatic negotiations, during which the SAS remained on standby for action. Eventually, Vince and the rest of A Squadron, along with B and D Squadrons, were given their marching orders. It was the largest mobilization of the Regiment since World War II, but as he flew out for Saudi Arabia after enjoying Christmas with his wife and two daughters, Vince had no more idea of the role the Regiment was to play than anyone else.

There were plans to use the SAS in its traditional role as a raiding force behind Iraqi lines. There were also tentative plans based around the possibility of rescuing British hostages being held both in Iraq and Kuwait, and plans for the Regiment to forge ahead of the Allied advance when it was eventually launched, disrupting Iraqi supply lines and communications. The commander of the *Desert Storm* operation, General Norman Schwarzkopf, however, was not a great fan of special forces and had no immediate requirement for the SAS, despite its reputation as the British Army's foremost exponent of desert warfare and the fact that it had conducted extensive training exercises in the area.

When Vince arrived in the Saudi desert he was kept busy with his troop, organizing their equipment and training with the Pinkies (Land Rovers) to ensure they were ready to go wherever they were asked to go, at a moment's notice. They were to enjoy a lengthy period of desert acclimatization not normally afforded to SAS troops on operation. It slowly became clear, however, that there would be a very specific role for the SAS desert raiders to play.

At the end of November and beginning of December, Saddam began test firing his Scud long-range ballistic missiles. The ageing Soviet designs had been improved by the Iraqis to extend their range to almost 400 miles (644km). The missiles fell harmlessly in the wasteland of the Iraqi desert, but they had been fired, quite deliberately, in the direction of Tel Aviv. Saddam had demonstrated that should the coalition forces think about trying to drive him out of Kuwait, he had a weapon with which he could not only deliver high-explosive, poison gas or chemical warheads into the coalition's rear echelon, he could also hit Israel. The Israelis, naturally, would then retaliate with their own missiles, and the prospect of the Iraq/Kuwait situation escalating into a far greater Arab/Israeli war was a very uncomfortable notion. Israel signalled its intentions by test firing one of its own long-range missiles into the Mediterranean Sea and deploying its missile batteries, undoubtedly equipped with nuclear warheads, pointing in the direction of Baghdad.

Clearly, Saddam's Scud threat had to be eliminated. While a deadline for his withdrawal from Kuwait was issued – he was warned that if he didn't leave by 15 January the coalition forces, with backing from the UN, would move against him – satellites and reconnaissance aircraft desperately searched for the mobile Scud launchers. They proved to be highly elusive. America attempted to persuade the Israelis to stay out of the confrontation and supplied them with batteries of Patriot missiles that were supposedly capable of destroying a Scud in flight. The Patriots, however, could never boast a 100 per cent success rate, and if just one Scud delivered a chemical or gas warhead to a densely populated area of Tel Aviv, it would cause thousands of deaths. Israel's subsequent reaction to such an attack didn't take much imagination.

The only possible solution to the Scud threat was to insert covert reconnaissance teams on the ground, placing them in the areas where the missiles would have to be based to have any chance of reaching Israel. The teams would not only identify Scud sites and Scuds in transit to call in air strikes, they would also have a search and destroy brief.

The day after the withdrawal deadline expired, the first coalition air strikes were launched against Iraq. The day after that, Iraq launched eight Scuds against Israel. The missiles did not cause the carnage that had been feared, but they demonstrated Saddam's willingness to follow through on his threat. The task of the SAS teams in what had become known as 'Scud Alley', a vast expanse of Western Iraq stretching south of Highway 10 to the Saudi Arabian border, became even more urgent.

Vince Phillips was drafted into one such anti-Scud patrol, code-named Bravo Two Zero. A great deal has been said and written about this particular patrol, mainly because it was the one that went wrong. The debates will rage forever about whether they were supplied with inadequate intelligence before their departure, whether they had the right kit, whether they should have taken vehicles with them as other patrols did and whether the right decisions were made on the ground. None of that really matters now. As they prepared to be infiltrated into Iraq by Chinook on the evening of 22 January, they had made their choices and were ready for their mission. They were experienced, well-trained SAS soldiers who knew their own abilities and limitations and knew what was expected of them. The eight-man patrol was as ready to go as they would ever be. The one thing that they didn't really have on their side was luck.

Vince was second-in-command of the patrol and, like the others, looking forward to doing his bit to eliminate the Scuds. When the Chinook dropped them off at the LZ they immediately set off to put as much distance between themselves and the LZ as quickly as possible, heading for their designated area of operations. As always on such patrols, each man was carrying a load heavy enough to flatten a pack mule. Four of them carried M16s with M203 grenade launchers, while the others had Minimis, a very effective light machine-gun with a high rate of fire. Each man also carried a disposable LAW 80 rocket launcher and they were all weighed down with ammunition and demolition charges.

They made their way north towards a petroleum pipeline close to a ridge that was to be their designated RV, the place where they would gather should they become separated in an emergency. It was hard going and the temperature in the desert hovered around freezing – this was to be the worst winter weather experienced in the region for many years. They trekked for about 12 miles (19km) until they located their RV and from there identified their primary reconnaissance target, one of the Main Supply Routes (MSRs) out of Baghdad. They found a small cleft in a rocky outcrop, a cave nestled in a wadi that would serve as an ideal LUP during the daylight hours, providing them with shelter from the elements as well as a good hiding place.

The terrain around the LUP was mainly flat and featureless, although a quick check in the darkness identified some kind of settlement only about a mile away, with a water tower clearly visible above a cluster of darkened buildings. Once they had stowed their kit in the cave, they attempted to check in with base by radio. Try as they might, they could not make contact. Believing the radio to be faulty, they had no choice but to follow their 'lost-comms' drill and head back to the helicopter LZ the next night to pick up a new set.

When dawn broke, they checked out their surroundings by daylight. To their horror there was a military camp practically on their doorstep. It had not been marked on their maps. Although scheduled to be out in the field for 14 days, it was clear that they could not stay there. They would have to wait out the daylight hours in the cave and then move out after darkness. From the cave they could see traffic moving on the MSR, but there was no movement in their vicinity until that afternoon, when a boy tending his goats wandered into the wadi and spotted them. He took one look, turned and ran. It would surely only be a matter of time before someone from the camp came to investigate. Now they would have to get out fast in broad daylight.

Taking a detour to avoid being spotted from the Iraqi camp, they then made a bee-line for the helicopter LZ. They marched fast, building up a sweat but glad to be on the move. For a while, it looked like they might have put enough ground between themselves and the camp for anyone checking out the boy's story to dismiss it as a childish fantasy. Then they heard the unmistakeable sound of a tracked vehicle rumbling up a small ridge to their left. They assumed a defensive position and Vince knelt with the shoulder-launched LAW ready to fire. An armoured personnel carrier (APC) crested the ridge and trundled down the incline towards them. Vince fired. A rocket from one of the others also hit the APC and it ground to a halt. Then a truck appeared and that too was immobilized with a rocket, but there was now another APC and a detachment of troops closing on them. The patrol was too exposed simply to turn and run, so they attacked. One half of the patrol advanced under covering fire from Vince and his group, then Vince got to his feet and charged forward with his men. The hail of fire from the Minimis, M16s and grenade launchers drove off the Iraqis, despite the fact that they had the patrol heavily outnumbered.

Their action gave the SAS soldiers the breathing space they needed to try to make good their escape. They made off fast, but soon came under fire from a group of infantry disgorging from two trucks that pulled up in the distance to the east. They changed direction but began to be targeted by, of all things, a battery of anti-aircraft guns. Ditching their Bergens so that they could move faster, they ran on, shaking off their pursuers as darkness began to close in. Running without the Bergen suited Vince. Running was his sport. He had run in army cross-country teams ever since he first joined up. He had been a member of the Para RAOC team that had won the Welsh 3,000m event in 1976 and had competed in marathons for the British Army. He had picked up an injury to his leg during the firefight, but if they had to run, he was fit enough to keep running all night.

With no sign of anyone in immediate pursuit, they stopped for a breather, sucking in the cold night air as they gathered together to discuss their options. They would be expected to head south for Saudi Arabia. Instead, they would take the longer route to Syria, over 75 miles (121km) to the west, in the hope of shaking off anyone who might still be tailing them. They were now drenched with sweat that was chilling on their clothes and bodies in the freezing night air. They marched on into the darkness, stopping every hour for five minutes to take a drink and rest. As the night progressed, the group became more spaced out. Vince's injury became progressively worse and he began to slow up. One of the others was also beginning to suffer from dehydration. At the next stop, the column was rejigged so that the two slower men were marching second and third in line to ensure that they did not fall behind.

In the darkness, however, the group became more and more strung out and eventually the three in front could see no trace of those behind. As the icy wind began to blow through rain, they had to keep moving to try to stay warm. Before long, the rain turned to driving snow. Vince's injury, exacerbated by the intense cold, now left him intensely frustrated at not being able to move as quickly as he wanted. The other two, however, were no better off. As dawn broke, with snow still falling, they found themselves out in the open, with no cover to be found anywhere nearby. Huddling together in a rut in the ground they shivered as snow settled on their clothes and they tried to rest. They would be easy targets if they were spotted marching during the day, so they hunkered down and prayed for darkness to come so that they could move on again.

The desert cold is intense and Vince and the others were unlucky enough to be experiencing the most extreme conditions anyone could remember in that area. They now faced far greater danger from the environment than they did from the enemy. Even under favourable conditions, when you are not fleeing for your life from heavily armed pursuers, the cold can be a killer. On exercise with the Regiment in Norway, I was part of a patrol that forded a river before continuing along a mossy path towards our objective at the head of a valley. It was bitterly cold, but there was no snow, just a light, penetrating rain that seemed to chill your very bones. After a few hours, I started to grumble. Knowing me, my friends took this as some kind of joke and ignored me. Then I started to complain, loudly, moaning about being wet, being cold and being in Norway in general. This wasn't like me and it was annoying for everyone, but apart from the odd request for me to shut my trap, they let it go. Then I started babbling a load of nonsense and, when one of the patrol saw me stumble he immediately realized what was happening. I was suffering the onset of hypothermia. Disorientated and confused, I was helped into a sleeping bag with one of the others hugging me tight to provide some body warmth. They made a hot drink for me and we rested up until I appeared to have returned to normal. Without their help, I would have been in serious trouble, my core body temperature would have dropped and, drained of energy, I would have slipped into a sleep from which I would never have woken. This was the peril that now faced Vince and the other members of Bravo Two Zero.

When they deemed it dark enough to continue, Vince and the others dragged themselves to their feet and forced their legs to start carrying them forward once again, heads bowed against the wind and rain. The further they marched, the greater the distance that developed between the three. Vince stumbled on, keeping up as best he could. When they stopped to rest, the other two looked round to find that Vince was nowhere in sight. They searched for over an hour, calling to him, their voices carried off into the night by the howling wind. They never found him. Vince had wandered off course and died from hypothermia.

Any man who is prepared to put his life on the line serving his country is a brave man. Any man who is prepared to go into combat behind enemy lines, completely isolated from the support that is enjoyed by most conventional soldiers, is a hero. Vince Phillips was one of those men.

AFTERWORD

Several of the men I have written about in this book have died since leaving the army. Some of those deaths are recorded in the relevant chapters of the book. Where this is not the case, I have noted a few details about their later lives below. It would not be wise of me, however, to provide an update on the lives of a number of those who have featured in this book. Some are still involved in sensitive work, and others could do without being directly identified in such a way in print.

BRONCO LANE

Bronco is still very active and travels widely giving presentations and demonstrations about his experiences as a mountaineer.

LOFTY LARGE

When he retired from the army, Lofty set up his own transport business and later went back to Oman to work for the SAF as a transport officer. Once back home in Hereford, he started his own driving school, wrote three books about his military career and took part in a TV documentary, in which we returned to the Koemba River in Borneo. Sadly,

Lofty died in 2006 after a long illness. He was a great friend and I will always miss him.

KEVIN WALSH

After a remarkable military career, in which he faced up to and overcame all kinds of dangers, Kevin fell ill and succumbed to cancer in 1986.

TALAIASI LABALABA

For his brave actions at Mirbat, Laba was awarded a posthumous MID to add to the British Empire Medal (BEM) he'd been awarded while serving with the Royal Irish Rangers. His funeral service in the small churchyard of St Martin's Church in Hereford was one of the most moving I have ever witnessed; the most poignant moment was the singing of a Fijian hymn, unaccompanied, by the numerous fellow Fijians who had gathered from all over the UK, and elsewhere, to bid farewell and pay their respects to their friend and colleague.

Laba is buried next to Tommy Tobin. The inscription on Laba's headstone reads: 'No greater love hath any man than he should lay down his life for his friend.'

In his native Fiji, Laba is regarded as a military hero. There is a memorial to him, dedicated by B Squadron in 1998, alongside the Wesleyan Chapel in his home village of Nawaka, where many of his family still live. His elderly mother, Torika Canau Laudola, now nearly 90, and sister, Merewarita, are immensely proud of him and a framed photograph of Laba stands in prime position in their home. They always give a warm welcome to his friends from the Regiment who visit on trips home to the island.

When HRH Prince Charles visited Fiji in 2005, he requested a meeting with Laba's family. His mother was unfortunately not well enough, being badly crippled, but Merewarita was able to meet privately with the prince, something that she greatly appreciated.

Laba was a thoroughly good man; he is remembered not only for his courage and professionalism, but for his great sense of humour, constant cheerfulness and kindness. He was a good Christian and family-loving man whose character embodied the motto of the Great Seal of Fiji: *REREVAKA NA KALOU KA DAGA NA TUI* (Fear God and Honour the King).

PETE LOVEDAY

After Pete retired from his civilian job with the Regiment, he settled down to enjoy his retirement with his family. Sadly, he developed cancer and died in 2002.

IN MEMORIAM

Blair 'Paddy' Mayne 1915–55
Don 'Lofty' Large 1930–2006
Kevin Walsh 1938–1986
Reg Tayler 1940–2004
Talaiasi Labalaba 1942–72
Tommy Palmer 1951–83
Vince Phillips 1955–91
Alfie Tasker 1930–2003
Pete Loveday 1931–2002
Iain 'Jock' Thomson 1939–2004
Steve Callan 1941–83
Tommy Tobin 1947–72
Gavin John Hamilton 1953–82

The 20 men I've written about are representative of the soldiers of the SAS, past and present. Over the years, I served with so many outstanding soldiers, any of whom could have been included in my list of unsung heroes, men like:

Roy Ball
Sir Peter de la Billière
Ken Connor
Bill Farley
Keith Farnes
Fred Fearnley
Clive 'Dusty' Grey
Reg 'Brummie' Hassall
Alan 'Spike' Hoe
Henry Lee
Robin Letts
Eddie 'Geordie' Lillicoe
The Lock brothers, Colin and Joe
Fred Marafano
Colin 'Paddy' Millikin
Steve Moores
Tom Morrell
Mel Parry

Bert Perkins
Richard 'Duke' Pirie
Wally Poxon
Mick Reeves
Joe Schofield
Rover Slater
Ian 'Tanky' Smith
Alec Spence
Aubrey 'Taff' Springles
Geordie Tindale
Dick Tubnan
Bob Turnbull
Jim Vakatali
Johnny Watts
John Wildman
Glen Williams
John Woodhouse

Each of these, in his own way, contributed a great deal to the history and success of the Regiment. I might also have included Captain Robert Nairac, whom I met on a tour in Northern Ireland. He was not a member of the SAS, but had the attributes of any special forces soldier: courage, professionalism, tenacity and a friendly nature.

APPENDICES

RANKS AT END OF SERVICE/TIME OF DEATH

Steve Callan	WO2 Squadron Sergeant-Major
Gavin Hamilton	Captain
Talaiasi Labalaba	Sergeant
Michael Lane	Major
Don Large	WO2 Squadron Sergeant-Major
Pete Loveday	Sergeant
Paddy Mayne	Lieutenant-Colonel
Len Owens	Sergeant
Tommy Palmer	Sergeant
John Partridge	Staff Sergeant
Vince Phillips	Sergeant
Bob Podesta	Staff Sergeant
Sekonaia Takavesi	Staff Sergeant
Alfie Tasker	WO2 Squadron Sergeant-Major
Reg Tayler	WO1 Regimental Sergeant-Major
Iain Thomson	Sergeant
Tommy Tobin	Trooper
Mick Tyler	Sergeant
Kevin Walsh	WO2 Squadron Sergeant-Major
Pete Winner	Staff Sergeant

SAS SQUADRON TROOPS

Mountain Troop

Mountain Troop is responsible for all aspects of mountaineering and skiing. New members with no previous experience will be taught the basics of climbing and Arctic tactics. Many SAS individuals attend courses in Europe, among the best of which is the German Alpine Guides course in Bavaria. The Regiment annually selects two Mountain Troop soldiers to attend the year-long course. Six months is spent on skiing and six on mountaineering.

Normally one of the squadrons will be committed to the NATO winter exercise in Norway.

Air Troop

Previously known as 'Free-fall Troop.' Every SAS soldier is required to be parachute-trained before he can enter a squadron. Air Troop extends beyond these normal static-line procedures and practises HAHO (High-Altitude High-Opening) jumps. This allows the men to glide some 30km on to a target. Air Troop also uses unusual entry methods, including micro-lights and power-kites.

There is an Air Troop with each squadron, normally referred to as the 'Prima Donnas'. Their tasks are more individual, as they are normally only involved with the rest of the squadron in the path-finding role, going in ahead of the main force to secure and mark a drop zone or landing area.

Mobility Troop

Often previously referred to as 'Land Rover Troop', Mobility Troop operates using a variety of vehicles, of which the SAS 'Pink Panther' or 'Pinkie' is best known. The Regiment decided to paint their vehicles a dusky pink when an old aircraft, shot down during World War II, was found in the middle of the desert – the sand had burnished it pink.

Other vehicles used by Mobility Troop include KTM 350 and Honda 250 motorbikes; the Honda is preferred as it is very quiet.

Courses for members of Mobility Troop cover several weeks with the REME (Royal Electrical and Mechanical Engineers), learning basic mechanical fault-finding and training in cross-country conditions.

Amphibious Troop

Previously known as 'Boat Troop', Amphibious Troop concentrates on all water insertion methods. These include diving and even swimming ashore on a surf-board. In recent years, members of the SBS (Special Boat Service) have been stationed at Hereford and joined with the SAS in cross-training. Several operations have been jointly carried out using the SBS for actual water insertion and during the Falklands War they demonstrated how truly professional they are.

CHRONOLOGY

World War II	1939–1945
The Korean War	1950–53
The Malayan Campaign	1950–57
Suez Crisis	1956
The Jebel Akhdar – Northern Oman	1958–59
Borneo Campaign	1962–66
South Yemen (Aden)	1964–68
Southern Oman (Dhofar)	1971–76
Battle of Mirbat	19 July 1972
Northern Ireland	1969 onwards
Iranian Embassy Siege	1980
The Falklands War	1982
First Gulf War	1991

GLOSSARY OF ABBREVIATIONS

APC Armoured Personnel Carrier
ASFA Allied Special Forces Association
AWOL Absent Without Leave
BAOR British Army of the Rhine
BAS British Antarctic Survey
BATT British Army Training Team
BD Battledress
BEF British Expeditionary Force
BEM British Empire Medal
BFBT British Forces Borneo Territories
BP British Petroleum
CCO Clandestine Communist Organization
CCTV Closed-Circuit Television
CO Commanding Officer
COG Combined Operations Group
CP Close Protection
CQB Close-Quarters Battle
CRW Counter-Revolutionary Warfare
CTs Communist Terrorists
DG Dhofar Gendarmerie
DPRK Democratic People's Republic of Korea
DSO Distinguished Service Order
DZ Drop Zone
EOKA *Ethniki Organosis Kyprion Agoniston* (National Organization of Cypriot Fighters)
FLOSY Front for the Liberation of Occupied South Yemen
FRA Federal Regular Army
FSA Federation of South Arabia
GHQ General Headquarters
GPMG General-Purpose Machine-Gun
GPS Global Positioning System
GSM General Service Medal
HAHO High-Altitude High-Opening parachute jump
HALO High-Altitude Low-Opening parachute jump
HEAT High-Explosive Anti-Tank
HMG Heavy Machine-Gun
HQ Headquarters
IRA Irish Republican Army
JLSS Jungle Line Supply System
JSIU Joint Services Interrogation Unit
KAF Kuwait Air Force
KNF Kuwait Naval Force
LAW Light Anti-Armour Weapon
LRDG Long Range Desert Group
LUP Lying-Up Position
LZ Landing Zone
MBE Member of the British Empire
MC Military Cross
MID Mention In Dispatches
MM Military Medal
MOD Ministry of Defence
MSR Main Supply Route

MSTA Medical Support and Training Advisor
NAAFI Navy, Army and Air Force Institutes
NKNA North Kalimantan National Army
NLF National Liberation Front
OP Observation Post
OPEC Organization of Petroleum Exporting Countries
PLUTO Pipeline Under The Ocean
POW Prisoner Of War
PVA (Chinese) People's Volunteer Army
QGM Queen's Gallantry Medal
QRF Quick Reaction Force
R&R Rest & Recuperation
RA Royal Artillery
RAF Royal Air Force
RAMC Royal Army Medical Corps
RAOC Royal Army Ordnance Corps
REME Royal Electrical and Mechanical Engineers
RoK Republic of Korea
RPG Rocket-Propelled Grenade
RSM Regimental Sergeant-Major
RTU'd Returned to Unit
RUC Royal Ulster Constabulary
RV Rendezvous
SAF Sultan's Armed Forces
SARBE Surface to Air Rescue Beacon
SBS Special Boat Squadron (renamed the Special Boat Service in 1987)
SEP Surrendered Enemy Personnel
SGTG South Georgia Task Group
SLR Self-Loading Rifle (the British L1A1)
SMG Submachine-Gun
SOAF Sultan of Oman's Air Force
SOE Special Operations Executive
SOPs Standard Operating Procedures
SRN State Registered Nurse
SRS Special Raiding Squadron
TA Territorial Army
TWATT Terrorist Weapons and Tactics Team
UN United Nations
UNITA *União Nacional para a Independência Total de Angola* (National Union for the Total Independence of Angola)
VC Victoria Cross

INDEX